A JOHNSON SAMPLER

A
JOHNSON
SAMPLER

EDITED BY
HENRY DARCY CURWEN

A NONPAREIL BOOK
DAVID R. GODINE, PUBLISHER
BOSTON

This is a *Nonpareil Book,* first published in 2002 by

DAVID R. GODINE, *Publisher*
Post Office Box 450
Jaffrey, New Hampshire 03452
www.godine.com

LIBRARY OF CONGRESS
CATALOGING-IN-PUBLICATION DATA

Johnson, Samuel, 1709–1784
A Johnson sampler /
edited by Henry Darcy Curwen.
p. cm.
Includes bibliographical references and index.
ISBN 1–56792–130–2 (softcover : alk. paper)
I. Curwen, Henry Darcy. II. Title.
PR3522.C8   2001
828'609—dc21   00–037148

FIRST EDITION
Printed in Canada

To
ELWYN AND ELIZABETH SIMMONS
without whose generosity this work could have
remained a retired man's perpetual project

Preface

Books about Samuel Johnson are always being published, always will be, for Johnson is an ever fresh study to the scholar and the specialist. But this book is not *about* Johnson; it *is* Johnson. Nor is it Johnson the moralist, the Grand Cham, the literary critic, the lexicographer, or the philosopher. It is Johnson the forthright, clearheaded human being who made Dr. Maclean of Mull exclaim, "This man is just a hogshead of sense!" The *Sampler* is intended for the layman, for the kind of man who could go through life and perhaps never hear of Sam Johnson, much less read anything that he wrote.

This book grew, in fact, out of my thirty-year experience with such individuals—English classes of seventeen-year-old boys who *had* to read Boswell and who at the outset could not have cared less for Boswell, or Johnson, or the whole Johnson circle. Invariably, however, Johnson caught them. Within a week many were making up their own lists of the Johnsonisms that especially impressed them—wasting time with "a set of wretched un-idea'd girls," "no settling a point of precedency between a louse and a flea," "a woman's preaching is like a dog's walking on its hinder legs," "That fellow seems to me to possess but one idea, and that is a wrong one." These collections began, I am afraid, as good ammunition, as razor-sharp or hammer-blunt "cutdowns"—to use the schoolboy phrase—with which to subdue or macerate in argument their friends and companions. They memorized a lot of Johnson and made use of him, too.

Soon they became conscious of that other Johnson—the observer of life as men live life. They ran through the poems "London" and "The Vanity of Human Wishes" like so many Jack Horners, each pulling out plums to his taste. They noted, "This mournful truth is everywhere expressed/ Slow rises worth by poverty depressed." It echoes Gray's "Chill penury . . ." Most could quote the somber end of Charles XII: "He left a name at which the world turned pale/ To point a moral or adorn a tale." And Johnson's social wisdom: "a man should never tell stories to his disadvantage . . . people will remember them," or "Only a fool marries for love," or "Never speak of a man in his presence," or "I speak to a lord as I would expect the lord to speak to me were I a lord and he Sam Johnson." These and dozens like them the boys would at least ponder; and they would even accept from Johnson principles which, if offered by their fathers, they would immediately reject.

The father of such a boy was so startled that he wrote to find out what was happening to his son at school. The boy, unread and unashamed, came home for Christmas vacation and spent much time in the kitchen perched on a high stool reading gems from Johnson to his wondering mother and half-jeering sister. Unread though he was, he was well on the way to becoming a Johnsonian.

Then, of course, there was the Johnson of *The Rambler* and *The Idler*, of *Rasselas*, and of *A Journey*. Even this Johnson many of the boys would take, although each became expert in swiftly discarding all but the gold that caught his eye. It was not all fools' gold, either. This book is made up of exactly the Johnson that these boys would pick out and linger over.

Johnson, in fact, has much to say to our age, and he says it better than most of our modern thinkers. He covers a wider area, too. He could; he got around. With equal relish he talked to Bet Flint, whom he characterized as "generally a slut and a drunkard, occasionally a whore and a thief," and to King George the Third. Johnson did indeed "with extensive view/ Survey mankind from

China to Peru." This volume of his own words offers, in easily
manageable form, some of the wisdom he distilled from his observations.

Perhaps at first view he looks alien to our poor, inward-looking,
excuse-making age. He kept his mind clear of cant—of the mean-
ingless thinking that makes Eliot call us hollow men. To his
age he was, perhaps, in a major way what Will Rogers was to
ours. He was so honest that he would not fool even himself.
For instance, when a man was quoted as saying that Johnson's
Irene was one of the great plays of the century, "If Pot says so,
Pot lies," was Johnson's crusher. Again, Boswell with considerable ingenuity was trying one evening to defend a lady whose
divorce for adultery was the talk of London. At last Johnson
cut through the fog of words: "The woman's a whore, and
there's an end on 't."

He discusses everything under the sun except history, which
he hated—education, business, price fixing, "profitable con-
tacts," corrupt politics, marriage, law and punishments, and
from innumerable angles man's place in the universe and his
relationship with his fellow men and with God. He does it, too,
in sharp sentences as effective as the short stabbing sword of
the Roman legionary, or in magnificent periods whose sonorous
rhythms catch the general reader and whose careful architecture
delights the scholar. He always makes sense and usually makes
it in a most arresting way.

This book is not meant to be read consecutively from page
one to the end. It can be, of course; and any section, read in
order, gives an organized idea of Johnson's thinking on the
subject. But it can be opened anywhere and read with pleasure
and profit, in snippets or in pages. The introductory essays to
each section can, without much loss, be left unread. They are
no more than sketchy maps of the journey ahead: Johnson
speaks very adequately for himself. It does not contain all of
Johnson, but it may contain, in its limited way, much of the
best of Johnson. For teacher, preacher, public speaker, for the

scholar and student of the eighteenth century, it could be a valuable reference book. It is with this use in view that the work has been indexed.

I have tried to let the excerpts stand on their own, with a minimum of annotation and explanation, though occasionally I have identified the speaker or the situation (these brief notes precede the Johnson excerpt and are printed in italics). The sources of the quotations are indicated clearly enough for all practical purposes (a key is included at the back of the book). The reader wishing to look them up in their larger context will have no trouble finding them; and by a kind of induced serendipity, in seeking them he may come upon other passages that are more to his purpose. Every man hammers out truth on his own anvil; every reader of Johnson finds his own special treasures. Then, of course, there is always the possibility that the reader, once exposed to Johnson's own words, will be tempted to read for himself in *The Idler, Rasselas, A Journey to the Western Islands of Scotland,* the poems, some of *The Lives,* and even *The Rambler.* If he does, he is bound to be caught; and when he is caught, he enters a very special fellowship. The sun, which was once said never to set on the British Empire, never sets today on the fellowship of Johnson lovers.

It was at such a gathering, immediately after the toast to "the immortal memory," that my wife whispered, "This is such a *pleasant* lunacy." Lunacy, indeed! But in that moment she was caught. Since then she has gladly seen our substance go out for books which we cannot afford, has wandered through the horrid purlieus of Birmingham looking for Stourbridge School, has spent in the mists and gales of Skye weeks of vacation that might have been spent more comfortably in easier climes, and has gone to the church of St. Clement Danes, not to hear the bells sound out "Oranges and lemons" over the busiest section of London, but to sit in the balcony over the pulpit where our hero used to sit. My own interest has yielded double pleasure because of hers.

My thanks are due also to F. L. Lucas, Kings College, Cambridge University, James L. Clifford of Columbia University, W. Jackson Bate of Harvard University, Edward A. Bloom of Brown University, and David M. K. McKibbin of the Boston Athenaeum for their help in finding and verifying passages for me. It is hard to assess my debt to the late Myron R. Williams. For forty years he taught Boswell to his senior classes at The Phillips Exeter Academy. To each boy in his classes he would give a printed leaflet—three small pages—which contained some of the best of Johnson. It whetted the appetite of his students for more. I am sure that this leaflet was the seed from which this volume grew.

Exeter, New Hampshire   Henry Darcy Curwen
March 1963

Contents

A Johnson Sampler

Herculean strength and a Stentorian voice,
Of wit a fund, of words a countless choice;
In learning rather various than profound,
In truth intrepid, in religion sound;
A trembling form and a distorted sight,
But firm in judgement and in genius bright;
In controversy seldom known to spare,
But humble as the publican in prayer;
To more than merited his kindness, kind,
And though in manners harsh, of friendly mind;
Deep tinged with Melancholy's blackest shade,
And though prepared to die, of death afraid—
Such Johnson was: of him with justice vain,
When will this nation see his like again?

Memoirs of Richard Cumberland, Esq. (London, 1807)

Introduction

A Mrs. Cotterell one day asked Samuel Johnson to introduce her to a celebrated writer. "Dearest Madam," he replied, "you had better let it alone; the best part of every author is in general to be found in his book, I assure you."[1] This statement is not true of Johnson. Johnson the man is greater than Johnson the writer. In *The Rambler*, he writes: "A transition from an author's book to his conversation, is too often like an entrance into a large city, after a distant prospect. Remotely, we see nothing but spires of temples and turrets of palaces, and imagine it the residence of splendour, grandeur, and magnificence; but, when we have passed the gates, we find it perplexed with narrow passages, disgraced with despicable cottages, embarrassed with obstructions, and clouded with smoke."[2] Nor is this statement true of Johnson. His talk was as sensible and as pithy and as well constructed as his writings. Indeed, Johnson today is perhaps as well remembered for what he said when he was idling as he is for what he wrote when he was working.

Yet what Johnson wrote cannot be lightly considered. His *Life of Savage* was the best biography in English up to its time and set the pattern for Boswell's greater work. His *Rasselas* was translated into most, if not all, of the modern languages,[3] and was read with pleasure well into the nineteenth century. The *English Dictionary* would have been a monumental achievement for any man. The *Lives of the Poets* is a delight to the

[1] Bos. 21 July 1763 (n).   [2] Ram. 14.   [3] Bos. April 1759.

well-read layman and a goldmine to the scholar. Johnson's critical views of Shakespeare, so sound and so free from pedantic ingenuity, are today coming again into honor.

Johnson, however—great man though he was—would really have to be called a literary hack, but a hack touched with genius. It would be difficult to show that he ever wrote for the love of writing. Until he got his pension, he wrote only to earn bread for the day that was passing over him—no more willingly than most men work at their callings, and often less so. A craftsman, he wrote with a craftsman's speed and a craftsman's sureness. He told Dr. Burney that he never wrote any of his works that were printed twice over;[4] some he did not even read over before sending them off to the printer.[5] He would write anything—reviews, biography, criticism, dedications, political pamphlets, poetry, drama, epitaphs, sermons. Yet, whatever it was, it bore the Johnson stamp and was—Mrs. Thrale once wrote him—"as good as a journey to Rome, exactly."[6] But he would write only for a price. Walpole quotes Johnson as saying that "nothing excites a man to write but necessity."[7] A clergyman, an old acquaintance, applied to him for help in composing a sermon for a particular occasion. "I will write a sermon for thee," said Johnson, "but thou must pay me for it." (His customary fee for a sermon was two guineas.[8])

Nothing shows his habitual procrastination and his unwillingness to write as his long delay in producing his edition of Shakespeare. He issued proposals in June 1756,[9] promising that the work would be published by or before Christmas 1757. By then, however, he had not got through the second volume. Nor did he finish the work until 1767—nine years late; and even then Boswell wrote, "His throes in bringing it forth had been severe and remittent; and at last we may almost conclude

4 Bos. 1729(n).   5 Bos. 1758, Bos. 12 April 1776.
6 Bos. 5 April 1776(n).   7 Bos. 5 April 1776(n).
8 Hawkins.   9 Bos. (Hill-Powell, I, App. G).

that the Caesarian operation was performed by the knife of Churchill, whose upbraiding satire, I dare say, made Johnson's friends urge him to dispatch."[10]

It is easy to think of Johnson's writings as only an insignificant part of his fame. They are more than that, even today; and in his own day he was famous for his works and his critical opinions. Johnson's wit, his talk, his good fortune in having Boswell as his biographer, all contribute to his present stature. But we must not forget that it was his *Rambler* that made Boswell seek him out;[11] that his *Rasselas* spread his fame through Europe; that his *Dictionary* won him his academic honors and probably his pension; and that his *Lives of the Poets* gives him authority among scholars today.

Johnson's life is, in a subdued way, a success story in the American manner—the story of success won over the impediments of poverty, defective schooling, ill health, and temperament.

Samuel Johnson was the elder son of Michael Johnson, a bookseller of Lichfield, England. He was born on 18 September 1709; he died seventy-five years later. Thus he was an almost exact contemporary of Benjamin Franklin, whom—oddly enough—he never met. Sarah Johnson, his mother, came of an ancient yeoman family. She claimed higher social rank than her husband, but Michael was no inconsiderable figure in his community. He was respected for his learning; he served as sheriff of the county, was a justice of the peace, and was comfortable enough in his circumstances to own a not unimposing residence in the middle of the city and to lose a considerable sum of money in a parchment-manufacturing venture.

Young Samuel's birth was a difficult one. According to his own account, he was almost dead at birth and could not cry for some time;[12] and the male midwife gave his attention rather to Mrs. Johnson. The late Dr. Peter Pineo Chase believed that

[10] Bos. 1756.   [11] Bos. 25 June 1763.   [12] Miss Boothby.

many of Johnson's physical and spiritual peculiarities in later life stemmed from this experience, for they look like the usual results of infant anoxia.[13] More certain is the origin of his scrofula, which, Dr. Swinfen said, he contracted from his wet nurse.[14] The morbid melancholy which, before he was twenty, became chronic hypochondria, he inherited from his father.[15] Thus, before the infant Samuel was properly settled in his cradle, he had in him the seeds of most of his later afflictions.

He attended the Lichfield School and the grammar school at Stourbridge. At Stourbridge he lived with "Parson" Ford, his mother's nephew, who urged him to learn all that he could about all things. He was sixteen when he left Stourbridge.[16] Since there was no money to send him on to either university, he stayed at home and read "as chance threw books in his way"; but what he read was "not voyages and travel, but all literature, all ancient authors, all manly."[17] He was to say later that his "great period of study was from twelve to eighteen,"[18] and again when he was in his mid-fifties, "I knew almost as much at eighteen as I do now."[19] Then in the fall of 1728 came a chance for him to enter Pembroke College, Oxford. With what financial support he entered is not clear, but, whatever it was, it did not carry him through. In the fall of 1731 he left without a degree; shortly afterward his father died, leaving Johnson about £20. Johnson now saw that he had to make his own fortune: "Meanwhile, let me take care that the powers of my mind may not be debilitated by poverty, and that indigence do not force me into any criminal act."[20] He went to Birmingham, found his way into some desultory literary labors, and did a translation of A Voyage to Abyssinia by Father Lobo, a Portuguese Jesuit.[21] This task foreshadowed the Johnson of later years—the inertia, the procrastination, the rush to meet the deadline; and in the

---

[13] Chase, p. 376.   [14] Bos. 1712.   [15] Bos. 1709.
[16] Bos. 1725.   [17] Bos. 1725–1728.   [18] Tour.
[19] Bos. 21 July 1763.   [20] Bos. 1731.   [21] Bos. 1733.

book itself, the skepticism, the stately style, and the sound good sense.[22]

By 1733, then, the pattern of what was to be Johnson's life and career had already appeared. His short term as usher in the grammar school at Market Bosworth, his marriage to a widow twice his age, his attempt to set up a boarding school at Edial, near Lichfield—these were but steps on the way to his career as a man of letters in London. The ushership ended in "an aversion and even a degree of horrour" for that way of earning a living.[23] The marriage, with all its ups and downs, was to do much over a long period of struggle and poverty to make tolerable, at least, a life that was radically wretched. The school at Edial gave him a companion for his migration to London and a lifelong friend, David Garrick.

In 1736, carrying a letter of introduction from his steadfast friend Gilbert Walmsley to a Reverend Mr. Colson and three acts of a tragedy which he had started, and leaving behind him in Lichfield a wife he could not support and a record to date of dismal failure, Johnson went up to London. He and Garrick, Garrick once said when both were famous and Garrick wealthy, "rode and tied"—a method of travel certainly a step above trudging the highway. Johnson said he had but two pence halfpenny in his pocket, "and thou, Davy, with three half-pence in thine."[24] Spiritually at least Johnson took up residence in Grub Street, which later he was to define in his *Dictionary* as "much inhabited by writers of small histories, dictionaries, and temporary poems." How he lived in London in this period is not so important as the fact that he could later explain in detail how to live without being contemptible on £30 a year.[25]

In 1737 he returned to Lichfield to finish his tragedy *Irene* and to take his wife back to London. The next year he was employed regularly by Edward Cave, founder and owner of *The*

[22] Bos. 1733.
[24] Bos. 1737(n).
[23] Bos. 1733.
[25] Bos. 1737.

Gentleman's Magazine, and entered finally upon a life in which he worked during some of his best years as "a mere literary labourer for gain not glory, merely to obtain an honest support."[26]

How slowly now the tide of recognition and modest prosperity came in to float him off the flats of anonymity and poverty! In 1738 he wrote and published his poem "London," an imitation of the Third Satire of Juvenal.[27] It purported to do for the literary man in London what Juvenal had done for the same in Rome. In much of it one can read Johnson's own experience. Perhaps the most often quoted couplet indicates the tenor of the whole:

> This mournful truth is everywhere confess'd,
> Slow rises worth by poverty depress'd.

The poem appeared without Johnson's name, but it won for him the praise and attention of Alexander Pope, who tried to get the author an M.A. from Dublin, to qualify him for the headmastership of a school. Nothing came of the effort.[28] Seven years later there appeared his *Life of Savage,* again anonymously.[29] For "London" Johnson had received ten guineas; for *Savage* he got fifteen.[30] Three years after this—Johnson had now been in London ten years—a group of booksellers contracted with him for the compiling of a dictionary of the English language. The price stipulated was £1575, out of which Johnson was to meet all costs. The Plan or Prospectus Johnson addressed to Lord Chesterfield, not out of deep policy, but to gain a few days' delay for a task that was overdue.[31] Normally, however, he might have expected the patronage and perhaps some financial help from Chesterfield. He got neither. Later,

[26] Bos. May 1738.   [27] Bos. 1738.
[28] Bos. 1738.   [29] Bos. Spring 1738.
[30] Bos. Feb. 1744(n). [31] Bos. Autumn 1747.

Chesterfield attempted to make some slight amends for his neglect. Johnson repelled these late advances in a letter that has been rather pretentiously called "the death-knell of patronage."[32]

Johnson had optimistically believed that he could complete the *Dictionary* in three years. "But," said Dr. Adams, "the French Academy, which consists of forty members, took forty years to compile their Dictionary." Johnson replied: "Sir, thus it is. This is the proportion. Let me see; forty times forty is sixteen hundred. As three to sixteen hundred, so is the proportion of an Englishman to a Frenchman."[33] Actually the task thus hopefully entered upon was to take eight weary years. During this period he published a second imitation of Juvenal, "The Vanity of Human Wishes," for which he received fifteen guineas.[34] Garrick, by now famous as an actor and producer, put the tragedy *Irene* on the stage. Although it was really no success, Johnson received, first and last, nearly £300 from it.[35] In 1750 he undertook a biweekly series of periodical essays after the manner of *The Spectator* of Addison and Steele. He called them *The Rambler* and wrote, in all, two hundred and eight of them.[36] The essays were little noticed at first, the sale running to no more than five hundred copies an issue.[37] By 1760, however, they were in high favor; when they were collected and bound, Johnson lived to see ten editions published in London in addition to those published in Dublin and Edinburgh. Each edition was of twelve hundred and fifty copies.[38] For the essays as they came out, Johnson received but two guineas each.[39] In the spring of 1752, Mrs. Johnson died, leaving her husband desolate,[40] but he had no time for the luxury of idle grief. He was already three years behind with the *Dic-*

[32] Bos. 1754.
[33] Bos. 1748.
[34] Bos. January 1749.
[35] Bos. February 1749 and n.
[36] Bos. March 1750.
[37] Murphy.
[38] Bos. 1750.
[39] Bos. 1750(n).
[40] Bos. 17 March 1752.

tionary, and the contract price of fifteen hundred guineas, which seemed so large at the beginning, now looked less and less adequate.

The publication of the *Dictionary* in 1755 was a kind of watershed in Johnson's life. The work, to be sure, did nothing for him financially. He had overdrawn the stipulated £1575 by over £100, but had been forgiven the overdraft.[41] Within a year he was arrested for a debt of under £6 and had to be rescued by Richardson.[42] The death of his mother in 1759 caught him, as always, without money. He set to work and in a week wrote *Rasselas*. With the £100 which he got for it he defrayed the expenses of his mother's funeral and paid the few debts that she left. But his life now assumes a different aspect. He was known; he was "Dictionary Johnson." He had been granted an M.A. by Oxford.[43] In mid-1762 he was granted a pension of £300 a year by the government, "solely as a reward of his literary merit,"[44] and from now on, this "most indolent man in Britain"[45] was relieved of the labor of writing. He once told Boswell that he "always felt an inclination to do nothing."[45] But now he could, in his own words, "fold his legs and have his talk out."[46] In May 1763 he met Boswell. In February 1764 he founded the Club. In 1765 he was surprised to receive the unexpected compliment of a doctorate of laws from Dublin;[47] he had to wait ten more years before he received a similar degree from Oxford and became "Doctor Johnson."[48] And in this same year, 1765, he was introduced into the household of the Thrales.[49] The pension, the Club, and the Thrales were to dictate the course of his life.

But before he could settle completely into idleness, he still had one piece of business to finish. He had not done his edition

[41] Murphy.
[42] Murphy.
[43] Bos. 28 Nov. 1754.
[44] Bos. 1762.
[45] Bos. 2 Aug. 1763.
[46] Bos. 31 March 1773.
[47] Bos. July 1765.
[48] Bos. 1775.
[49] Bos. Summer 1765.

of Shakespeare, and there was fear among his friends that he
never would. In June 1758 a Dr. Grainger wrote to Dr. Burney,
"I have several times called on Johnson to pay him part of your
subscriptions: I say part because he never thinks of working if
he has a couple of guineas in his pocket."[50] In 1763 a young
bookseller took him a subscription and offered the subscriber's
address, that it might be properly inserted in the printed list
of subscribers. "*I shall print no list of subscribers*," said Johnson with great abruptness; then more complacently, "I have
two very cogent reasons for not printing any list of subscribers;
—one, that I have lost all the names,—the other, that I have
spent the money."[51] His friends' concern for his reputation
was greater even than Johnson's inertia. Still nothing happened.
Then Charles Churchill in a satire, "The Ghosts," wrote,

> He for subscribers bates his hook,
> And takes their cash; but where's the book?
> No matter where; wise fear, we know,
> Forbids the robbing of a foe;
> But what, to serve our private ends,
> Forbids the cheating of our friends?[52]

At last, in October 1765, the Shakespeare appeared. Johnson
now was free.

It can truthfully be said that never again did he write unless
he wanted to, and he rarely wanted to. Boswell ventured to ask
him if he did not think it wrong to live in idleness and not
make use of his great talents.[53] He owned that it was bad but
continued to do nothing. "I have been trying to cure my laziness all my life, and could not do it," he said to Boswell when
they were eating lotus at Dunvegan.[54] "I am not quite idle,"

---

[50] Bos. 1756(n).
[52] Bos. 1756.
[54] Tour 20 September.

[51] Bos. May 1781.
[53] Bos. 24 May 1763.

he said on another occasion to Boswell and Goldsmith. "I made one line [of poetry] t'other day; but I make no more."[55] And Mrs. Thrale in a letter wrote, "Don't sit making verses that will never be written." But he did not merely sit. He was already famous for his talk. He had through the years acquired a remarkable fund of information. He was one of the most widely read men in a well-read age. He had an unusually retentive memory. He made it "a constant rule to talk as well as he could both as to sentiment and expression," and at all times he was ready for conversation.[56] Boswell early noted that "the extraordinary vigor and vivacity of his conversation constituted one of the first features of his character."[57] And his talk attracted and held the attention. "In general," Hannah More quotes an old acquaintance of Johnson as saying, "you can tell what a man to whom you are speaking will say next. This you can never do of Johnson."[58] A Mrs. Beresford, who was traveling to Oxford in the same coach with Johnson exclaimed, "How he does talk! Every sentence is an essay."[59] Johnson himself, Boswell once remarked, after hearing part of Boswell's journal, "was delighted on review to find that his conversation teemed with point and imagery."[60]

Hence, when Goldsmith and Boswell were one day urging him to give the world more of his work, he answered, "a man is to have part of his life to himself . . . A physician, who has practised long in a great city, may be excused if he retires to a small town, and takes less practice. Now, Sir, the good I can do by my conversation bears the same proportion to the good I can do by my writings, that the practice of a physician retired to a small town, does to his practice in a great city."[61] And in *Rambler* No. 87 he wrote: "Every man of genius has some arts of fixing attention peculiar to himself, by which, honestly ex-

[55] Bos. Spring 1766 and n.
[57] Bos. (Hill-Powell, I, 26).
[59] Bos. 3 June 1784.
[61] Bos. Spring 1766.

[56] Bos. November 1783.
[58] Bos. 20 Dec. 1784(n).
[60] Bos. 10 April 1778.

erted, he may benefit mankind." Johnson's genius now was to be his talk.

As early as the mid-fifties, Johnson had become something of a public oracle. Dr. Maxwell, whose acquaintance with him began in 1754, wrote: "About 12 o'clock I commonly visited him and frequently found him in bed . . . He generally had a levee of morning visitors, chiefly men of letters, and sometimes learned ladies." And again, "Few persons quitted his company without perceiving themselves wiser and better than before."[62] A William Bowles said, "Dr. Johnson's method of conversation was calculated to excite attention and to amuse or instruct . . . without wearying or confusing his company."[63] Yet all his hearers were not so charmed. A Mrs. Harris of Salisbury said, "his conversation is the same as his writing, but a dreadful voice and manner. He is certainly amusing as a novelty, but . . . is beyond all description awkward, and more beastly in his dress and person . . . He feeds nastily and ferociously, and eats quantities most unthankfully."[64] This sounds like Chesterfield's "respectable Hottentot."

The Literary Club was his arena. The Club dined once a month and supped every Friday at the Turk's Head on Gerrard Street. Among the original members were Sir Joshua Reynolds, Oliver Goldsmith, Edmund Burke, Topham Beauclerk, Bennett Langton, and Sir John Hawkins. Boswell, Bishop Percy, and others came in later.[65] The original number was nine—nine, Sir John Hawkins supposes, because Johnson considered that a *clubable* number. It was soon increased to twelve, later to thirty-five. The talk ranged over all creation. Some members, Johnson once half-objected, talked from books. He did not, nor—said he—did Boswell.[66] That the talk was vigorous is shown by Boswell's once remarking with considerable relish that

[62] Bos. 1770. [63] Bos. September 1783.
[64] Bos. (Hill-Powell, II, App. B). [65] Bos. February 1764 and n.
[66] Tour 3 November(n).

Johnson had the previous evening tossed and gored several persons;[67] and he recorded in detail quarrels between Johnson and Dr. Percy, Johnson and Beauclerk, Johnson and Goldsmith. Johnson was the autocrat, a monarch in a body that, Goldsmith objected, should be a republic;[68] one who, after an all-night session, could sit, his face glowing with meridian splendor.

The Club, of course, was a masculine group. Mrs. Thrale provided the stage for Johnson in a more social, if not more sociable, world. Hester Lynch Salusbury Thrale, wife of the wealthy brewer Henry Thrale, gave Johnson after the death of Mrs. Johnson such endearing elegance of female companionship as he had never enjoyed in his own home. She and her husband provided apartments for him in their residences at Southwark and Streatham. They took him with them on their travels to Brighton, Bath, Wales, France. When Johnson was ill, Mrs. Thrale comforted him; when he was sunk in melancholy, she supported him. If she was flattered by the great man's affection, he was no less pleased with the consideration which he enjoyed as part of the Thrale household. Certainly he found there a peace quite impossible amidst the strange crew of indigents that he sheltered in his home, his Seraglio Boswell called them.[69]

Mrs. Thrale was a quick, intelligent, nearly learned woman —a "light-blue stocking," A. Edward Newton called her. Her dinners were splendid; her drawing room, with Johnson perhaps as the magnet, was a salon frequented by many of the Johnson circle, by the Burneys, Hannah More, Mrs. Knowles, Arthur Murphy, and others known in their day for their wit and learning, in our day for their association with Johnson. For us the importance of this association with the Thrales is not so much that it gave companionship and domestic comfort to the lonely Johnson as that so many who met Johnson there recorded his talk and left such full memorials of him. Of these Mrs. Thrale

[67] Bos. Summer 1768.　　[68] Bos. 7 May 1773.　　[69] Bos. 21 Nov. 1778.

(later Mrs. Piozzi), Fanny Burney (later Mme. D'Arblay), and Hannah More are perhaps, outside of Boswell, the most often quoted. In sheer bulk they exceed Boswell—but it is doubtful whether any one else devoted himself so completely to recording Johnson. One evening at the Thrales' Johnson spoke of resolution as being a requisite for excellence in conversation. "Now, I want it. I throw up the game upon losing a trick." Said Boswell, "I don't know, Sir, how this may be; but I am sure you beat other people's cards out of their hands." As Johnson continued to talk, Boswell, fixed in admiration, said to Mrs. Thrale, "O, for short-hand to take this down!" "You'll carry it all in your head," said she; "a long head is as good as short-hand."[70]

About two months after meeting Johnson, Boswell had spoken to him about a trip to the Highlands and the Hebrides —a trip which impressed Voltaire as foolhardy as an attempt to reach the North Pole.[71] In August 1773 Johnson met Boswell in Edinburgh, and the two started out on the long-projected tour. For Johnson it was a remarkable feat. He was sixty-four, essentially a city man. After leaving Inverness, the two traveled on horseback. The ways were rough, the accommodations at times crude by any standards. The weather was foul; sometimes they were actually in danger of their lives. But Johnson saw a different system of life—the old feudal system which was already passing. He talked with Flora Macdonald, for whom he felt such a romantic admiration.[72] He enjoyed respect and hospitality wherever he went. And he saw, first and last, as he told Richard Cumberland, "more gentlemen than shoes." It was late in November when he left Boswell at Blackshiels and took the coach for London. Early in 1775 there appeared his *Journey to the Western Islands of Scotland*, a very interesting work, more Johnson than Scotland. Boswell, indeed,

[70] Bos. 21 March 1783.   [71] Bos. 21 July 1763.
[72] Tour 12 September.

observed that a great part of what was in the book was in his mind before he left London.[73] The book was, on the whole, well received and the sale "was sufficiently quick."[74] But a second edition was not printed until Boswell's *Tour to the Hebrides* appeared in 1785.

Within the next two years Johnson was at work again—this time on what can properly be called his labor of love. In May 1777 he undertook to write for a syndicate of booksellers a number of brief biographical sketches of poets whose works the group was to publish. The price agreed upon was £200. The work thus lightly entered upon extended to four volumes, took four years to complete, and today is regarded as Johnson's most characteristic and best work—"the richest, most beautiful, and indeed the most perfect production of Johnson's pen," is Boswell's probably justified estimate.[75] Johnson himself wrote in a letter to his friend Edmund Hector of Birmingham: "I know not that I have written any thing more generally commended than the *Lives of the Poets*; and have found the world willing enough to caress me, if my health invited me to be in much company."[76]

It was well that Johnson could savor this late triumph. He was soon to be beset with the woes that go with old age—bereavement, estrangement, ill health. He completed the *Lives* in March 1781. In April Henry Thrale died, and Johnson "looked for the last time upon a face that for fifteen years had never been turned on [him] but with respect and benignity."[77] In October 1782 Mrs. Thrale closed Streatham. In January 1783 Johnson was writing of Mrs. Thrale's "diminution of regard" for him.[78] In June 1784, in the face of all opposition, Mrs. Thrale married the Italian musician Piozzi. Johnson's reaction to the news was an unpardonably savage letter—written

[73] Bos. 17 April 1778.
[74] Bos. 25 Feb. 1775.
[75] Bos. 3 May 1777.
[76] Bos. 21 March 1782.
[77] Bos. 4 April 1781.
[78] Letter to Mrs. T., 19 June 1783.

probably on the spur of the moment.[79] Mrs. Thrale, in her answer, begged "the conclusion of a correspondence which I can no longer bear to continue."[80] She then went abroad with her husband.

Meanwhile his old household companions, Dr. Levett and Mrs. Williams, had died. Johnson had known Levett for forty years, had given him an apartment in his house, regarded him highly as a friend and as a physician. Levett died in January 1782,[81] Mrs. Williams in September 1783.[82] She had been a friend of Mrs. Johnson and had taken residence with the Johnsons while awaiting an operation for cataracts. When the failure of the operation left her totally blind, she stayed on as long as she lived. "I have lost a companion," Johnson wrote to Langton, "to whom I have had recourse for domestic amusement for thirty years, and whose variety of knowledge was never exhausted."[83] These deaths and the marriage of Mrs. Thrale left him a lonely, sick old man.

His physical disorders multiplied upon him; he had asthma, gout, intermittent colds. Late in 1783 he was threatened with a painful surgical operation for sarcocele.[84] Gout he could endure with some equanimity. "By representing gout as an antagonist to the palsy, you have . . . made it welcome," he wrote to Dr. Mudge.[85] In mid-June of 1783 he suffered what promised to be the most serious blow of all, a paralytic stroke. "It has pleased God this morning," he wrote to Edmund Allen, "to deprive me of the powers of speech; and as I do not know that it may be his further good pleasure to deprive me soon of my senses, I request you will on the receipt of this note, come to me, and act for me, as the exigencies of my case may require."[86] He made a remarkable recovery. In December he

[79] Letter to Mrs. T., 2 July 1784. [80] Letter to John., 4 July 1784.
[81] Bos. 17 Jan. 1782. [82] Bos. September 1783.
[83] Bos. 1751(n). [84] Bos. September 1783.
[85] Bos. 29 Sept. 1783. [86] Bos. 17 June 1783.

established a club at the Essex Head.[87] In June he went on a visit to Oxford. In the summer he visited Ashbourne; in October he was in Lichfield for the last time; in mid-November he returned to London. On 13 December 1784 he died. He was buried in the south transept of Westminster Abbey near David Garrick, the man with whom, when both were young, he had set out from Lichfield to seek his fortune in London.

Shortly before he died, Reynolds said, "His work is almost done, and well he has done it"—manly praise which the great man would have liked to hear. More striking, perhaps, was the remark of William Gerard Hamilton, known in history as "Single-speech Hamilton": "He has made a chasm, which not only nothing can fill up, but which nothing has a tendency to fill up.—Johnson is dead. Let us go to the next best:—there is nobody;—no man can be said to put you in mind of Johnson."[88]

[87] Bos. December 1783.   [88] Bos. 20 Dec. 1784.

On Conversation and Talk

Every thing he says is as correct as a second edition.
Humphrey, John. Misc.

With Johnson, talk—or conversation, for he made a sharp distinction between the two—was serious business, a hard-won acquirement. In his lighter moments he could speak of the best conversation as being that in which there was "no competition, no vanity";[1] but he really didn't mean it. He could also quote Tom Tyers, who said of him, "You are like a ghost: you never speak till you are spoken to."[2] But when he did speak, he jumped at once into combat: conversation was a battle in which "one or the other will come off superiour."[3] Furthermore, he believed that a man entering the contest must talk "as if impelled by fullness of knowledge or vivacity of imagination."[4] Conversation must inform; something must be discussed; there must be leisure. There was hardly any topic, "if not one of the great truths of Religion and Morality, that he might not have been incited to argue, either for or against."[5] And Johnson himself said, "I dogmatize and am contradicted, and in this conflict of opinions and sentiments I find delight."[6]

He "made it a constant rule to talk as well as he could both as to sentiment and expression, by which means, what had been originally effort became familiar and easy."[7] An interesting

[1] Bos. 14 April 1775.　　　　[2] Bos. 17 April 1778.
[3] Bos. March 1776.　　　　　[4] Bos. 7 April 1778.
[5] Bos. 7 April 1776.　　[6] Hawkins.　　[7] Bos. 1783.

example, not perhaps of ease but of simple statement of a complicated matter, is his statement about infinite number. "Numeration," he said, "is certainly infinite, for eternity might be employed in adding unit to unit; but every number is in itself finite, as the possibility of doubling it easily proves: besides, stop at what point you will, you will find yourself as far from infinitude as ever."[8]

And his talk was conclusive.[9] With surprising frequency he ended a topic with an epigram so clear and comprehensive as to make further discussion unnecessary, or with a figure so bizarre as to end the matter; Goldsmith remarked, "when his pistol misses fire, he knocks you down with the butt end of it."[10] A tiresome young man who wanted to acquire learning came to Johnson for help. It soon became apparent that he was a perambulating vacuum. When Johnson spoke of biology and the division of animals into oviparous and viviparous, the young man asked, "And this cat here, Sir, pray in what class is she?" The great man's patience was at an end. "Sir, you would do well to look for some person capable of explaining such matters to you, and not come to us to know whether or not a cat lays eggs."[11]

Occasionally, of course, he did not get the last word. Goldsmith one day said he could write the fable of the little fishes that saw birds flying overhead and prayed Jupiter to change them into birds. "The skill," he said, "consists in making them talk like little fishes." At this he perceived Johnson shaking with laughter. "Why, Dr. Johnson," he continued, "this is not so easy as you seem to think; for if you were to make little fishes talk, they would talk like whales."[12]

Sometimes the neatly aimed salvo did not demolish the target; then Johnson would wade in with bludgeon and dynamite. Always skeptical, but most skeptical about any person's finding

[8] Pioz. Anec.   [9] Bos. May 1776.   [10] Bos. October 1769.
[11] Pioz. Anec.   [12] Bos. 27 April 1773.

happiness in this life, he was aroused when a friend asserted that his wife's sister was really happy. "If your sister-in-law is really the contented being she professes herself, Sir," answered Johnson, "her life gives the lie to every research of humanity; for she is happy without health, without beauty, without money, and without understanding." Mrs. Thrale expostulated. "I tell you, the woman is ugly, and sickly, and foolish, and poor; and would it not make a man hang himself to hear such a creature say it was happy?"[13] The butt end of the pistol twice applied.

When Boswell and Johnson were on Skye, MacLeod of Ulinish was so struck with Johnson's wide knowledge and his speech that he exclaimed, "It is music to hear this man speak."[14] Baretti wrote in the margin of a letter which Johnson had written to Mrs. Thrale on the death of her husband, "His trade was wisdom."[15] And another friend, William Gerard Hamilton, said, "If you can contrive to have his fair opinion on a subject . . . it is wisdom itself, not only convincing but overpowering."[16]

Most men think indistinctly, and therefore cannot speak with exactness. [Pref. Dict.

It is common for people to talk from books, to retail the sentiments of others and not their own; in short to converse without originality of thinking . . . I do not talk from books. [Tour 4 November

Talking of conversation, he said: "There must, in the first place, be knowledge, there must be materials; in the second place, there must be a command of words; in the third place,

---

[13] Pioz. Anec.
[15] Bos. 15 Sept. 1777(n).
[14] Tour 23 September.
[16] Bos. May 1781.

there must be imagination, to place things in such views as they are not commonly seen in; and in the fourth place, there must be presence of mind, and a resolution that is not to be overcome by failures. This last is an essential requisite; for want of it many people do not excel in conversation." [Bos. 21 March 1783

Wit, you know, is the unexpected copulation of ideas, the discovery of some occult relation between images in appearance remote from each other; an effusion of wit, therefore, presupposes an accumulation of knowledge; a memory stored with notions, which the imagination may cull out to compose new assemblages. [Ram. 194

The foundation . . . must be laid by reading. General principles must be had from books, which, however, must be brought to the test of real life. [Bos. 1775

Asked if, at a friend's house, there had been good conversation, Johnson answered:

No, Sir; we had *talk* enough, but no *conversation*; there was nothing *discussed*. [Bos. 1783

I observed once that Solander was a man of great parts who talked from a full mind. "It may be so," said Mr. Johnson, "but you cannot know yet. The pump works well, to be sure; but how are we to decide in so short an acquaintance whether it is supplied by a spring or a reservoir?" [Pioz. Anec.

. . . depend upon it, Sir, it is when you come close to a man in conversation that you discover what his real abilities are; to make a speech in a publick assembly is a knack. [Bos. March–April 1783

After the exercises which the health of the body requires,

and which have themselves a natural tendency to actuate and
invigorate the mind, the most eligible amusement for a rational
being seems to be that interchange of thoughts which is practised in free and easy conversation; where suspicion is banished
by experience, and emulation by benevolence; where every man
speaks with no other restraint than unwillingness to offend,
and hears with no other disposition than desire to be pleased.
[Ram. 89

When I [Boswell] complained of having dined at a splendid
table without hearing one sentence of conversation worthy of
being remembered, he said, "Sir, there is seldom any such conversation." *Boswell*. "Why then meet at table?" *Johnson*.
"Why to eat and drink together, and to promote kindness;
and, Sir, this is better done when there is no solid conversation; for when there is, people differ in opinion, and get into
bad humour, or some of the company who are not capable of
such conversation, are left out, and feel themselves uneasy. It
was for this reason, Sir Robert Walpole said, he always talked
bawdy at his table, because in that all could join." [Bos. May
1776

Dr. Adams told us, that in some of the Colleges at Oxford,
the fellows had excluded the students from social intercourse
with them in the common room. *Johnson*. "They are in the
right, Sir, for there can be no real conversation amongst them,
no fair exertion of mind amongst them, if the young men are
by; for a man who has a character does not choose to stake it
in their presence." *Boswell*. "But, Sir, may there not be very
good conversation without a contest for superiority?" *Johnson*.
"No animated conversation, Sir, for it cannot be but one or
other will come off superiour. I do not mean that the victor
must have the better of the argument, for he may take the
weak side; but his superiority of parts and knowledge will nec-

essarily appear: and he to whom he thus shews himself superiour is lessened in the eyes of the young men." [Bos. 20
March 1776

My dear friend, clear your *mind* of cant. You may *talk* as
other people do: you may say to a man, "Sir, I am your most
humble servant." You are *not* his most humble servant. You
may say, "These are sad times; it is a melancholy thing to be
reserved to such times." You don't mind the times. You tell a
man, "I am sorry you had such bad weather the last day of
your journey, and were so much wet." You don't care six-pence
whether he was wet or dry. You may *talk* in this manner; it is
a mode of talking in Society: but don't *think* foolishly. [Bos.
15 May 1783

"Dear Doctor," said he one day to a common acquaintance,
who lamented the tender state of his *inside*, "do not be like
the spider, man; and spin conversation thus incessantly out of
thy own bowels." [Pioz. Anec.

Concerning the conversational powers of a gentleman:

He talked to me at club one day . . . concerning Catiline's
conspiracy—so I withdrew my attention, and thought about
Tom Thumb. [Pioz. Anec.

*Asked what he thought of a Mr. Macklin's conversation, John-
son replied:*

I think, Sir, it is a constant renovation of hope, and an un-
varied succession of disappointment. [Steevens, John. Misc.

That is the happiest conversation where there is no competition, no vanity, but a calm, quiet interchange of sentiments.
[Bos. 14 April 1775

To be contradicted, in order to force you to talk, is mighty unpleasing. You *shine*, indeed; but it is by being *ground*. [Bos. 24 April 1779

Sir, there is nothing by which a man exasperates most people more, than by displaying a superiour ability or brilliance in conversation. They seem pleased at the time; but their envy makes them curse him at their hearts. [Bos. March–April 1783

The most active imagination will be sometimes torpid under the frigid influence of melancholy, and sometimes occasions will be wanting to tempt the mind, however volatile, to sallies and excursions. Nothing was ever said with uncommon felicity, but by the co-operation of chance; and, therefore, wit as well as valour must be content to share its honours with fortune. [Idl. 58

For my own part, I think it is more disgraceful never to try to speak, than to try it and fail; as it is more disgraceful not to fight, than to fight and be beaten. [Bos. 5 April 1775

Goldsmith . . . was not a social man. He never exchanged mind with you. [Bos. 11 April 1776

There are men whose powers operate only at leisure and in retirement, and whose intellectual vigour deserts them in conversation. [L.P., Dryden

Of a man who sat silent the whole evening in the midst of a brilliant society:

"Sir," said he, "the conversation overflowed, and drowned him." [Bos. 1770

Of a pretty woman:

She says nothing . . . a talking blackamoor were better than a white creature who adds nothing to life, and by sitting down before one thus desperately silent, takes away the confidence one should have in the company of her chair if she were once out of it. [Pioz. Anec.

If (said he) I had no duties, and no reference to futurity, I would spend my life in driving briskly in a post-chaise with a pretty woman; but she should be one who could understand me, and would add something to the conversation. [Bos. 19 Sept. 1777

Of a man who had spent a life in business, had acquired a fortune, was now invited to parties, and "had no conversation":

Man commonly cannot be successful in different ways. This gentleman has spent, in getting four thousand pounds a year, the time in which he might have learnt to talk; and now he cannot talk. [Bos. 1 April 1781

. . . such is the laxity of Highland conversation that the inquirer is kept in continual suspense, and by a kind of intellectual retrogradation knows less as he hears more. [Journey, Skye

. . . conscious dullness has little right to be prolix. [Idl. 1

Taylor was an instance how far impudence could carry ignorance. [Bos. 24 April 1779

Questioning is not the mode of conversation among gentlemen. [Bos. 25 March 1776

He that never thinks, never can be wise. Perpetual levity must end in ignorance; and intemperance, though it may fire the spirits for an hour, will make life short or miserable. [Ras. 17

. . . gaiety must be recommended by higher qualities . . . mirth can never please long but as the efflorescence of a mind loved for its luxuriance, but esteemed for its usefulness. [Ram. 141

At night [Tom] has a new feast for his intellects; he always runs to a disputing society, or a speaking club, where he half hears what, if he had heard the whole, he would but half understand; goes home pleased with the consciousness of a day well spent, lies down full of ideas, and rises in the morning empty as before. [Idl. 48

To Boswell, who remarked that it would be terrible if Johnson could not get quickly back from Harwich to London:

Don't, Sir, accustom yourself to use big words for little matters. It would *not* be *terrible,* though I *were* to be detained some time here. [Bos. 6 Aug. 1763

Speaking of Goldsmith:

He was not an agreeable companion, for he talked always for fame. A man who does so never can be pleasing. The man who talks to unburthen his mind is the man to delight you. An eminent friend of ours is not so agreeable as the variety of his knowledge would otherwise make him, because he talks partly from ostentation. [Bos. 7 April 1778

Of an eminent author:

He is not a pleasant man. His conversation is neither instructive nor brilliant. He does not talk as if impelled by any fullness of knowledge or vivacity of imagination . . . He talks with no wish either to inform or to hear, but only because he thinks it does not become [him] to sit in a company and say nothing. [Bos. 8 May 1778

Some people . . . tell you that they let themselves down to
the capacity of their hearers. I never do that. I speak uniformly,
in as intelligible manner as I can. [Bos. 27 March 1775

[People] consider it as a compliment to be talked to as if
they are wiser than they are. So true is this, Sir, that Baxter
made it a rule in every sermon that he preached, to say something that was above the capacity of his audience. [Bos. March
1783

Thus wit, too copiously poured out, agitates the hearer with
emotions rather violent than pleasing; every one shrinks from
the force of its oppression, the company sits intranced and
overpowered; all are astonished, but nobody is pleased. [Idl. 34

On his friend Beauclerk's wit:
. . . every thing comes from him so easily. It appears to me
that I labour, when I say a good thing. [Tour 21 August

*To Mrs. Thrale, who remarked that a certain woman would
grieve at the disappointment of a friend's losing an estate which
she had long expected to receive:*
"She will suffer as much, perhaps," said he, "as your horse
did when your cow miscarried." [Pioz. Anec.

I [Mrs. Thrale] professed myself sincerely grieved when accumulated distresses crushed Sir George Colebrook's family;
and I was so. "Your own prosperity," said he, "may possibly
have so far increased the natural tenderness of your heart, that
for aught I know you *may* be a *little sorry*; but it is sufficient
for a plain man if he does not laugh when he sees a fine new
house tumble down all on a sudden, and a snug cottage stand
by ready to receive the owner, whose birth entitled him to do

nothing better, and whose limbs are left him to go to work again with." [Pioz. Anec.

Dr. Burney having remarked that Mr. Garrick was beginning to look old, he said, "Why, Sir, you are not to wonder at that; no man's face has had more wear and tear." [Bos. 18 Dec. 1775

On another occasion, when he was musing over the fire in our drawing-room at Streatham, a young gentleman called to him suddenly, and I suppose he thought disrespectfully, in these words: Mr. Johnson, Would you advise me to marry? "I would advise no man to marry, Sir (returns for answer in a very angry tone Dr. Johnson), who is not likely to propagate understanding." [Pioz. Anec.

[Primogeniture] makes but one fool in the family. [Lucas, p. 94

To a tiresome young man of untimely levity:

What provokes your risibility, Sir? Have I said anything that you understand? Then I ask pardon of the rest of the company. [Cumberland, Johnsoniana

To Boswell, who was asking too many questions about him:

Sir, you have but two topicks, yourself and me. I am sick of both. [Bos. May 1776

Johnson . . . argued for some time with a pertinacious gentleman; his opponent, who had talked in a very puzzling manner, happened to say, "I don't understand you, Sir": upon which Johnson observed, "Sir, I have found you an argument; but I am not obliged to find you an understanding." [Bos. June 1784

Dr. Johnson being asked by a lady why he so constantly gave money to beggars, replied with great feeling, "Madam, to enable them to beg on." [Cooke, John. Misc.

Dr. Johnson was observed by a musical friend of his to be extremely inattentive at a concert, whilst a celebrated solo player was running up the divisions and subdivisions of notes on his violin. His friend, to induce him to take notice, told him how extremely difficult it was. "Difficult do you call it, Sir?" replied the Doctor: "I wish it were impossible." [Seward, Johnsoniana

To Boswell, who said that music affected him with such dejection that he was ready to weep or with such resolution that he was inclined to rush into battle:

I would never hear it, if it made me such a fool. [Bos. 23 Sept. 1777

To a company which very much admired the line "Who rules o'er freemen should himself be free," Johnson answered:

I cannot agree . . . It might as well be said, "Who drives fat oxen should himself be fat." [Bos. June 1784

Asked why he did not answer newspaper abuse:

. . . the eagle will not catch flies. [Pioz. Anec.

Asked why he had wrongly defined pastern as the knee of a horse, Johnson said:

Ignorance, Madam, pure ignorance. [Bos. August 1755

Mrs. Digby told me that when she lived in London with her sister Mrs. Brooke, they were every now and then honoured by the visits of Dr. Johnson. He called on them one day soon after the publication of his immortal dictionary. The two ladies paid him due compliments on the occasion. Amongst other topics of praise they very much commended the omission of all *naughty* words. "What, my dears! then you have been looking for them?" said the moralist. [Best, John. Misc.

Dr. Adams once insisted that Chesterfield was affable and easy of access to literary men:

"Sir (said Johnson), that is not Lord Chesterfield; he is the proudest man this day existing." "No (said Dr. Adams), there is one person, at least, as proud; I think, by your own account, you are the prouder man of the two." "But mine (replied Johnson, instantly) was *defensive* pride." [Bos. 1754

A gentleman [probably Boswell] having to some of the usual arguments for drinking added this: "You know, Sir, drinking drives away care, and makes us forget whatever is disagreeable. Would not you allow a man to drink for that reason?" *Johnson.* "Yes, Sir, if he sat next to *you.*" [Bos. April 1772

Johnson attacked the Americans with intemperate vehemence of abuse. I said something in their favour; and added, that I was always sorry when he talked on that subject. This, it seems, exasperated him; though he said nothing at the time. The cloud was charged with sulphureous vapour, which was afterwards to burst in thunder. We talked of a gentleman who was running out his fortune in London; and I said, "We must get him out of it. All his friends must quarrel with him, and that will soon drive him away." *Johnson.* "Nay, Sir, we'll send *you* to him. If your company does not drive a man out of his house, nothing will." This was a horrible shock, for which there was no visible cause. I afterwards asked him why he had said so harsh a thing. *Johnson.* "Because, Sir, you made me angry about the Americans." *Boswell.* "But why did you not take your revenge directly?" *Johnson* (smiling). "Because, Sir, I had nothing ready. A man cannot strike till he has his weapons." This was a candid and pleasant confession. [Bos. 18 April 1778

It was said that Foote had been horsewhipped by a Dublin apothecary for mimicking him on the stage. Garrick remarked:

"Nobody ever thought it *worth his while* to quarrel with him in London." "I am glad," said Johnson, "to find that the *man is rising in the world*." [Murphy

One evening Boswell said he thought it hard that six students, Methodists, were expelled from Oxford for publicly praying and exhorting. Answered Johnson:

Sir, that expulsion was extremely just and proper. What have they to do at an university who are not willing to be taught, but will presume to teach? . . . I believe they might be good beings; but they were not fit to be at the University of Oxford. A cow is a very good animal in the field; but we turn her out of a garden. [Bos. 15 April 1772

Asked by a Scotsman what he thought of his country:

"That is a very vile country, to be sure, Sir" (returned Dr. Johnson). "Well, sir," replies the other, somewhat mortified, "God made it." "Certainly he did" (answers Mr. Johnson again); "but we must always remember that he made it for Scotchmen, and comparisons are odious, Mr. S——; but God made hell." [Pioz. Anec.

A Mrs. Bruce said one evening:

"Dr. Johnson, you tell us in your Dictionary that in England oats are given to horses; but that in Scotland they support the people. Now, Sir, I can assure you, that in Scotland we give oats to our horses, as well as you do to yours in England . . ." "I am very glad, Madam, to find that you treat your horses as well as you treat yourselves." [Stockdale, John. Misc.

A young gentleman at dinner one evening resolved to bait the bear:

"Now Dr. Johnson, do not look so glum, but be a little gay and lively, like others: what would you give, old gentleman, to be as young and sprightly as I am?" "Why, Sir," said he, "I think I would almost be content to be as foolish." [Cradock, John. Misc.

One of Dr. Johnson's rudest speeches was to a pompous gentleman coming out of Lichfield Cathedral, who said, "Dr. Johnson, we have had a most excellent discourse today." "That may be," said Johnson; "but, it is impossible that you should know it." [Cradock, John. Misc.

Dr. Johnson called one morning on Mr. West (the painter) to converse with him on American affairs. After some time Mr. West said that he had a young American (Gilbert Stuart) living with him, from whom he might derive some information, and introduced Stuart. The conversation continued (Stuart being thus invited to take a part in it), when the Doctor observed to Mr. West that the young man spoke very good English; and turning to Stuart rudely asked him where he had learned it. Stuart very promptly replied, "Sir, I can better tell you where I did not learn it—it was not from your dictionary." Johnson seemed aware of his own abruptness, and was not offended. [Stuart, John. Misc.

A Mr. Grattan, writing vehemently in the newspaper about freedom for Ireland, stated:

"We will persevere till there is not one link of the English chain to clank upon the rags of the meanest beggar in Ireland." "Nay, Sir (said Johnson), don't you perceive that one link cannot clank?" [Bos. June 1784

To a Thames boatman who, as was the custom of the day on the river, attacked him with some coarse raillery:

Sir, your wife, *under pretense of keeping a bawdy house,* is a receiver of stolen goods. [Bos. 1780 (end)

A man remarked one evening that the king's congé d'élire, his preference in the election of a bishop, was only a strong recommendation:

Sir (replied Johnson, who overheard him), it is such a recommendation, as if I should throw you out a two-pair-of-stairs window, and recommend to you to fall soft. [Bos. June 1784

Andrew Millar, the publisher of the Dictionary, finally succeeded in extracting the last part of the book from Johnson:

When the messenger who carried the last sheet to Millar returned, Johnson asked him, "Well, what did he say?" "Sir (answered the messenger), he said, thank GOD I have done with him." "I am glad (replied Johnson, with a smile), that he thanks GOD for any thing." [Bos. April 1755

It is appropriate to end this section, and to introduce the others, with Boswell's tribute to the power of Johnson's own talk:

He had a loud voice, and a slow deliberate utterance which no doubt gave some additional weight to the sterling metal of his conversation. Lord Pembroke said once to me at Wilton, with a happy pleasantry and some truth, that "Dr. Johnson's sayings would not appear so extraordinary, were it not for his *bow-wow way*": but I admit the truth of this only on some occasions. The *Messiah,* played upon the *Canterbury organ,* is more sublime than when played upon an inferior instrument; but very slight musick will seem grand, when conveyed to the ear through that majestick medium. *While therefore Dr. John-*

son's sayings are read, let his manner be taken along with them. Let it however be observed, that the sayings themselves are generally great; that, though he might be an ordinary composer at times, he was for the most part a Handel. [Tour (beg.)

On Reading and Writing

*What is written without effort is in general read
without pleasure.*

Seward, John. Misc.

In a paper read to the Johnson Society in Lichfield in 1960,
Sir William Haley, editor of The Times, said that Johnson was
essentially a journalist, that he wrote under the rowelings of
necessity, that he wrote about anything and everything, that
he gave little time to correcting or amending his copy, and
that, once he was done with it, he was done. One can well
believe that Johnson was unconsciously writing of himself when
he said of Dryden: "He wrote, as he tells us, with little consideration. When necessity or occasion called upon him, he
poured out what the present moment happened to supply, and
once it had passed to press, ejected it from his mind. For when
he had no pecuniary interest, he had no further solicitude."[1]

In going to London to seek a living, he took up writing as
a trade, just as he had taken up schoolmastering as a trade; and
in a short while he could work with a craftsman's speed. He
says himself that in an hour he could write three columns
(1350 words) of the "Parliamentary Debates" for The Gentleman's Magazine.[2] He wrote forty-eight pages of the Life of
Savage in a single sitting;[3] he wrote Rasselas in the evenings of
a single week.[4] Each Rambler was written "just as they were

[1] L.P., Dryden.
[2] Lucas.
[3] Bos. Spring 1744.
[4] Bos. April 1759.

wanted for the press," and he would send a portion as it was done and write "the remainder while the former part of it was printing."[5] He was always ready to turn out what was needed —an essay, an epitaph, a literary review, a dedication, a sermon, even a dictionary. Writing was his trade; and when he had reached the comparative affluence of his pension, he retired. He would talk, but he would not write—except once. The Lives of the Poets, which he began as a literary chore, he did as a labor of love. A syndicate of forty booksellers wanted to put out an elegant and uniform edition of the English poets; and "to stamp the reputation of this edition superior to anything that had gone before," they asked Johnson to write a concise account of the life of each author. He specified a price of two hundred guineas and went to work "with a mind full of matter." He started the project in 1777. In 1779 it was half done; not until 1781 was it completed. In the end, far from being a series of concise accounts, the whole—printed separately— comprised fifty-two considerable essays and over nineteen hundred pages in four volumes.

One also gets the idea that reading for Johnson was not much more pleasurable than writing. Physically, of course, it was difficult. He had no vision in one eye and no more than defective vision in the other. He could say that "the progress which the understanding makes through a book has more pain than pleasure in it."[6] Yet Adam Smith, "than whom," Boswell says, "few were better judges on the subject," used to declare that Johnson knew more books than any man alive. He read, as he did most things, violently. "He had a peculiar facility in seizing at once what was valuable in any book, without submitting to the labour of perusing it from beginning to end."[7] Furthermore, he did his reading in a most desultory way. But Mrs. Knowles said, "He knows how to read better than anyone

[5] Bos. April 1776.   [6] Bos. May 1783.
[7] Bos. 1729.

... he gets at the substance of a book directly; he tears out the heart of it."[8]

The important thing, however, is not that he read but that he remembered. And it is equally important that—to quote his own words—he learned "by commerce with mankind to reduce his speculations to practice, and accommodate his knowledge to the purposes of life."[9] His reading was always relevant.

We must read what the world reads at the moment. [Bos. 29 April 1778

... if a man begins to read in the middle of a book, and feels an inclination to go on, let him not quit it, to go to the beginning. He may, perhaps, not feel again the inclination. [Bos. April 1776

A Mr. Croft advised a pupil to read to the end whatever books he should begin:

This is surely a strange advice; you may as well resolve that whatever men you happen to get acquainted with, you are to keep them for life. A book may be good for nothing; or there may be only one thing in it worth knowing; are we to read it all through? [Bos. 15 June 1784

Books, says Bacon, can never teach the use of books. [Ram. 137

Alas . . . how few books are there of which one ever can arrive at the *last* page! Was there ever yet any thing written by mere man that was wished longer by its readers, excepting Don Quixote, Robinson Crusoe, and the Pilgrim's Progress? [Pioz. Anec.

[8] Bos. April 1778.　　　　[9] Ram. 137.

What is read with delight is commonly retained, because pleasure always secures attention; but the books which are consulted by occasional necessity, and perused with impatience, seldom leave any traces on the mind. [Idl. 74

[Works of fiction] are written chiefly to the young, the ignorant, and the idle, to whom they serve as lectures of conduct and introductions into life. They are the entertainment of minds unfurnished with ideas, and therefore easily susceptible of impression; not fixed by principles, and therefore easily following the current of fancy; not informed by experience, and consequently open to every false suggestion and partial account. [Ram. 4

Mr. Elphinston talked of a new book that was much admired, and asked Dr. Johnson if he had read it. *Johnson.* "I have looked into it." "What (said Elphinston), have you not read it through?" "No, Sir; do *you* read books *through?*" [Bos. 19 April 1773

Books are faithful repositories, which may be awhile neglected or forgotten; but when they are opened again, will again impart their instruction: memory, once interrupted, is not to be recalled. Written learning is a fixed luminary which, after the cloud that had hidden it has passed away, is again bright in its proper station. Tradition is but a meteor which, if once it falls, cannot be rekindled. [Journey, Ostig

Dictionaries are like watches: the worst is better than none, and the best cannot be expected to go quite true. [Pioz. Anec.

Obscurity and clearness are relative terms: to some readers scarce any book is easy, to others not many are difficult. [Adv. 58

[Many books are] produced, where just and noble sentiments are degraded and obscured.

Words, therefore, as well as things, claim the care of an
author . . . every man . . . has often found himself deficient in
the power of expression, big with ideas which he could not
utter, obliged to ransack his memory for terms adequate to his
conceptions, and at last unable to impress upon his reader the
image existing in his own mind. [Adv. 138

I am not yet so lost in lexicography as to forget that 'words
are the daughters of earth, and that things are the sons of
heaven.' [Pref. Dict.

Originally there were not [synonyms in the language]; but
by using words negligently, or in poetry, one word comes to be
confounded with another. [Bos. 18 April 1783

. . . a mean or common thought, expressed in pompous
diction, generally pleases more than a new or noble sentiment
delivered in a low or vulgar language . . . Words become low
by the occasions to which they are applied, or the general
character of them who use them. [Ram. 168

There may possibly be books without a polished language,
but there can be no polished language without books. [Journey,
Ostig

A man may write at any time if he will set himself doggedly
to it. [Tour 16 August

The importance of writing letters with propriety justly claims
to be considered with care, since, next to the power of pleasing
with his presence, every man would wish to be able to give
delight at a distance. This great art should be diligently taught,

the rather because of these letters which are most useful, and by which the general business of life is transacted, there are no examples easily to be found. [Pref. Preceptor

The following paragraph, from the life of Edmund Smith, Hesketh Pearson calls "the best single passage in British biography":

Having formed his plan, and collected materials, [Smith] declared that a few months would complete his design [a tragedy on Lady Jane Grey]; and, that he might pursue his work with less frequent avocations, he was, in June 1710, invited by Mr. George Ducket to his house at Gartham, in Wiltshire. Here he found such opportunities for indulgence as did not much forward his studies, and particularly some strong ale too delicious to be resisted. He eat and drank till he found himself plethorick; and then, resolving to ease himself by evacuation, he wrote to an apothecary in the neighbourhood a prescription of a purge so forcible, that the apothecary thought it his duty to delay it till he had given notice of its danger. Smith, not pleased with the contradiction of a shopman, and boastful of his own knowledge, treated the notice with rude contempt, and swallowed his own medicine, which, in July 1710, brought him to the grave. He was buried in Gartham. [L.P., Smith

The art of the writer . . . is attained by slow degrees. [Idl. 25

Read over your compositions, and where ever you meet with a passage which you think is particularly fine, strike it out. [Bos. 30 April 1773

Composition is, for the most part, an effort of slow diligence and steady perseverance, to which the mind is dragged by necessity or resolution, and from which the attention is every moment starting to more delightful amusements. [Adv. 138

To fix the thoughts by writing, and subject them to frequent examinations and reviews, is the best method of enabling the mind to detect its own sophisms, and keep it on guard against the fallacies which it practises on others: in conversation we naturally diffuse our thoughts, and in writing we contract them; method is the excellence of writing, and unconstraint the grace of conversation.

To read, write, and converse in due proportions, is, therefore, the business of a man of letters. [Adv. 85

Dr. William Dodd, before he was hanged for forgery, published "The Convict's Address." Seward expressed doubt that it was Dodd's own work because it had a great deal more force of mind than anything known to be his:

Depend upon it, Sir, when a man knows he is to be hanged in a fortnight, it concentrates his mind wonderfully. [Bos. 19 Sept. 1777

To a person praising Johnson's impartiality in his reports of the debates:

That is not quite true. I saved appearances tolerably well, but I took care that the Whig dogs should not have the best of it. [Murphy

He that merely makes a book from books may be useful, but can scarcely be great. [L.P., Butler

In all pointed sentences some degree of accuracy must be sacrificed to conciseness. [Brav. Engl. Soldier

In writing, as in life, faults are endured without disgust when they are associated with transcendent merit. [Ram. 158

Precept has generally been posterior to performance. The art of composing works of genius has never been taught but by the example of those who performed it by natural vigour of imagination and rectitude of judgement. [Ram. 152

No man practises so well as he writes. I have, all my life long, been lying till noon; yet I tell young men, and tell them with great sincerity, that nobody who does not rise early will ever do any good. [Tour 14 September

Whoever wishes to attain an English style, familiar but not coarse, and elegant but not ostentatious, must give his days and nights to the volumes of Addison. [L.P., Addison

Depend upon it; no author was ever written down but by himself. [Hawkins

Scarcely anything awakens attention like a tale of cruelty. The writer of news never fails in the intermission of action to tell how the enemies murdered children and ravished virgins; and, if the scene of action be somewhat distant, scalps half the inhabitants of a province. [Idl. 30

A story (says Johnson) should be a specimen of life and manners; but if the surrounding circumstances are false, as it is no more a representation of reality, it is no longer worthy our attention. [Pioz. Anec.

[Biography] should tell us [a man's] studies, his mode of living, the means by which he attained to excellence, and his opinion of his own works. [Tour 22 September

. . . nobody can write the life of a man but those who have eat and drunk and lived in social intercourse with him. [Bos. 31 March 1772

[Defer] publication, if not for nine years, according to the direction of Horace, yet till [the] fancy was cooled after the raptures of invention and the glare of novelty had ceased to dazzle the judgement. [Ram. 169

Truth like beauty varies its fashions, and is best recommended by different dresses to different minds; and he that recalls the attention of mankind to any part of learning which time has left behind it, may be truly said to advance the literature of his own age. [Idl. 85

Imagination is nothing without knowledge. [L.P., Butler

Sublimity is produced by aggregation, and littleness by dispersion. Great thoughts are always general and consist in positions not limited by exceptions, and in descriptions not descending to minuteness . . . Those writers who lay on the watch for novelty could have little hope of greatness; for great things cannot have escaped former observation. Their attempts were always analytick; they broke every image into fragments; and could no more represent, by their slender conceits and laboured particularities, the prospect of nature or the scenes of life than he, who dissects a sunbeam with a prism, can exhibit the wide effulgence of a summer noon. [L.P., Cowley

One of the amusements of idleness is reading without the fatigue of close attention, and the world therefore swarms with writers whose wish is not to be studied, but to be read. [Idl. 30

Grubstreet: The name of a street near Moorfields, London, much inhabited by writers of small histories, dictionaries, and temporary poems; whence any mean production is called grubstreet. [Dict.

No man but a blockhead ever wrote, except for money. [Bos. 5 April 1776

Dull: Not exhilarating, not delightful; as, *to make diction-aries is* DULL *work.* [Dict.

I look upon this [his edition of Shakespeare] as I did upon the dictionary; it is all work, and my inducement to it is not love or desire of fame but the want of money, which is the only motive of writing that I know of. [Hawkins

Lexicographer: A writer of dictionaries; a harmless drudge . . . [Dict.

Poetaster: A vile petty poet.
Poetess: A she poet. [Dict.

Genius is shewn only by invention. [Idl. 40

I allow you may have pleasure from writing, after it is over, if you have written well; but you don't go willingly to it again. [Bos. 1 May 1783

The promises of authors are like the vows of lovers. [L.P., Addison

I know not whether more is to be dreaded from streets filled with soldiers accustomed to plunder, or from garrets filled with scribblers accustomed to lie. [Idl. 30

But though it should happen that the writer finds no . . . faults in his performance, he is still to remember, that he looks upon it with partial eyes: and . . . he will be afraid of deciding too hastily in his own favour, or of allowing himself to contemplate with too much complacence treasure that has not yet been brought to the test, nor passed the only trial that can stamp its value. [Adv. 138

Nothing is more disgusting than a narrative spangled with conceits. [L.P., Cowley

The only end of writing is to enable the readers better to enjoy life, or better to endure it. [Review, A *Free Inquiry*

Books without the knowledge of life are useless . . . for what should books teach but the art of *living?* [Pioz. Anec.

Of an Irish painter whom he knew in Birmingham:

This man . . . was a very sensible man . . . a man of a great deal of knowledge of the world, fresh from life, not strained through books. [Bos. 1737

Some seem always to read with the microscope of criticism. [Ram. 176

Criticism is a study by which men grow important and formidable at very small expence . . . No genius was ever blasted by the breath of criticks. [Idl. 60

Attack is the re-action. I never think I have hit hard, unless it rebounds. [Bos. 2 April 1775

I would rather be attacked than unnoticed. For the worst thing you can do to an authour is to be silent as to his works. [Bos. 26 March 1779

Abuse is often of service: there is nothing so dangerous to an author as silence; his name, like a shuttlecock, must be beat backward and forward, or it falls to the ground. [Murphy

. . . criticism is a goddess easy of access and forward of advance, who will meet the slow, and encourage the timorous; the want of meaning she supplies with words, and the want of spirit she recompenses with malignity. [Idl. 60

Few characters can bear the microscopick scrutiny of wit quickened by anger; and perhaps the best advice to authors would be that they should keep out of the way of one another. [L.P., Rowe

I hope, however, the criticks will let me be at peace; for though I do not much fear their skill and strength, I am a little afraid of myself, and would not willingly feel so much ill-will in my bosom as literary quarrels are apt to excite.   [Letter to Thos. Warton, Bos. 1 Feb. 1755

Therefore the man who is asked by an authour, what he thinks of his work, is put to the torture, and is not obliged to speak the truth; so that what he says is not to be considered as his opinion; yet he has said it, and cannot retract it; and this authour, when mankind are hunting him with a cannister at his tail, can say, "I would not have published, had not Johnson, or Reynolds, or Musgrave, or some other good judge commended the work." Yet I consider it as a very difficult question in conscience, whether one should advise a man not to publish a work, if profit be his object . . . you have only your own opinion, and the publick may think very differently. [Bos. 23 April 1778

Of Edwards' criticism of Warburton:

Nay, [Edwards] has given him some smart hits to be sure; but there is no proportion between the two men. . . . A fly, Sir, may sting a stately horse and make him wince; but one is but an insect, and the other is a horse still. [Bos. 1754(n)

Goldsmith seemed jealous of the success of Beattie's "Essay on Truth":

"Here's such a stir (said he) about a fellow that has written one book, and I have written many." Ah, Doctor (says his friend), there go two-and-forty sixpences you know to one guinea. [Pioz. Anec.

Authors and lovers always suffer some infatuation, from which only absence can set them free. [Ram. 169

A publick performer is so much in the power of the spectators, that all unnecessary severity is restrained by that general law of humanity which forbids us to be cruel where there is nothing to be feared.

In every new performer something must be pardoned. [Idl. 25

[Actors are] studious to please yet afraid to fail. [Prol. Opening Drury Lane

What is good only because it pleases cannot be pronounced good till it has been found to please. [L.P., Dryden

> The stage but echoes back the public voice;
> The drama's laws the drama's patrons give,
> For we that live to please must please to live.
> [Prol. Opening Drury Lane

From the publick, and only from the publick, is [the writer] to await a confirmation of his claim, and a final justification of self-esteem; but the publick is not easily persuaded to favour an author. [Adv. 138

After the failure of his play Irene:

A man (said he) who writes a book, thinks himself wiser or wittier than the rest of mankind; he supposes that he can instruct or amuse them, and the publick to whom he appeals, must, after all, be the judges of his pretensions. [Bos. Feb. 1749

Sir, in my early years I read very hard. It is a sad reflection, but a true one, that I knew almost as much at eighteen as I do now. [Bos. 21 July 1763

No man reads long together with a folio on his table. Books . . . that you may carry to the fire, and hold readily in your hand are the most useful, after all. . . . Such books form the mass of general and easy reading. [Hawkins, Johnsoniana

. . . *a corrupt society has many laws;* I know not whether it is not equally true, that *an ignorant age has many books.* When the treasures of ancient knowledge lie unexamined, and original authors are neglected and forgotten, compilers and plagiaries are encouraged, who give us again what we had before, and grow great by setting before us what our own sloth had hidden from our view. [Idl. 85

The business of a poet . . . is to examine, not the individual, but the species; to remark general properties and large appearances: he does not number the streaks of the tulip, or describe the different shades of the verdure of the forest. He is to exhibit in his portraits of nature such prominent and striking features as recall the original to every mind; and must neglect the minuter discriminations, which one may have remarked, and another have neglected, for those characteristics which are alike obvious to vigilance and carelessness. [Ras. 10

No poem should be long of which the purpose is only to strike the fancy, without enlightening the understanding by precept, ratiocination, or narrative. A blaze first pleases, then tires the sight. [L.P., Fenton

Asked the definition of poetry:

Why, Sir, it is much easier to say what it is not. We all *know* what light is; but it is not easy to *tell* what it is. [Bos. 12 April 1776

Asked his opinion about Dido and its author:

Sir, I never did the man an injury; yet he would read his tragedy to me. [Nichols, John. Misc.

Of the histories of Highland peoples:

We soon found what memorials were to be expected from an illiterate people, whose whole time is a series of distress; where every morning is labouring with expedients for the evening; and where all mental pains or pleasure arose from the dread of winter, the expectation of spring, the caprices of their chiefs, and the motions of the neighbouring clans; where there was neither shame from ignorance, nor pride in knowledge; neither curiosity to inquire, nor vanity to communicate. [Journey, Ostig

"It is a shame [Boswell remarked] that authors are not now better patronized." "No, sir [was Johnson's answer]. If learning cannot support a man, if he must sit with his hands across till somebody feeds him, it is as to him a bad thing, and it is better as it is. With patronage, what flattery! what falsehood! . . . in patronage, he must say what pleases his patron, and it is an equal chance whether that be truth or falsehood." [Tour 19 August

Johnson's famous letter to the Earl of Chesterfield, dated 7 Feb. 1755:

My Lord:

I have been lately informed by the proprietor of the World, that two papers in which my Dictionary is recommended to

the publick, were written by your Lordship. To be
tinguished, is an honour which, being very little accu
to favours from the great, I know not well how to rece
in what terms to acknowledge.

When, upon some slight encouragement, I first visited your
Lordship, I was overpowered, like the rest of mankind, by the
enchantment of your address; and could not forbear to wish
that I might boast myself *Le vainqueur du vainqueur de la
terre;*—that I might obtain that regard for which I saw the
world contending; but I found my attendance so little encouraged, that neither pride nor modesty would suffer me to
continue it. When I had once addressed your Lordship in
publick, I had exhausted all the art of pleasing which a retired
and uncourtly scholar can possess. I had done all that I could;
and no man is well pleased to have his all neglected, be it ever
so little.

Seven years, my Lord, have now past, since I waited in your
outward rooms, or was repulsed from your door; during which
time I have been pushing on my work through difficulties, of
which it is useless to complain, and have brought it, at last,
to the verge of publication, without one act of assistance, one
word of encouragement, or one smile of favour. Such treatment
I did not expect, for I never had a Patron before.

The shepherd in Virgil grew at last acquainted with Love,
and found him a native of the rocks.

Is not a Patron, my Lord, one who looks with unconcern on
a man struggling for life in the water, and, when he has reached
ground, encumbers him with help? The notice which you have
been pleased to take of my labours, had it been early, had been
kind; but it has been delayed till I am indifferent, and cannot
enjoy it; till I am solitary, and cannot impart it; till I am
known, and do not want it. I hope it is no very cynical asperity
not to confess obligations where no benefit has been received,
or to be unwilling that the Publick should consider me as

owing that to a Patron, which Providence has enabled me to do for myself.

Having carried on my work thus far with so little obligation to any favourer of learning, I shall not be disappointed though I should conclude it, if less be possible, with less; for I have been long wakened from that dream of hope, in which I once boasted myself with so much exultation,

My Lord,
Your Lordship's most humble,
Most obedient servant,
SAM. JOHNSON
[Bos. 1754

*In 1761 James Macpherson published what he said were trans-
lations of the poems of an ancient Gaelic poet, Ossian. Johnson
denied the authenticity of the poems and wrote the following
answer to a now-lost public letter from Macpherson:*

MR. JAMES MACPHERSON:

I received your foolish and impudent letter. Any violence offered me I shall do my best to repel; and what I cannot do for myself, the law shall do for me. I hope I shall never be deterred from detecting what I think a cheat, by the menaces of a ruffian.

What would you have me retract? I thought your book an imposture; I think it an imposture still. For this opinion I have given my reasons to the publick, which I here dare you to refute. Your rage I defy. Your abilities, since your Homer, are not so formidable; and what I hear of your morals inclines me to pay regard not to what you shall say, but to what you shall prove. You may print this if you will.

SAM. JOHNSON
[Bos. 20 Jan. 1775

. . . if you are to have but one book with you upon a journey, let it be a book of science. When you have read through a book of entertainment, you know it, and it can do no more for you; but a book of science is inexhaustible. [Tour 31 August(n)

In perusing a corrupted piece, [the editor] must have before him all possibilities of meaning, with all possibilities of expression. Such must be his comprehension of thought, and such his copiousness of language. Out of many readings possible, he must be able to select that which best suits with the state of opinions and the modes of language prevailing in every age, and with his authour's cast of thought, and turn of expression. Such must be his knowledge, and such his taste. Conjectural criticism demands more than humanity possesses, and he that exercises it with most praise has very frequent need of indulgence. Let us now be told no more of the dull duty of an editor. [Pref. Shakespeare

All works that describe manners require notes in sixty or seventy years or less. [For the Defense, p. 169

I have always suspected that the reading is right, which requires many words to prove it wrong; and the emendation wrong, that cannot without so much labour appear to be right. The justness of a happy restoration strikes at once, and the moral precept may be well applied to criticism, *quod dubitas ne feceris.* [Pref. Shakespeare

Of Thomas Gray:

In the character of his Elegy I rejoice to concur with the common reader; for, by the common sense of readers uncorrupted with literary prejudices, after all the refinements of subtilty and the dogmatism of learning, must be finally decided all claim to poetical honors. The Churchyard abounds with images which find a mirror in every mind, and with sentiments

to which every bosom returns an echo. The four stanzas beginning, "Yet even these bones," are to me original: I have never
seen the notions in any other place; yet he that reads them
here persuades himself that he has always felt them. Had Gray
written often thus, it had been vain to blame, and useless to
praise him. [L.P., Gray

Of an ode that was enjoying popular favor:

Bolder words and more timorous meaning, I think never
were brought together. [Bos. Oct. 1780

Old age will shew . . . that much of the book now before us
has no other use than to perplex the scrupulous and to shake
the weak, to encourage impious presumption, or stimulate idle
curiosity. . . . The shame is to impose words for ideas upon
ourselves or others. To imagine that we are going forward
when we are only turning around. [Review, A *Free Inquiry*

Of Macpherson's Ossian:

The Scots have something to plead for their easy reception
of an improbable fiction; they are seduced by their fondness
for their supposed ancestors. A Scotsman must be a very sturdy
moralist who does not love Scotland better than truth; he will
always love it better than inquiry; and if falsehood flatters his
vanity, will not be very diligent to detect it. [Tour, Ostig

[Chesterfield's *Letters*] teach the morals of a whore, and the
manners of a dancing master. [Bos. 1754

Of Pope's Essay on Man:

Never were penury of knowledge and vulgarity of sentiment
so happily disguised. The reader feels his mind full though
he learns nothing; and, when he meets it in its new array, no
longer knows the talk of his mother and his nurse. [L.P., Pope

... a gentleman of eminence in literature had got into a bad style of poetry of late. "He puts (said he) a very common thing in a strange dress till he does not know it himself, and thinks other people do not know it." . . . For example, he'd write thus:

> "Hermit hoar, in solemn cell,
>   Wearing out life's evening gray."

Gray evening is common enough; but *evening gray* he'd think fine.—Stay—we'll make out the stanza:

> "Hermit hoar, in solemn cell,
>   Wearing out life's evening gray;
> Smite thy bosom, sage, and tell,
>   What is bliss? and which the way?"

Boswell. "But why smite his bosom, Sir?" *Johnson.* "Why, to shew he was in earnest" (smiling). He at an after period added the following stanza:

> "Thus I spoke, and speaking sigh'd;
>   —Scarce repress'd the starting tear;—
> When the smiling sage reply'd—
>   —Come, my lad, and drink some beer."
>   [Bos. 18 Sept. 1777

When a well-known author published his poems in the year 1777: Such a one's verses are come out, said I [Mrs. Thrale]: "Yes (replied Johnson), and this frost has struck them in again. Here are some lines I have written to ridicule them: but remember that I love the fellow dearly, now—for all I laugh at him.

> "Wheresoe'er I turn my view,
> All is strange, yet nothing new:
> Endless labour all along,
> Endless labour to be wrong;

> Phrase that Time has flung away;
> Uncouth words in disarray,
> Trick'd in antique ruff and bonnet,
> Ode, and elegy, and sonnet."
>
> [Pioz. Anec.

Hearing some verses praised more than he thought they deserved, Johnson observed that "they were founded on a trivial conceit," ill expressed and ill explained. One might as well say:

> If the man who turnips cries,
> Cry not when his father dies,
> 'Tis a proof that he had rather
> Have a turnip than his father.
>
> [Pioz. Anec.

. . . when one was reading his tragedy "Irene" to a company . . . [Johnson] left the room; and somebody having asked him the reason of this, he replied, "Sir, I thought it had been better." [Bos. 1780

"I was told," wrote Sir Walter Scott, "that a gentleman called Pot, or some such name, was introduced to him as a particular admirer of his. The Doctor growled and took no further notice. "He admires in especial your 'Irene' as the finest tragedy of modern times"; to which the Doctor replied, "If Pot says so, Pot lies!" [Bos. 1780(n)

Of Harwood's Liberal Translation of the New Testament:

The passage that first caught [Johnson's] eye was from that sublime apostrophe in St. John upon the raising of Lazarus, "Jesus wept"; which Harwood had conceitedly rendered, "and Jesus, the Saviour of the world, burst into a flood of tears." He contemptuously threw aside the book, exclaiming, "Puppy!" [Wickens, John. Misc.

Of Goldsmith's She Stoops to Conquer:

I know of no comedy for many years that has so much exhilarated an audience, and has answered so much the great end of comedy—making an audience merry. [Bos. 29 April 1773

Jonas Hanway published a successful work, Travels in Persia, and followed it with a less successful Eight Days' Journey from London to Portsmouth:

Jonas . . . acquired some reputation by travelling abroad, but lost it all by travelling at home. [Bos. 1770

Of a popular poem:

It had indeed the beauty of a bubble: the colours are gay (said he), but the substance slight. [Pioz. Anec.

Sometimes the reader is suddenly ravished with a sonorous sentence of which, when the noise is past, the meaning does not long remain. [Review, *Court of Augustus*

Of Lycidas:

Where there is leisure for fiction, there is little grief. [L.P., Milton

In answer to Boswell, who was speaking of Sheridan's enthusiasm for the advancement of eloquence:

I bring his declamation to a point. I ask him a plain question, "What do you mean to teach?" Besides, Sir, what influence can Mr. Sheridan have upon the language of this great country, by his narrow exertions? Sir, it is burning a farthing candle at Dover, to shew a light at Calais. [Bos. 28 July 1763

Miss Seward said that he had made poetry of no value by his criticism. "Why, my dear lady," replied he, "if silver is dirty, it is not the less valuable for a good scouring." [Parker, John. Misc.

To a poet nothing can be useless. Whatever is beautiful, and whatever is dreadful, must be familiar to his imagination: he must be conversant with all that is awfully vast or elegantly little. [Ras. 10

Of William Collins:

He affected the obsolete when it was not worthy of revival; and he puts his words out of the common order, seeming to think, with some later candidates for fame, that not to write prose is certainly to write poetry. [L.P., Collins

The genius of Shakespeare was not to be depressed by the weight of poverty, nor limited by the narrow conversation to which men in want are inevitably condemned; the incumbrances of his fortune were shaken from his mind, *as dewdrops from a lion's mane.* [Pref. Shakespeare

He that has read Shakespeare with attention will perhaps find little new in the crowded world. [Dedic. Lennox Shakespeare

Comparing Young's description of night to one by Shakespeare, Johnson said to Mrs. Thrale:

Young froths, and foams, and bubbles sometimes very vigorously; but we must not compare the noise made by your teakettle here with the roaring of the ocean. [Pioz. Anec.

The merit of Shakespeare is such as the ignorant can take in and the learned add nothing to it. [Windham Diary

Notes are often necessary, but they are necessary evils. Let him, that is yet unacquainted with the powers of Shakespeare, and who desires to feel the highest pleasure the drama can give, read every play from the first scene to the last, with utter negligence of all his commentators. When his fancy is once on the wing, let it not stoop at correction or explanation. [Pref. Shakespeare

[I am] only maintaining that Congreve has one finer passage than any that can be found in Shakespeare. Sir, a man may have no more than ten guineas in the world, but he may have those ten guineas in one piece; and so may have a finer piece than a man who has ten thousand pounds: but then he has only one ten-guinea piece. [Bos. 16 Oct. 1769

It is not to be inferred, that of this poetical vigour Pope had only a little, because Dryden had more; for every other writer since Milton must give place to Pope; and even of Dryden it must be said, that, if he has brighter paragraphs, he has not better poems. Dryden's performances were always hasty, either excited by some external occasion, or extorted by domestick necessity; he composed without consideration, and published without correction. What his mind could supply at call, or gather in one excursion, was all that he sought, and all that he gave. The dilatory caution of Pope enabled him to condense his sentiments, to multiply his images, and to accumulate all that study might produce, or chance might supply. If the flights of Dryden, therefore, are higher, Pope continues longer on the wing. If of Dryden's fire the blaze is brighter, of Pope's the heat is more regular and constant. Dryden often surpasses expectation, and Pope never falls below it. Dryden is read with frequent astonishment, and Pope with perpetual delight. [L.P., Pope

On Teaching and Learning

*Wealth is nothing but as it is bestowed, and
knowledge nothing but as it is communicated.*
Ras. 35

What Johnson said about education and related matters—
like what he said about so many other things—depended
largely on the time, the place, and the stimulus. How much of
it was unconscious rationalization of his own spotty education
is hard to say. Some certainly was. But he had a vivid memory
of his schooldays, a sharp appreciation of his teachers, and decided ideas on the whole learning process as it touches most
boys. His ideas are valid even now; and they make sense. His
judgments of his teachers are especially interesting.

At Lichfield Grammar School he commenced Latin with a
Mr. Hawkins. Then he moved up to a Mr. Hunter, who flogged
his boys unmercifully. For Johnson, at least, this stringent
method worked. Asked years later how he acquired so accurate
a knowledge of Latin, he answered, "My master whipt me very
well. Without that, Sir, I should have done nothing."[1]

But his schooling was irregular. He depended largely on a
memory "so tenacious that he never forgot anything that he
either read or heard." In his last school—at Stourbridge—he
was under a Mr. Wentworth, a man who "saw that I did not
reverence him; and that he should get no honour by me. I had
brought enough with me, to carry me through . . . Yet he

[1] Bos. 1719–1725.

taught me a great deal."[2] He was sixteen when he left Stourbridge.

He next settled down to two years of desultory reading in his father's shop—idling apparently; there was no money to send him on to the university. But he was reading "not voyages and travels, but all literature, all the ancient writers and all manly; though but little Greek, only some of Anacreon and Hesiod."[3] He dipped into hundreds of books and so developed the habit of pecking, rather than studying, that in later years, when a man insisted on knowing whether he had finished a book, Johnson could retort tartly, "Do you read books through?"[4]

At nineteen he entered Oxford. Looking back from the age of fifty, he could say, "It is a sad reflection, but a true one, that I knew almost as much at eighteen as I do now. My judgement, to be sure, was not so good; but I had all the facts."[5] His learning, though, he had acquired "by fits and starts, by violent inruptions into the field of knowledge."[6] But he had managed to get a good education, and he knew what a good education should be, although he himself could never have undergone the methodical plodding which so much conventional education demands of less able boys. And he hated pedants, dusty scholars in whose veins ran not blood but printer's ink, and whose passions had been damped down by judgment so nicely balanced that it stopped all action. "Books without knowledge of life," he told Mrs. Thrale, "are useless; for what should books teach but the art of living."[7] For books he would willingly have substituted learning. In view of what can happen to a young man after the cursus in the best boarding schools and ivied colleges, Johnson's characterization of The Macdonald, whose brother was to entertain Johnson and Boswell on Skye, perhaps

2 Bos. 1725–1728.
4 Bos. April 1773.
6 Bos. 1736.
3 Bos. 1725–1728.
5 Bos. July 1763.
7 Pioz. Anec.

sums up what schooling not infrequently does: "He was . . . one not tamed into insignificance by an Eton education."[8]

Much of this, then, a reader must keep in mind when he encounters Johnson's dogmatic statements about education. It might be added that he never had children. Still, a farmer never laid an egg, but he knows more about the process than hens do.

Integrity without knowledge is weak and useless, and knowledge without integrity is dangerous and dreadful. [Ras. 41

I believe it may be sometimes found that a *little learning* is to a poor man a *dangerous thing*. But such is the condition of humanity, that we easily see, or quickly feel the wrong, but cannot always distinguish the right. Whatever knowledge is superfluous, in irremediable poverty, is hurtful, but the difficulty is to determine when poverty is irremediable, and at what point superfluity begins. Gross ignorance every man has found equally dangerous with perverted knowledge. [Review, A *Free Inquiry*

When a king asked Euclid, the mathematician, whether he could not explain his art to him in a more compendious manner? he was answered, That there was no royal way to geometry. Other things might be seized by might, or purchased with money, but knowledge is to be gained only by study, and study must be prosecuted only in retirement. [Ram. 7

I am always afraid of determining on the side of envy and cruelty. The privileges of education may sometimes be improperly bestowed, but I shall always fear to withhold them, lest I should be yielding to the suggestions of pride while I persuade myself that I am following the maxims of policy; and under

8 Tour 2 September(n).

the appearance of salutary restraints, should be indulging the lust of dominion, and that malevolence which delights in seeing others depressed. [Review, A *Free Inquiry*

Vulgar and inactive minds confound familiarity and knowledge, and conceive themselves informed of the whole nature of things when they are shewn their form and told their use; but the speculatist, who is not content with superficial views, harasses himself with fruitless curiosity, and still as he inquires more, perceives only that he knows less. [Idl. 36

Curiosity is one of the permanent and certain characteristics of the vigorous intellect. Every advance into knowledge opens new prospects, and produces new incitements to further progress. All the attainments possible in our present state are evidently inadequate to our capacities of enjoyment; conquest serves no purpose but that of kindling ambition, discovery has no effect but of raising expectation; the gratification of one desire encourages another; and, after all our labours, studies, and inquiries, we are continually at the same distance from the completion of our schemes, have still some wish importunate to be satisfied, and the same faculty restless and turbulent for want of its enjoyment. [Ram. 103

Ignorance is a subject for pity—not for laughter. [Croker, John. Misc.

To be ignorant is painful; but it is dangerous to quiet our uneasiness by the delusive opiate of hasty persuasion. [Journey, Ostig

He that knows which way to direct his view, sees much in little time. [Letter to Baretti, 10 June 1761

He that voluntarily continues ignorance is guilty of all the crimes that ignorance produces; as to him that should extinguish the tapers of a light-house might fairly be imputed the calamities of ship wrecks. [Letter to Drummond, Aug. 1776

Biography is, of the various kinds of narrative writing, that which is most eagerly read, and most easily applied to the purposes of life. [Idl. 84

Knowledge is certainly one of the means of pleasure, as is confessed by the natural desire every mind feels of increasing its ideas. Ignorance is mere privation, by which nothing can be produced; it is a vacuity in which the soul sits motionless and torpid for want of attraction; and, without knowing why, we always rejoice when we learn, and grieve when we forget. I am therefore inclined to conclude, that if nothing counteracts the natural consequences of learning, we grow more happy as our minds take a wider range. [Ras. 11

Of whatever we see we always wish to know; always congratulate ourselves when we know that of which we see another to be ignorant. Take therefore all opportunities of learning, however remote the matter is from common life or common conversation. Look in Herschel's telescope; go into a chemist's laboratory; if you see a manufacturer at work, remark his operations. By this activity of attention you will find in every place diversion and improvement. [Letter to Susanna Thrale, March 1784

To know any thing we must know its effects; to see men, we must see their works. [Ras. 30

The true art of memory is the art of attention. [Idl. 74

He that enlarges his curiosity after the works of nature,

demonstrably multiplies the inlets to happiness; and, therefore, the younger part of my readers . . . must excuse me for calling upon them, to make use at once of the spring of the year, and the spring of life; . . . and to remember that a blighted spring makes a barren year, and that the vernal flowers, however beautiful and gay, are only intended by nature as preparatives to autumnal fruits. [Ram. 5

Time may be employed to more advantage from nineteen to twenty-four almost in any way than in travelling; when you set travelling against mere negation, against doing nothing, it is better, to be sure; but how much more would a young man improve were he to study during those years. Indeed, if a young man is wild, and must run after women and bad company, it is better this should be done abroad, as, on his return, he can break off such connections, and begin at home a new man, with a character to form, and acquaintances to make. How little does travelling supply to the conversation of any man who has travelled? how little to Beauclerk? . . . I never but once heard him talk of what he had seen, and that was of a large serpent in one of the Pyramids of Egypt. [Bos. 13 May 1778

The use of travelling is to regulate imagination by reality, and, instead of thinking how things may be, to see them as they are. [Pioz. Anec.

As we see more, we become possessed of more certainties, and consequently gain more principles of reasoning, and found a wider basis of analogy. [Journey, Anoch

All travel has its advantages. If the traveller visits better countries, he may learn to improve his own, and if fortune carries him to worse, he may learn to enjoy it. [Journey, Mull

That wonder is the effect of ignorance, has been often observed . . . Wonder is a pause of reason, a sudden cessation of the mental progress, which lasts only while the understanding is fixed upon some single idea, and is at an end when it recovers force enough to divide the object into its parts, or mark the intermediate gradations from the first agent to the last consequence. [Ram. 137

As the Spanish proverb says, "He, who would bring home the wealth of the Indies, must carry the wealth of the Indies with him." So it is in travelling; a man must carry knowledge with him, if he would bring home knowledge. [Bos. 17 April 1778

When we are alone, we are not always busy; the labour of excogitation is too violent to last long. [Ras. 44

Of the difference between English and Scotch education:

. . . if from the first he did not come out a scholar, he was fit for nothing at all; whereas (he added) in the last a boy is always taught something that may be of use to him; and he who is not able to read a page of Tully will be able to become a surveyor, or to lay out a garden. [Seward, John. Misc.

Dr. Johnson was extremely averse to the present . . . mode of educating children, so as to make them what foolish mothers call "elegant young men." He said to some lady who asked him what she should teach her son early in life, "Madam, to read, to write, to count; grammar, writing, arithmetic; three things which, if not taught in very early life, are seldom or ever taught to any purpose, and without the knowledge of which no superstructure of learning or of knowledge can be built." [Seward, John. Misc.

A mother tells her infant, that *two and two make four*; the child remembers the proposition, and is able to count four to all the purposes of life, till the course of his education brings him among philosophers, who fright him from his former knowledge, by telling him, that four is a certain aggregate of units; that all numbers being only the repetition of an unit, which, though not a number itself, is the parent, root, or original of all number, *four* is the denomination assigned to a certain number of such repetitions. The only danger is, lest, when he first hears these dreadful sounds, the pupil should run away: if he has but the courage to stay till the conclusion, he will find that, when speculation has done its worst, two and two still make four. [Idl. 36

One day a Mrs. Gastrel set a little girl to repeat to him Cato's soliloquy, which she went through very correctly. The Doctor, after a pause, asked the child . . . the meaning of "bane and antidote," which she was unable to give. Mrs. Gastrel said, "You cannot expect so young a child to know the meaning of such words." He then said, "My dear, how many pence are there in *sixpence?*" "I cannot tell, Sir," was the half-terrified reply. On this, addressing himself to Mrs. Gastrel, he said, "Now, my dear lady, can any thing be more ridiculous than to teach a child Cato's soliloquy, who does not know how many pence there are in sixpence?" [Parker, John. Misc.

Raphael, in return to Adam's inquiries into the courses of the stars and the revolutions of heaven, counsels him to withdraw his mind from idle speculations, and employ his faculties upon nearer . . . objects, the survey of his own life, the subjection of his passions, the knowledge of duties which must daily be performed, and the detection of dangers which must daily be incurred.

This angelic counsel every man of letters should always have before him. He that devotes himself to retired study naturally sinks from omission to forgetfulness of social duties; he must be therefore sometimes awakened and recalled to the general condition of mankind.

I am far from any intention to limit curiosity, or confine the labours of learning to arts of immediate and necessary use. . . .

But the distant hope of being one day useful or eminent, ought not to mislead us too far from that study which is equally requisite to the great and mean, to the celebrated and the obscure; the art of moderating the desires, of repressing the appetites, and of conciliating or retaining the favour of mankind. [Ram. 180

I hate by-roads in education . . . Endeavouring to make children prematurely wise is useless labour. Suppose they have more knowledge at five or six years old than other children, what use can be made of it? It will be lost before it is wanted . . . Too much is expected from precocity, and too little performed. [Bos. 1775

. . . read diligently; they who do not read can have nothing to think and little to say. When you can get proper company, talk freely and cheerfully; it is often by talking that we come to know the value of what we read, to separate it with distinctness, and fix it in the memory. [Letter to Hester Maria Thrale, July 1780

It has been observed, by long experience, that late springs produce the greatest plenty. [Ram. 111

Learn (said he) that there is propriety or impropriety in every thing how slight soever, and get at the general principles of dress and of behaviour; if you then transgress them, you will at least know that they are not observed. [Pioz. Anec.

. . . who was ever able to convince himself by arguments, that he had chosen for his son that mode of instruction to which his understanding was best adapted, or by which he would most easily be made wise or virtuous? [Ram. 184

He begins to reproach himself with neglect of George's education, and censures . . . that deviation by the indulgence of which he has left uncultivated such a fertile mind. I advised him to let the child alone . . . that the matter was not great, whether he could read at the end of four years or five, and that I thought it not proper to harass a tender mind with the violence of attention. [Letter to Mrs. T., May 1776

[In the learning of Latin] do not be very particular about method; any method will do if there be but diligence. [Letter to Geo. Strahan, March 1763

It has been told that in the art of education [Milton] performed wonders; and a formidable list is given of the authors, Greek and Latin, that were read in Aldersgate-street by youth between ten and fifteen or sixteen years of age. Those who tell or receive these stories should consider, that nobody can be taught faster than he can learn. The speed of the horseman must be limited by the power of his horse. Every man, that has ever undertaken to instruct others, can tell what slow advances he has been able to make, and how much patience it requires to recall vagrant inattention, to stimulate sluggish indifference, and to rectify absurd misapprehension. [L.P., Milton

The Guardian directs one of his pupils *to think with the wise, but speak with the vulgar.* This is a precept specious enough, but not always practicable. Difference of thoughts will produce difference of language. He that thinks with more extent than another will want words of larger meaning; he that thinks with more subtility will seek for terms of more nice discrimination; and where is the wonder, since words are but the images of things, that he who never knew the original should not know the copies?

Yet vanity inclines us to find faults any where rather than in ourselves. He that reads and grows no wiser, seldom suspects his own deficiency; but complains of hard words and obscure sentences, and asks why books are written which cannot be understood? [Idl. 70

Knowledge always desires increase: it is like fire, which must first be kindled by some external agent, but which will afterwards propagate itself. [Letter to Drummond, Aug. 1776

Men advanced far in knowledge do not love to repeat the elements of their art. [Ras. 46

Sir, it is no matter what you teach [children] first, any more than what leg you shall put into your breeches first. Sir, you may stand disputing which is best to put in first, but in the mean time your breech is bare. Sir, while you are considering which of two things you should teach your child first, another boy has learnt them both. [Bos. 26 July 1763

. . . young people should have *positive* not general rules given for their direction. "My mother (said he) was always telling me that I did not *behave* myself properly; that I should endeavour to learn behaviour, and such cant: but when I replied, that she ought to tell me what to do, and what to avoid, her admonitions were commonly, for that time at least, at an end." [Pioz. Anec.

I am always for getting a boy forward in his learning; for that is a sure good. I would let him read at first *any* English book which happens to engage his attention; because you have done a great deal when you have brought him to have entertainment from a book. He'll get better books afterwards. [Bos. 16 April 1779.

Example is more efficacious than precept. [Ras. 30

Poor people's children, dear Lady, never respect them. I did not respect my own mother, though I loved her. One day, when in anger she called me a puppy, I asked her if she knew what they called a puppy's mother. [Pioz. Anec.

Johnson advised me to-night not to *refine* in the education of my children. "Life (said he) will not bear refinement: you must do as other people do. [Bos. 16 Sept. 1777

People are not born with a particular genius for particular employments or studies; for it would be like saying that a man could see a great way east, but could not [see] west. [Genius] is good sense applied with diligence to what was at first a mere accident, and which, by great application, grew to be called, by the generality of mankind, a particular genius. [Miss Reynolds

Genius is nothing more than knowing the use of tools, but there must be tools for it to use. [D'Arblay Diary

. . . it is not sufficiently considered, that men more frequently require to be reminded than informed. [Ram. 2

At one [school] I learnt much in the school, but little from the master; in the other, I learnt much from the master, but little in the school. [Bos. 1725

. . . as I advanced towards manhood, I lost much of the reverence with which I had been used to look on my instructors; because, when the lessons were ended, I did not find them wiser or better than common men. [Ras. 8

A boy should never be sent to Eton or Westminster school before he is twelve years old at least; for if in his years of babyhood he 'scapes that general and transcendent knowledge without which life is perpetually put to a stand, he will never get it at public school, where if he does not learn Latin and Greek, he learns nothing . . . there was too much stress laid upon literature as indispensably necessary: there is surely no need that every body should be a scholar, no call that every one should square the circle. [Pioz. Anec.

. . . we must own that neither a dull boy, nor an idle boy, will do so well at a great school as at a [small] private one. For at a great school there are always boys enough to do well easily, who are sufficient to keep up the credit of the school; and after whipping being tried to no purpose the dull or idle boys are left at the end of class, having the appearance of going through the course, but learning nothing at all. Such boys may do good at a private school, where constant attention is paid to them, and they are watched. So that the question of publick or private education is not properly a general one; but whether one or the other is best for *my son*. [Tour 22 August

. . . no man was ever great by imitation. [Ras. 10

More is learned in publick [large boarding] than in private schools, from emulation; there is the collision of mind with mind, or the radiation of many minds pointing to one centre. [Bos. 1775

Of monks—could be said of schoolboys:

Their time is regularly distributed; one duty succeeds another; so that they are not left open to the distraction of unguided choice, nor lost in the shades of listless inactivity. [Ras. 47

Of a boy whose father proposed to send him to a great public school to cure him of shyness:

This is a preposterous expedient for removing his infirmity; such a disposition should be cultivated in the shade. Placing him at a publick school is forcing an owl upon day. [Bos. June 1784

Of a fifteen-year-old boy who had a manner at once sullen and sheepish:

That lad (says Mr. Johnson) looks like the son of a schoolmaster; which (added he) is one of the very worst conditions of childhood: such a boy has no father, or worse than none; he never can reflect on his parent but the reflection brings to his mind some idea of pain inflicted, or of sorrow suffered. [Pioz. Anec.

No cause more frequently produces bashfulness than too high an opinion of our own importance. He that imagines an assembly filled with his merit, panting with expectation, and hushed with attention, easily terrifies himself with the dread of disappointing them, and strains his imagination in pursuit of some thing that may vindicate the veracity of fame, and shew that his reputation was not gained by chance. He considers, that what he shall say or do will never be forgotten; that renown or infamy is suspended upon every syllable, and that nothing ought to fall from him which will not bear the test of time. Under such solicitude, who can wonder that the mind is overwhelmed. [Ram. 159

The seeds of knowledge may be planted in solitude, but must be cultivated in public. [Ram. 168

Sir . . . a desire of knowledge is the natural feeling of mankind; and every human being, whose mind is not debauched, will be willing to give all that he has to get knowledge. [Bos. 30 July 1763

The discipline of a school is military. There must be either unbounded license or absolute authority. The master, who punishes, not only consults the future happiness of him who is the immediate subject of correction; but he propagates obedience through the whole school; and establishes regularity by exemplary justice. The victorious obstinacy of a single boy would make his future endeavours of reformation or instruction totally ineffectual. Obstinacy, therefore, must never be victorious. [Bos. 11 April 1772

A nurse made of common mould will have a pride in overpowering a child's reluctance. There are few minds to which tyranny is not delightful; power is nothing but as it is felt, and the delight of superiority is proportionate to the resistance overcome. [Bos. 1719–1725(n)

There is now less flogging in our great schools than formerly, but then less is learned there; so that what the boys get at one end, they lose at the other. [Bos. 1775

Though he was attentive to the peace of children in general, no man had a stronger contempt than he for such parents as openly confess that they cannot govern their children . . . Such people, for the most part, multiply prohibitions till obedience becomes impossible, and authority seems absurd; and never suspect that they tease their family, their friends, and themselves, only because conversation runs low and something must be said. [Pioz. Anec.

No science [knowledge] can be communicated to mortal creatures without attention from the scholar; no attention can be obtained from children without the infliction of pain, and pain is never remembered without resentment. [Pioz. Anec.

I would rather . . . have the rod to be the general terrour to all, to make them learn, than tell a child, if you do thus or thus, you will be more esteemed than your brothers or sisters. The rod produces an effect which terminates in itself. A child is afraid of being whipped, and gets his task, and there's an end on't; whereas, by exciting emulation and comparisons of superiority, you lay the foundation of lasting mischief; you make brothers and sisters hate each other. [Bos. 1719–1725

The grammar schools [in Scotland] are not generally well supplied; for the character of a school-master, being there less honourable than in England, is seldom accepted by men who are capable to adorn it, and where the school has been defi- cient, the college can effect little. [Journey, Auchinleck

Reproof should not exhaust its power upon petty failings. [Idl. 25

The care of the critick should be to distinguish error from inability, faults of inexperience from defects of nature. [Idl. 25

Mankind have a great aversion to intellectual labour; but even supposing knowledge to be easily attainable, more people would be content to be ignorant than would take even a little trouble to acquire it. [Bos. 24 May 1763

Daily business adds no more to wisdom than daily lessons to the learning of the teacher . . . The greater part of human minds never endeavour their own improvement. Opinions once received from instruction, or settled by whatever accident, are seldom recalled to examination; having been once supposed to be right, they are never discovered to be erroneous, for no application is made of any thing that time may present, either to shake or to confirm them . . . They that are wise at thirty-three are very little wiser at forty-five. [Letter to Mrs. T., Aug. 1775

The mind is seldom quickened to very vigorous operations but by pain, or the dread of pain. [Idl. 18

The chief art of learning, as Locke has observed, is to attempt but little at a time. The widest excursions of the mind are made by short flights frequently repeated; the most lofty fabrics of science are formed by the continued accumulation of single propositions. [Ram. 137

People have now-a-days . . . got a strange opinion that every thing should be taught by lectures. Now, I cannot see that lectures can do so much good as reading the books from which the lectures are taken. I know nothing that can be best taught by lectures, except where experiments are to be shewn. You may teach chymistry by lectures,—You might teach making of shoes by lectures! [Bos. Feb. 1776

Lectures were once useful; but now, when all can read, and books are so numerous, lectures are unnecessary. If your attention fails, and you miss a part of a lecture, it is lost; you cannot go back as you do upon a book. [Bos. 15 April 1781

You can never be wise unless you love reading. [Bos. 25 Sept. 1770

. . . the size of a man's understanding might always be justly measured by his mirth. [Pioz. Anec.

No place affords a more striking conviction of the vanity of human hopes, than a public library. [Ram. 106

When I was at Oxford, an old gentleman said to me, "Young man, ply your book diligently now, and acquire a stock of knowledge; for when years come upon you, you will find that poring upon books will be but an irksome task." [Bos. 21 July 1763

To the strongest and quickest mind it is far easier to learn than to invent . . . The man whose genius qualifies him for great undertakings, must at least be content to learn from books the present state of human knowledge. [Ram. 154

False hopes and false terrours are equally to be avoided. Every man, who proposes to grow eminent by learning, should carry in his mind, at once the difficulty of excellence and the force of industry; and remember, that fame is not conferred but as the recompense of labour, and that labour vigorously continued has not often failed of its reward. [Ram. 25

To count is a modern practice; the ancient method was to guess; and when numbers are guessed they are always magnified. [Journey, Ostig

Knowledge is of two kinds. We know a subject ourselves, or we know where we can find information upon it. [Bos. 18 April 1775

Between falsehood and useless truth there is little difference. As gold which he cannot spend will make no man rich, so knowledge which he cannot apply will make no man wise. [Idl. 84

What is read twice is commonly better remembered than what is transcribed. [Idl. 74

That the vulgar express their thoughts clearly is far from true; and what perspicuity can be found among them proceeds not from the easiness of their language, but the shallowness of their thoughts. [Idl. 70

To help the ignorant commonly requires much patience, for the ignorant are always trying to be cunning. [Tour 17 September(n)

Distinction is not always made between the faults which require speedy and violent eradication, and those which gradually drop away in the progression of life. Vicious solicitations of appetite, if not checked, will grow more importunate; and mean arts of profit and ambition will gather strength in the mind, if they are not suppressed. But the mistaken notions of superiority, desires of useless show, pride in little accomplishments, and all the train of vanity will be brushed away by the wing of Time. [Idl. 25

[Teachers of morality] discourse like angels, but they live like men. [Ras. 18

> Deign on the passing world to turn thine eyes,
> And pause awhile from Letters to be wise;
> There mark what ills the scholar's life assail,
> Toil, envy, want, the patron, and the gaol.
> [Van. H. Wishes

To be grave of mien and slow of utterance; to look with solicitude and speak with hesitation, is attainable at will; but the shew of wisdom is ridiculous when there is nothing to cause doubt, as that of valour where there is nothing to be feared. [Idl. 51

An English or Irish doctorate cannot be obtained by a very young man, and it is reasonable to suppose, what is likewise by experience commonly found to be true, that he who is by age qualified to be a doctor, has in so much time gained learning sufficient not to disgrace the title, or wit sufficient not to desire it. [Journey, Aberdeen

There is no employment in which men are more easily betrayed to indecency and impatience, than in that of teaching; in which they necessarily converse with those who are their inferiours in the relation by which they are connected, and whom it may be sometimes proper to treat with that dignity which too often swells into arrogance; and to restrain with such authority as not every man has learned to separate from tyranny . . . [The teacher] is inclined to wonder that what he comprehends himself is not equally clear to others; and often reproaches the intellects of his auditors, when he ought to blame the confusion of his own ideas, and the improprieties of his own language. He reiterates, therefore, his positions without elucidation, and enforces his assertions by his frown, when he finds arguments less easy to be supplied. Thus forgetting that he has to do with men, whose passions are perhaps equally turbulent with his own, he transfers by degrees to his instruction the prejudices which are first raised by his behaviour; and having forced upon his pupils an hatred of their teacher, he sees it quickly terminate in a contempt of the precept. [Sermon VIII

It is, however, not necessary that a man . . . [discover] some truth unknown before; he may be sufficiently useful, by only diversifying the surface of knowledge, and luring the mind by a new appearance to a second view of those beauties which it passed over inattentively before . . . and, perhaps, truth is often more successfully propagated by men of moderate abilities, who, adopting the opinions of others, have no care but to explain them clearly, than by . . . curious searchers, who exact from their readers powers equal to their own, and if their fabricks of science be strong, take no care to render them accessible. [Adv. 137

. . . the learning of the recluse often fails him; nothing but long habit and frequent experiments confer the power of changing a position into various forms, presenting it in different points of view, connecting it with known and granted truths, fortifying it with intelligible arguments, and illustrating it with apt similitudes; and he, therefore, who has collected his knowledge in solitude, must learn its application by mixing with mankind. [Adv. 89

A friend's erudition was commended one day as equally deep and strong—"He will not talk, Sir (was the reply), so his learning does us no good, and his wit, if he has it, gives us no pleasure: out of all his boasted stores I never heard him force but one word, and that word was *Richard*. [Pioz. Anec.

Knowledge is nothing to him who is not known by others to possess it. [Adv. 85

But though learning may be conferred by solitude, its application must be attained by general converse. He has learned to no purpose, that is not able to teach; and he will always teach unsuccessfully, who cannot recommend his sentiments by his diction or address.

Even the acquisition of knowledge is much facilitated by the advantages of society: he that never compares his notions with those of others, readily acquiesces in his first thoughts, and very seldom discovers the objections which may be raised against his opinions; he, therefore, often thinks himself in possession of truth, when he is only fondling an errour long since exploded. He that has neither companions nor rivals in his studies, will always applaud his own progress, and think highly of his performances, because he knows not that others have equalled or excelled him. And I am afraid it may be added, that the student who withdraws himself from the world, will soon feel that ardour extinguished which praise or emulation had enkindled, and take the advantage of secrecy to sleep, rather than to labour. [Adv. 126

I have passed my time in study without experience . . . I have missed the endearing elegance of female friendship, and the happy commerce of domestic tenderness. [Ras. 46

He is a scholar undoubtedly Sir (replied Dr. Johnson), but remember that he would run from the world, and that it is not the world's business to run after him. I hate a fellow whom pride, or cowardice, or laziness drives into a corner, and who does nothing when he is there but sit and *growl*; let him come out as I do, and *bark*. [Pioz. Anec.

A ready man is made by conversation. He that buries himself among his manuscripts, "besprent . . . with learned dust," and wears out his days and nights in perpetual research and solitary meditation, is too apt to lose in his elocution what he adds to his wisdom; and when he comes into the world, to appear overloaded with his own notions, like a man armed with weapons which he cannot wield. He has no facility of inculcating his speculations, of adapting himself to the various degrees of intellect which the accidents of conversation will present; but will talk to most unintelligibly, and to all unpleasantly. [Adv. 85

Pedantry is the unseasonable ostentation of learning. [Ram. 173

When he had opportunities of mingling with mankind, he cleared himself . . . from great part of his scholastick rust. [L.P., Broome

Of the sage in Rasselas:
The prince soon found that this was one of the sages whom he should understand less as he heard him longer. [Ras. 22

To trifle agreeably is a secret which schools cannot impart; that gay negligence and vivacious levity, which charm down resistance . . . are never attainable by him who, having spent his first years among the dust of libraries, enters late into the gay world with an unpliant attention and established habits. [Ram. 173

. . . life is surely given us for higher purposes than to gather what our ancestors have wisely thrown away, and to learn what has no value, but because it has been forgotten. [Ram. 121

There is no snare more dangerous to busy and excursive minds, than the cobwebs of petty inquisitiveness, which entangle them in trivial employments and minute studies, and detain them in a middle state, between the tediousness of total inactivity, and the fatigue of laborious efforts, enchant them at once with ease and novelty, and vitiate them with the luxury of learning. The necessity of doing something, and the fear of undertaking much, sinks the historian to a genealogist, the philosopher to a journalist of the weather, and the mathematician to a constructor of dials. [Ram. 103

But such are the conceits of speculatists, who *strain* their *faculties* to find in a mine what lies upon the surface. [L.P., Prior

It will, I believe, be found invariably true, that learning was never decried by any learned man. [Adv. 85

It has been observed that the most studious are not always the most learned . . . it likewise frequently happens that the most recluse are not the most vigorous prosecutors of study. Many impose upon the world, and many upon themselves, by an appearance of severe and exemplary diligence, when they, in reality, give themselves up to the luxury of fancy, please their minds with regulating the past, or planning the future; place themselves at will in varied situations of happiness, and slumber away their days in voluntary visions . . . and, instead of pressing onward with a steady pace, delight themselves with momentary deviations, turn aside to pluck every flower, and repose in every shade.

There is nothing more fatal to a man whose business is to think. [Ram. 89

It is too common for those who have been bred to scholastic professions, and passed much of their time in academies where nothing but learning confers honours, to disregard every other qualification, and to imagine that they shall find mankind ready to pay homage to their knowledge, and to crowd about them for instruction. They therefore step out from their cells into the open world with all the confidence of authority and dignity of importance; they look round about them at once with ignorance and scorn on a race of beings to whom they are equally unknown and equally contemptible, but whose manners they must imitate, and with whose opinions they must comply, if they desire to pass their time happily among them. [Ram. 137

The general reproach with which ignorance revenges the superciliousness of learning, is that of pedantry; a censure which every man incurs who has at any time the misfortune to talk to those who cannot understand him, and by which the modest and timorous are sometimes frighted from the display of their acquisitions, and the exertion of their powers. [Ram. 173

... the miseries of life would be increased beyond all human power of endurance, if we were to enter the world with the same opinions as we carry from it. [Ram. 196

Such, however, is the state of the world, that the most obsequious slaves of pride, the most rapturous gazers upon wealth, the most officious of the whisperers of greatness, are collected from seminaries appropriated to the study of wisdom and of virtue, where it was intended that appetite should learn to be content with little, and that hope should aspire only to honours which no human power can give or take away. [Ram. 180

Nothing has so much exposed men of learning to contempt and ridicule, as their ignorance of things which are known to all but themselves. Those who have been taught to consider the institutions of the schools, as giving the last perfection to human abilities, are surprised to see men wrinkled with study, yet wanting to be instructed in the minute circumstances of propriety, or the necessary forms of daily transaction; and quickly shake off their reverence for modes of education, which they find to produce no ability above the rest of mankind. . . .

The student must learn by commerce with mankind to reduce his speculations to practice, and to accommodate his knowledge to the purposes of life. [Ram. 137

And as few men will endure the labour of intense meditation without necessity, he that has learned enough for his profit or his honour, seldom endeavours after further acquisitions. [Idl. 44

From the vexation of pupillage men commonly set themselves free about the middle of life, by shutting up avenues of intelligence, and resolving to rest in their present state; and they, whose ardour of inquiry continues longer, find themselves insensibly forsaken by their instructors. [Idl. 44

Man is not weak . . . knowledge is more than equivalent to force. The master of mechanics laughs at strength. [Ras. 13

As in life, so in study, it is dangerous to do more things than one at a time. [Pref. Preceptor

There is a vigilance of observation and accuracy of distinction which books and precepts cannot confer; from this almost all original and native excellence proceeds. [Pref. Shakespeare

Few minds will be long confined to severe and laborious meditation; and when a successful attack on knowledge has been made, the student recreates himself with the contemplation of his conquests, and forbears another incursion, till the new-acquired truth has become familiar, and his curiosity calls upon him for fresh gratifications. Whether the time of intermission is spent in company, or in solitude, in necessary business, or in voluntary levities, the understanding is equally abstracted from the object of inquiry; but perhaps if it be detained by occupations less pleasing, it returns again to study with greater alacrity, than when it is glutted with ideal pleasures, and surfeited with intemperance of application. He that will not suffer himself to be discouraged by fancied impossibilities, may sometimes find his abilities invigorated by the necessity of exerting them in short intervals, as the force of a current is increased by the contraction of its channel.

From some cause like this it has probably proceeded, that among those who have contributed to the advancement of learning, many have risen to eminence in opposition to all the obstacles which external circumstances could place in their way, amidst the tumult of business, the distresses of poverty, or the dissipations of a wandering and unsettled state. A great part of the life of Erasmus was one continual peregrination; ill supplied with the gifts of fortune, and led from city to city, and from kingdom to kingdom, by the hopes of patrons and preferment, hopes which always flattered and always deceived him; he yet found means, by unshaken constancy, and a vigilant improvement of those hours, which, in the midst of the most restless activity, will remain unengaged, to write more than another in the same condition would have hoped to read. Compelled by want to attendance and solicitation, and so much versed in common life, that he has transmitted to us the most perfect delineation of the manners of his age, he joined to his knowledge of the world, such application to books, that he will stand for ever in the first rank of literary heroes. How this proficiency was obtained he sufficiently discovers, by informing us, that the "Praise of Folly," one of his most celebrated performances, was composed by him on the road to Italy; *ne totum illud tempus, quo equo fuit insidendum, illiteratis fabulis tereretur,* lest the hours which he was obliged to spend on

horseback should be tattled away without regard to literature.
[Ram. 108

[Boswell] argued that a refinement of taste was a disadvantage, as they who have attained to it must be seldomer pleased
than those who have no nice discrimination, and are therefore
satisfied with every thing that comes in their way. *Johnson.*
"Nay, Sir; that is a paltry notion. Endeavour to be as perfect as
you can in every respect." [Bos. 30 June 1784

On Work, Wealth, and Their Opposites

There are few ways in which a man can be more innocently employed than in making money.
Bos. Mar. 1775

When Dr. Johnson commented on the ways by which men earned their bread, he usually spoke from considerable knowledge. He was curious about all manner of trades and callings. To the officers at Fort George he could talk with authority about the manufacture of gunpowder.[1] Mr. M'Queen, on Skye, thought him to have been trained in a mint,[2] then in a brewery. At Mrs. Thrale's he could discourse upon dancing so as to make a dancing-master believe he had taught the art. When a country clergyman complained to Mrs. Salusbury that his neighbors could talk of nothing but runts, she replied, "Oh, sir, Dr. Johnson would learn to talk about runts."[3]

He spent a week on a man-of-war as guest of a Captain Knight, and he left appalled by the conditions of a sailor's life.[4] His comments on the life of a professional soldier were based on what he had seen in the Scottish Highlands. He had a higher opinion of the clergyman's career than most men in orders.[5] Johnson had been a teacher[6] and had seriously con-

1 Tour 28 August.
3 Bos. May 1778.
5 Bos. April 1778.

2 Tour 16 September.
4 Pioz. Anec.
6 Bos. 1733.

sidered becoming a lawyer.[7] He probably thought of any one occupation as he did of writing—that a man could do it if he put himself doggedly to it.[8]

In the philosophical sense he was a good businessman; he knew what should be done, though, to be sure, he rarely did it for himself. As one of the executors of Thrale's will, he busied himself with the sale of the brewery, and what a generation earlier had been bought for £20,000 was sold for £135,000.[9] On the other hand, trading with the booksellers for his own works, he could scarcely have done worse. He got £1575[10] for the Dictionary—a seven years' task; and he paid out of that sum the cost of supplies and the wages of his helpers. He was an established and famous writer when he sold Rasselas for £100.[11] For the four volumes of the Lives of the Poets he got £300.[12] Very shortly afterward, Mrs. Thrale by contrast was to get 500 guineas for her Letters to and from Dr. Johnson and £50 more if the book went into a second edition;[13] and Murphy was to get £300 for his slight work, An Essay on the Life and Genius of Dr. Johnson.[14]

Yet it cannot be said that Johnson was indifferent to money. The woes of poverty and the comforts of wealth he knew intimately. For lack of lodging he had wandered about the streets of London.[15] He had been imprisoned once for debt, a petty matter of £5.[16] To protect himself from the condescension of the rich and the insolence of the proud he had developed what he called his "defensive pride."[17] On the other hand, he had for nearly twenty years enjoyed what luxury wealth could provide in the household of Henry Thrale.[18] He knew what money and what lack of it could do for a man. It is probable, how-

[7] Bos. 1738.
[8] Tour 16 August.
[9] Bos. April 1781.
[10] Bos. 1747.
[11] Bos. 1759.
[12] Bos. May 1777; Bos. 1781.
[13] Thraliana 26 Oct. 1787.
[14] Krutch, p. 456.
[15] Bos. 1744.
[16] Bos. 1756(n).
[17] Bos. 1754.
[18] Letter to Mrs. T., May 1779.

ever, that he was not merely arguing the other side when, in 1781, he said: "I have not observed that men of large fortune enjoy anything extraordinary that makes happiness. What has the Duke of Bedford? What has the Duke of Devonshire?"[19]

His own ideas of wealth were very modest. He not only lived himself but maintained a household of indigent dependants on his pension of £300. When efforts were made to have the Treasury grant him a further allowance so that he might enjoy the climate of Italy, he said that he would rather have his pension doubled than get an extra thousand pounds as an immediate gift. "For," said he, "though I might not live to receive as much as a thousand pounds, I would have the consciousness that I should pass the remainder of my life in splendor, how long soever it might be."[20] To anyone but Johnson, splendor on £600 a year would be modest splendor indeed.

In Johnson's whole attitude toward wealth there was a kind of philosophical balance. Without adopting the owl-eyed sententiousness of Mr. Micawber, he could say, "Whatever you have, spend less."[21] On the other hand, he advised a prospering tradesman to begin enjoying his wealth as soon as he could. For his work he accepted without question what the booksellers offered him[22]—it was little enough—and called them "generous men" and "patrons of literature."[23] Finally, he so husbanded his resources that he could "live rich,"[24] in his own meaning of the phrase, and yet leave a not inconsiderable estate of about £2000.[25]

Men are generally idle and ready to satisfy themselves and intimidate the industry of others by calling that impossible which is only difficult. [Boerhaave

[19] Bos. June 1781.
[20] Bos. June 1784.
[21] Letter to Bos., 7 Dec. 1782.
[22] Bos. April 1759(n).
[23] Bos. 1756.
[24] Bos. April 1778.
[25] Hawkins (postscript).

Many things difficult to design prove easy to performance.
[Ras. 13

Sir, the life of a parson, of a conscientious clergyman, is not
easy. I have always considered a clergyman as the father of a
larger family than he is able to maintain . . . No, Sir, I do not
envy a clergyman's life as an easy life, nor do I envy the clergyman who makes it an easy life. [Bos. 17 April 1778

A woman's preaching is like a dog's walking on his hinder
legs. It is not done well; but you are surprized to find it done at
all. [Bos. 31 July 1763

Stockjobber: A low wretch who gets money by buying and
selling shares in the funds. [Dict.

Broker: A factor . . . one who makes bargains for another.
"Brokers, who having no flocks of their own, set up and trade
with other men; buying here and selling there, and commonly
abusing both sides to make out a paultry bargain." [Dict.

It is the fate of those who toil at the lower employments of
life, to be rather driven by the fear of evil, than attracted by
the prospect of good; to be exposed to censure, without hope
of praise; to be disgraced by miscarriage, or punished for neglect, where success would have been without applause, and
diligence without reward. [Pref. Dict.

No man will be a sailor who has contrivance enough to get
himself into jail; for being in a ship is being in a jail, with the
chance of being drowned . . . A man in a jail has more room,
better food, and commonly better company. [Bos. 1759

Every man thinks meanly of himself for not having been a

soldier . . . were Socrates and Charles the Twelfth of Sweden both present in any company, and Socrates to say, "Follow me, and hear a lecture in philosophy"; and Charles, laying his hand on his sword, to say, "Follow me, and dethrone the Czar"; a man would be ashamed to follow Socrates. Sir, the impression is universal; yet it is strange. [Bos. 10 April 1778

I passed some years in the most contemptible of human stations, that of a soldier in time of peace . . . Wherever I came, I was for some time a stranger without curiosity, and afterwards an acquaintance without friendship. [Idl. 21

He was not displeased at the recollection of a sarcasm thrown on a whole profession at once; when a gentleman leaving the company, somebody who sate next Dr. Johnson asked him, who he was? "I cannot exactly tell you, Sir (replied he), and I would be loth to speak ill of any person who I do not know deserves it, but I am afraid he is an *attorney*." [Pioz. Anec.

Lawyers know life practically. A bookish man should always have them to converse with. They have what he wants [lacks]. [Bos. 17 April 1778

If . . . the profession you have chosen has some unexpected inconveniences, console yourself by reflecting that no profession is without them; and that all the importunities and perplexities of business are softness and luxury, compared with the incessant cravings of vacancy and the unsatisfactory expedients of idleness. [Bos. Aug. 1776

Scorn . . . to put your behaviour under the dominion of canters; never think it clever to call physic a mean study, or law a dry one; or ask a baby of seven years old which way *his genius* leads him, when we all know that a boy of seven years old has no *genius* for any thing except a peg-top and an apple-pye; but fix on some business where much money may be got and little virtue risqued; follow that business steadily, and do not live as Roger Ascham says the wits do, *Men know not how; and at last die obscurely, men mark not where.* [Pioz. Anec.

Everyone must have remarked what powers and prerogatives the vulgar imagine to be conferred by learning. A man of science is expected to excel the unlettered and unenlightened even on occasions where literature is of no use, and among weak minds loses part of his reverence by discovering no superiority in those parts of life where all are unavoidably equal. [Idl. 180

I do not call a gamester a dishonest man, but I call him an unsocial man, an unprofitable man. Gaming is a mode of transferring property without producing any intermediate good. Trade gives employment to numbers, and so produces intermediate good. [Bos. 6 April 1772

As to the rout that is made about people who are ruined by extravagance, it is no matter to the nation that some individuals suffer. When so much general productive exertion is the consequence of luxury, the nation does not care though there are debtors in gaol; nay they would not care though their creditors were there too. [Bos. May 1776

No man forgets his original trade; the rights of nations and of kings sink into questions of grammar if grammarians discuss them. [L.P., Milton

Politicks are now nothing more than means of rising in the world. With this sole view do men engage in politicks, and their whole conduct proceeds upon it. [Bos. 18 April 1775

To Barclay, who bought the Thrale brewery, advising him to continue his studies:

A mere literary man is a *dull* man; a man who is solely a man of business is a *selfish* man; but when literature and commerce are united, they make a *respectable* man. [Barclay, John. Misc.

But he that dares to think well of himself, will not always prove to be mistaken; and the good effects of his confidence will then appear in great attempts and great performances: if he should not fully complete his design, he will at least advance it so far as to leave an easier task for him that succeeds him; and even though he should wholly fail, he will fail with honour. [Adv. 81

It is the duty of every man to endeavour that something may be added by his industry to the hereditary aggregate of knowledge and happiness. To add much can indeed be the lot of few, but to add something, however little, every one may hope; and of every honest endeavour, it is certain that, however unsuccessful, it will be at last rewarded. [Ram. 129

In every great performance, perhaps in every great character, part is the gift of nature, part the contribution of accident, and part, very often not the greatest part, the effect of voluntary election and regular design. [King of Prussia

The business of life is carried on by a general co-operation; in which the part of any single man can be no more distinguished, than the effect of a particular drop when the meadows are floated by a summer shower: yet every drop increases the inundation, and every hand adds to the happiness or misery of mankind . . . truth is more often successfully propagated by men of moderate abilities, who, adopting the opinions of others, have no care but to explain them clearly. [Adv. 137

. . . he who does his best, however little, is always to be distinguished from him who does nothing. [Ram. 177

Nothing . . . will ever be attempted, if all possible objections must first be overcome. [Ras. 6

It is well observed by *Pythagoras,* that ability and necessity dwell near each other. [Idl. 80

Great powers cannot be exerted, but when great exigencies make them necessary. Great exigencies can happen but seldom, and therefore those qualities which have a claim to the veneration of mankind, lie hid, for the most part, like subterranean treasures, over which the foot passes as on common ground, till necessity breaks open the golden cavern. [Idl. 51

Nothing is to be expected from the workman whose tools are for ever to be sought. I was once told by a great master, that no man ever excelled in painting, who was eminently curious about pencils and colours. [Idl. 31

We are all ready to confess, that belief ought to be proportioned to evidence or probability: let any man, therefore, compare the number of those who have been . . . favoured by fortune, and of those who have failed of their expectations, and he will easily determine, with what justness he has registered himself in the lucky catalogue. [Adv. 69

The great end of prudence is to give cheerfulness to those hours which splendour cannot gild, and acclamation cannot exhilarate; those soft intervals of unbended amusement, in which a man shrinks to his natural dimensions, and throws aside the ornaments and disguises, which he feels in privacy to be useless incumbrances, and to lose all effect when they become familiar. To be happy at home is the ultimate result of all ambition, the end to which every enterprise and labour tends, and of which every desire prompts the prosecution. [Ram. 68

The trade [brewery] must be carried on by somebody who must be answerable for the debts contracted. This can be none but yourself . . . Do not be frighted. Trade could not be managed by those who manage it if it had much difficulty. Their great books are soon understood, and their language,

> If speech it may be called, that speech is none
> Distinguishable in number, mood, and tense

is understood with no very laborious application. [Letter to Mrs. T., 16 Nov. 1779

There is, indeed, no employment, however despicable, from which a man may not promise himself more than competence when he sees thousands . . . raised to dignity by no other merit than that of contributing to supply their neighbours with the means of sucking smoke through a tube of clay. [Adv. 67

"What is the reason that we are angry at a trader's having opulence?"—*Johnson.* "Why, sir, the reason is (though I don't undertake to prove that there is a reason), we see no qualities in trade that should entitle a man to superiority. We are not angry at a soldier's getting riches, because we see that he possesses qualities which we have not . . . we feel that he deserves the gold; but we cannot think that a fellow, by sitting all day at a desk, is entitled to get above us."—*Boswell.* "But sir, may we not suppose a merchant to be a man of an enlarged mind, such as Addison in the *Spectator* describes Sir Andrew Freeport to have been?"—*Johnson.* "Why, sir, we may suppose any fictitious character. We may suppose a philosophical day-labourer . . . A merchant may, perhaps, be a man of an enlarged mind;

but there is nothing in trade connected with an enlarged mind." [Tour 18 October

A fellow must do something, and what is so easy to a narrow mind as hoarding half-pence till they turn to sixpences? [Pioz. Anec.

The counting house of an accomplished merchant is a school of method where the great science may be learned of ranging particulars under generals, of bringing the different parts of a transaction together, and of showing at one view a long series of dealing and exchange. [Pref. Rolt's Comm'l. Dict.

Among the productions of mechanic art, many are of a form so different from that of their first materials, and many consist of parts so numerous and so nicely adapted to each other, that it is not possible to view them without amazement. But when we enter the shops of artificers, observe the various tools by which every operation is facilitated, and trace the progress of a manufacture through the different hands, that, in succession to each other, contribute to its perfection, we soon discover that every single man has an easy task, and that the extremes, however remote, of natural rudeness and artificial elegance are joined by a regular concatenation of effects, of which every one is introduced by that which precedes it, and equally introduces that which is to follow. [Ram. 137

If we estimate dignity by immediate usefulness, agriculture is undoubtedly the first and noblest science; yet we see the plough driven, the clod broken, the manure spread, the seeds scattered, and the harvest reaped, by men whom those that feed upon their industry will never be persuaded to admit into the same rank with heroes or with sages; and who, after all the confessions which truth may extort in favour of their occupation, must be content to fill up the lowest class of the commonwealth, to form the base of the pyramid of subordination, and lie buried in obscurity themselves, while they support all that is splendid, conspicuous, or exalted. (Ram. 145

Speaking of the cloistered life of a scholar:

About the same time of life [that] Meeke was left behind to feed on a fellowship, I went to London to get my living. [Bos. 21 Nov. 1754

He talked both of threshing and thatching. He said, it was very difficult to determine how to agree with a thresher. "If you pay him by the day's wages, he will thresh no more than he pleases; though, to be sure, the negligence of a thresher is more easily detected than that of most labourers, because he must always make a sound while he works. If you pay him by the piece, by the quantity of grain which he produces, he will thresh only while the grain comes freely, and, though he leaves a good deal in the ear, it is not worth while to thresh the straw over again; nor can you fix him to do it sufficiently, because it is so difficult to prove how much less a man threshes than he ought to do. Here then is a dilemma: but, for my part, I would engage him by the day. I would rather trust his idleness than his fraud." [Tour 28 September

. . . no man can see all with his own eyes, or do all with his own hands . . . whoever is engaged in multiplicity of business, must transact much by substitution, and leave something to hazard . . . he who attempts to do all, will waste his life doing little. [Idl. 19

Men unaccustomed to reason . . . think every enterprize impracticable which is extended beyond common effects . . . Many that presume to laugh at [visionaries] would consider a flight through the air of a winged chariot, and the movement of a mighty engine by the stream of water as equally the dreams of mechanick lunacy; and would hear, with equal negligence, of the union of the Thames and the Severn by a canal, and the scheme of Albuquerque, the viceroy of the Indies, who in the rage of hostility had contrived to make Egypt a barren desert, by turning the Nile into the Red Sea.

Those who have attempted much, have seldom failed to perform more than those who never deviate from the common roads of action . . . it is, therefore, just to encourage those who endeavour to enlarge the power of art, since they often succeed beyond expectation; and when they fail, may sometimes benefit the world even by their miscarriages. [Adv. 99

The present moment is never proper for the change, but there is always a time in view when all obstacles will be removed. [Idl. 21

A man accustomed to vicissitudes is not easily dejected. [Ras. 12

. . . as all must obey the call of immediate necessity, nothing that requires extensive views, or provides for distant consequences, will ever be performed. [Journey, Ostig

Many . . . find quiet shameful, and business dangerous, and therefore pass their lives between them, in bustle without business, and negligence without quiet. |Idl. 19

To confer duration is not always in our power. We must snatch the present moment, and employ it well, without too much solicitation for the future, and content ourselves with reflecting that our part is performed. He that waits for an opportunity to do much at once, may breathe out his life in idle wishes, and regrets, in the last hour, his useless intentions, and barren zeal. [Idl. 4

Where there is no hope, there can be no endeavour. [Ram. 110

Whatever facilitates our work is more than an omen; it is a cause of success. [Ras. 13

It would add much to human happiness, if an art could be taught of forgetting all of which the remembrance is at once useless and afflictive . . . that the mind might perform its functions without incumbrance, and the past no longer encroach upon the present.

Little can be done well to which the whole mind is not applied; the business of each day calls for the day to which it is assigned; and he will have no leisure to regret yesterday's vexations who resolves not to have a new subject of regret tomorrow. [Idl. 72

There would be few enterprises of great labour or hazard undertaken, if we had not the power of magnifying the advantages which we persuade ourselves to expect from them. [Ram. 2

There are few higher gratifications than that of reflection on surmounted evils, when they were not incurred nor protracted by our fault, and neither reproach us with cowardice nor guilt. [Ram. 203

I passed four months in the company of architects, whose whole business was to pursuade me to build a house. I told them that I had more room than I wanted, but could not get rid of their importunities. A new plan was brought me every morning; till at last my constancy was overpowered, and I began to build. The happiness of building lasted but a little while, for though I love to spend, I hate to be cheated; and I soon found, that to build is to be robbed. [Idl. 62

Labour is exercise continued to fatigue—exercise is labour used only while it produces pleasure. [Letter to Mrs. T., 23 June 1779

The natural progress of the works of men is from rudeness to convenience, from convenience to elegance, and from elegance to nicety. [Idl. 63

Whatever busies the mind without corrupting it, has at least this use, that it rescues the day from idleness, and he that is never idle will not often be vicious. [Ram. 177

Praise and money [are] the two powerful corrupters of mankind. [Bos. 1783

. . . the folly of projection [planning] is seldom the folly of a fool; it is commonly the ebullition of a capacious mind . . . Whatever is attempted without previous certainty of success, may be considered as a project, and amongst narrow minds may, therefore, expose its authour to censure and contempt. [Adv. 99

To strive with difficulties and to conquer them is the highest human felicity; the next is to strive and deserve to conquer: but he whose life has passed without a contest, and who can boast neither success nor merit, can survey himself only as a useless filler of existence; and if he is content with his own character, must owe his satisfaction to insensibility. [Adv. 111

No man is obliged to do as much as he can do. A man is to have part of his life to himself. [Bos. Spring 1766

There is no kind of idleness by which we are so easily seduced as that which dignifies itself by the appearance of business, and by making the loiterer imagine that he has something to do which must not be neglected, keeps him in perpetual agitation, and hurries him rapidly from place to place. [Idl. 48

. . . idleness is often covered by turbulence and hurry. [Idl. 31

. . . those who attempt nothing themselves think everything easily performed, and consider the unsuccessful always as criminal. [Idl. 1

. . . instead of rating the man by his performances, we rate too frequently the performance by the man. [Ram. 166

[Bustling] does not hasten us a bit. It is getting on horseback in a ship. All boys do it; and you [Boswell] are longer a boy than others. [Tour 13 October

The certainty that life cannot be long, and the probability that it will be much shorter than nature allows, ought to awaken every man to the active prosecution of whatever he is desirous to perform. It is true that no diligence can ascertain success; death may intercept the swiftest career; but he who is cut off in the execution of an honest undertaking, has at least the honour of falling in his rank, and has fought the battle, though he missed the victory .[Ram. 134

A man would never undertake great things, could he be amused with small. [Bos. 7 April 1778

To do nothing every man is ashamed; and to do much almost every man is unwilling or afraid. Innumerable expedients have therefore been invented to produce motion without labour, and employment without solicitude. [Idl. 48

Indolence is, therefore, one of the vices from which those whom it once infects are seldom reformed. Every other species of luxury operates upon some appetite that is quickly satiated, and requires some concurrence of art or accident which every place will not supply; but the desire of ease acts equally at all hours, and the longer it is indulged is the more increased. To do nothing is in every man's power; we can never want opportunity of omitting duties. [Ram. 155

The rest [the idle inhabitants of the Happy Valley], whose minds have no impression but of the present moment, are either corroded by malignant passions, or sit stupid in the gloom of perpetual vacancy. [Ras. 12

. . . it is the just doom of laziness and gluttony, to be inactive without ease, and drowsy without tranquillity. [Adv. 39

. . . whatever idleness may expect from time, its produce will be only in proportion to the diligence with which it has been used. He that floats lazily down the stream, in pursuit of something borne along by the same current, will indeed find himself move forward; but unless he lays his hand to the oar and increases his speed by his own labour, must be always at the same distance from that which he is following. [Adv. 69

There is nothing more common among this torpid generation than . . . murmurs at uneasiness which only vacancy and suspicion expose them to feel, and complaints of distresses which it is in their power to remove. Laziness is commonly associated with timidity. Either fear originally prohibits endeavours by infusing despair of success; or the frequent failure of irresolute struggles, and the constant desire of avoiding labour, impress by degrees false terrors on the mind. But fear, whether natural or acquired, when once it has full possession of the fancy, never fails to employ it upon visions of calamity, such as, if they are not dissipated by useful employment, will soon overcast it with horrors, and embitter life not only with those miseries by which all earthly beings are really more or less tormented, but with those which do not yet exist, and which can only be discerned by the perspicacity of cowardice. [Ram. 134

Idleness can never secure tranquillity; the call of reason and of conscience will pierce the closest pavilion of the sluggard; and though it may not have force to drive him from his down, will be loud enough to hinder him from sleep. [Ram. 134

Every man is, or hopes to be, an *Idler*. [Idl. 1

He that never labours may know the pains of idleness, but not the pleasures. [Idl. 9

[Johnson] made the common remark on the unhappiness which men who have led a busy life experience, when they retire in expectation of enjoying themselves at ease, and that they generally languish for want of their habitual occupation, and wish to return to it. He mentioned as strong an instance of this as can well be imagined. "An eminent tallow-chandler in London, who had acquired a considerable fortune, gave up the trade in favour of his foreman, and went to live at a country-house near town. He soon grew weary, and paid frequent visits to his old shop, where he desired they might let him know their *melting-days*, and he would come and assist them; which he accordingly did. Here, Sir, was a man, to whom the most disgusting circumstance in the business to which he had been used, was a relief from idleness." [Bos. 2 April 1775

All the performances of human art, at which we look with

praise or wonder, are instances of the resistless force of perseverance; it is by this that the quarry becomes a pyramid, and that distant countries are united with canals. If a man was to compare the effect of a single stroke of the pick-axe, or one impression of the spade, with the general design and last result, he would be overwhelmed by the sense of their disproportion; yet those petty operations, incessantly continued, in time surmount the greatest difficulties, and mountains are levelled, and oceans bounded, by the slender force of human beings. [Ram. 43

Perhaps no extensive and multifarious performance was ever effected within the term originally fixed in the undertaker's mind. He that runs against time has an antagonist not subject to casualties. [L.P., Pope

He is no wise man who will quit a certainty for an uncertainty. [Idl. 57

In proportion as perfection is more distinctly conceived, the pleasure of contemplating our own performance will be lessened. [Ram. 169

You must not neglect doing a thing immediately good, for fear of remote evil—from fear of its being abused. A man who has candles may sit up too late, which he would not do if he had not candles; but nobody will deny that the art of making candles, by which light is continued to us beyond the time that the sun gives us light, is a valuable art, and ought to be preserved. [Bos. 15 April 1772

Whatever is common is despised. Advertisements are now so numerous that they are very negligently perused, and it is therefore necessary to gain attention by magnificence of promises, and by eloquence sometimes sublime and sometimes pathetic.

Promise, large promise, is the soul of an advertisement. [Idl. 40

All imposture weakens confidence, and chills benevolence. [Ras. 44

If I accustom a servant to tell lies for me, have I not reason to apprehend that he will tell lies for himself? [Bos. 19 July 1763

Asked about the value of the Thrale brewery, which was to be sold, Johnson replied:

We are not here to sell a parcel of boilers and vats, but the potentiality of growing rich beyond the dreams of avarice. [Bos. 4 April 1781

A principal source of erroneous judgement was, viewing things partially and only on *one side*: as for instance, *fortune-hunters,* when they contemplated the fortunes *singly* and *separately,* it was a dazzling and tempting object; but when they came to possess the wives and their fortunes *together,* they began to suspect they had not made quite so good a bargain. [Bos. 1770

Greatness and littleness are terms merely comparative; and we err in our estimation of things because we measure them by some wrong standard . . . Man can only form a just estimate of his own actions, by making his power the test of his performance, by comparing what he does with what he can do. Whoever steadily perseveres in the exertion of all his faculties, does what is great with respect to himself; and what will not be despised by Him, who has given to all created beings their different abilities: he faithfully performs the task of life within whatever limits his labours may be confined, or how soon soever they may be forgotten. [Adv. 128

. . . idleness predominates in many lives where it is not suspected; for, being a vice which terminates in itself, it may be enjoyed without injury to others; and it is therefore not watched like fraud, which endangers property; or like pride, which naturally seeks its gratification in another's inferiority. Idleness is a silent and peaceful quality, that neither raises envy by ostentation, nor hatred by opposition; and therefore nobody is busy to censure or detect it. [Idl. 31

. . . labour, though unsuccessful, is more eligible than idleness; he that prosecutes a lawful purpose by lawful means, acts always with the approbation of his own reason; he is animated through the course of his endeavours by an expectation which, though not certain, he knows to be just; and is at last comforted in his disappointment, by the consciousness that he has not failed by his own fault. [Adv. 111

To be idle and to be poor, have always been reproaches, and therefore every man endeavours, with his utmost care, to hide his poverty from others, and his idleness from himself. [Idl. 17

. . . love of life . . . is necessary to the vigorous prosecution of any undertaking. [Ram. 59

Riches therefore, perhaps, do not so often produce crimes as incite accusers. [Ram. 172

Money, in whatever hands, will confer power. [Ram. 142

Wherever there is wealth there will be dependence and expectation, and wherever there is dependence there will be an emulation of servility. [Ram. 189

When I was running about this town a very poor fellow, I was a great arguer for the advantages of poverty; but I was, at

the same time, very sorry to be poor . . . Arguments which . . .
represent poverty as no evil, shew it to be evidently a great evil.
You never find people labouring to convince you that you may
live very happily upon a plentiful fortune. [Bos. 20 July 1763

When the power of birth and station ceases, no hope remains
but from the prevalence of money. Power and wealth supply
the place of each other. Power confers the ability of gratifying
our desire without the consent of others. Wealth enables us to
obtain the consent of others to our gratification. Power, simply
considered, whatever it confers on one, must take from another.
Wealth enables its owner to give to others, by taking only
from himself. Power pleases the violent and proud: wealth delights the placid and timorous. Youth therefore flies at power,
and age grovels after riches. [Journey, Ostig

Aspire not to public honours, enter not the palaces of kings;
thy wealth will set thee above insult, let thy moderation keep
thee below envy. [Ram. 190

Money, to be sure, of itself is of no use; for its only use is to
part with. [Bos. 20 July 1763

. . . fine clothes are good only as they supply the want of
other means of procuring respect. [Bos. 27 March 1776

[Wealth] is more useful for defence than acquisition, and is
not so much able to procure good as to exclude evil. [Ram. 53

Money *will* purchase occupation; it will purchase all the conveniences of life; it will purchase variety of company; it will
purchase all sorts of entertainment. [Bos. 17 Sept. 1777

Such . . . is the power of wealth that it commands the ear

of greatness and the eye of beauty, gives spirit to the dull and authority to the timorous, and leaves him from whom it departs, without virtue and without understanding, the sport of caprice, the scoff of insolence, the slave of meanness, and the pupil of ignorance. [Ram. 153

It has been long observed, that whatever is procured by skill or labour to the first possessor may be afterwards transferred for money; and that the man of wealth may partake all the acquisitions of courage without hazard, and all the products of industry without fatigue. [Ram. 193

Sir, riches do not gain hearty respect; they only procure external attention. A very rich man, from low beginnings, may buy his election in a borough; but, *ceteris paribus*, a man of family will be preferred . . . If gentlemen of family would allow the rich upstarts to spend their money profusely, which they are ready enough to do, and not vie with them in expence, the upstarts would soon be at an end, and the gentlemen would remain: but if the gentlemen will vie in expence with the upstarts, which is very foolish, they must be ruined. [Bos. 21 March 1772

The only great instance that I have ever known of the enjoyment of wealth was, that of Jamaica Dawkins, who, going to visit Palmyra, and hearing that the way was infested by robbers, hired a troop of Turkish horse to guard him. [Bos. 3 June 1781

It is observed of gold . . . that *to have it is to be in fear, and to want it is to be in sorrow*. There is no condition which is not disquieted either with the care of gaining or of keeping money; and the race of man may be divided . . . between those who are practising fraud, and those who are repelling it. [Ram. 131

He said, indeed that women were very difficult to be taught the proper manner of conferring pecuniary favours: that they always gave too much money or too little; for that they had an idea of delicacy accompanying their gifts, so that they generally rendered them either useless or ridiculous. [Pioz. Anec.

A man cannot make a bad use of his money, so far as regards Society, if he does not hoard it; for he either spends it or lends it out, Society has the benefit. It is in general better to spend money than to give it away; for industry is more promoted by spending money than by giving it away. A man who spends his money is sure he is doing good with it: he is not so sure when he gives it away [Bos. 23 March 1783

The great effect of money is to break property into small parts. In towns, he that has a shilling may have a piece of meat; but where there is no commerce, no man can eat mutton but by killing a sheep. [Journey, Ostig

. . . think not riches useless; there are purposes to which a wise man may be delighted to apply them; they may, by rational distribution to those who want them, ease the pains of helpless disease, still the throbs of restless anxiety, relieve innocence from oppression, and raise imbecility to cheerfulness and vigour. [Ram. 120

. . . wealth is nothing but as it is bestowed. [Ras. 35

Influence must ever be in proportion to property; and it is [right] that it should. [Tour 18 August

[Bluster] is wealthy without followers; he is magnificent without witnesses; he has birth without alliance, and influence without dignity. His neighbours scorn him as a brute; his dependents dread him as an oppressor; and he has only the gloomy comfort of reflecting, that if he is hated he is likewise feared. [Ram. 142

Getting money is not all a man's business: to cultivate kindness is a valuable part of the business of life. [Bos. 21 Sept. 1777

Depend upon it, this rage of trade will destroy itself. You and I shall not see it; but the time will come when there will be an end of it. Trade is like gaming. If a whole company are gamesters, play must cease; for there is nothing to be won. When all nations are traders, there is nothing to be gained by trade, and it will stop first where it is brought to the greatest perfection. Then the proprietors of land only will be the great men. [Tour 20 September

[Riches] very seldom make their owner rich. To be rich, is to have more than is desired, and more than is wanted; to have something which may be spent without reluctance, and scattered without care, with which the sudden demands of desire may be gratified, the casual freaks of fancy indulged, or the unexpected opportunities of benevolence improved. [Idl. 73

Money confounds subordination by overpowering the distinctions of rank and birth, and weakens authority by supplying power of resistance, or expedients for escape. [Journey, Ostig

. . . money and time are the heaviest burdens of life, and . . . the unhappiest of all mortals are those who have more of either than they know how to use. [Idl. 30

Every man is rich or poor, according to the proportion between his desires and enjoyments; any enlargement of wishes is therefore equally destructive to happiness with the diminution of possessions; and he that teaches another to long for what he never shall obtain, is no less an enemy to his quiet, than if he had robbed him of part of his patrimony. [Ram. 163

Asked by Boswell if he were not dissatisfied at having received so small a share of wealth, Johnson replied:

I have never complained of the world; nor do I think that I have reason to complain. It is rather to be wondered at that I have so much. My pension is more out of the usual course of things than any instances that I have known. Here, Sir, was a man avowedly no friend to the government at the time, who got a pension without asking for it. [Bos. May 1781

Nature makes us poor only when we want necessaries; but custom gives the name of poverty to want of superfluities. [Idl. 37

The desires of man increase with his acquisitions . . . no sooner are we supplied with every thing that nature can demand, than we sit down to contrive artificial appetites. [Idl. 30

Resolve not to be poor: whatever you have, spend less. Poverty is a great enemy to human happiness; it certainly destroys liberty, and it makes some virtues impracticable and others extremely difficult. [Bos. 7 Dec. 1782

The inevitable consequence of poverty is dependence. [L.P., Dryden

The poor and the busy have no time for sentimental sorrow. [Pioz. Anec.

A man guilty of poverty easily believes himself suspected. [Ram. 26

Want of money . . . is sometimes concealed . . . under a shew of thoughtless extravagance and gay neglect—while to a penetrating eye, none of these wretched veils suffice to keep the cruel truth from being seen. Poverty is *hic et ubique* . . . and if you do shut the jade out of the door, she will always contrive in some manner to poke her pale lean face in at the window. [Pioz. Anec.

I saw many poor whom I had supposed to live in affluence. Poverty has, in large cities, very different appearances; it is often concealed in splendour, and often in extravagance. It is the care of a very great part of mankind to conceal their indigence from the rest: they support themselves by temporary expedients, and every day is lost contriving for the morrow. [Ras. 25

. . . poverty, like many other miseries of life, is often little more than an imaginary calamity. Men often call themselves poor. not because they want necessaries, but because they have not more than they want. [Sermon V

The . . . oracles of our parsimonious ancestors have informed us, that the fatal waste of fortune is by small expences, by the profusion of sums too little singly to alarm our caution, and which we never suffer ourselves to consider together. Of the same kind is the prodigality of life; he that hopes to look back hereafter with satisfaction upon past years, must learn to know the present value of single minutes, and endeavour to let no particle of time fall useless to the ground. [Ram. 108

Of a friend, probably Langton:

He is ruining himself without pleasure. A man who loses at play, or who runs out his fortune at court, makes his estate less, in hopes of making it bigger . . . but it is a sad thing to pass through the quagmire of parsimony, to the gulph of ruin. To pass over the flowery path of extravagance is very well. [Bos. 12 May 1778

Do not accustom yourself to consider debt only as an inconvenience; you will find it a calamity. Poverty takes away so many means of doing good, and produces so much inability to resist evil, both natural and moral, that it is by all virtuous means to be avoided . . . Of riches it is not necessary to write the praise. Let it, however, be remembered, that he who has money to spare, has it always in his power to benefit others; and of such power a good man must always be desirous. [Bos. 3 June 1782

Do not think your estate your own, while any man can call upon you for money which you cannot pay . . . Let it be your first care not to be in any man's debt. [Bos. 7 Sept. 1782

. . . the creditor always shares the act, and often more than shares the guilt, of improper trust. [Idl. 22

Small debts are like small shot; they are rattling on every side, and can scarcely be escaped without a wound: great debts are like cannon; of loud noise, but little danger. [Bos. 1759

He, whose mind is engaged by the acquisition or improvement of a fortune, not only escapes the insipidity of indifference, and the tediousness of inactivity, but gains enjoyments wholly unknown to those, who live lazily on the toil of others; for life affords no higher pleasure than that of surmounting difficulties, passing from one step of success to another, forming new wishes, and seeing them gratified. He that labours in any great or laudable undertaking, has his fatigues first supported by hope, and afterwards rewarded by joy; he is always moving to a certain end, and when he has attained it, an end more distant invites him to a new pursuit. [Adv. 111

On Man as a Social Animal

Without intelligence man is not social; he is only gregarious.

Journey, Coll

Johnson was not only a sociable man; he prided himself on being a polite man.[1] Speaking one evening of Dr. Barnard, the Provost of Eton, he said, "He was the only man . . . that did justice to my good breeding; and you may observe that I am well-bred to a degree of needless scrupulosity. No man"—and Mrs. Thrale comments that he did not observe the amazement of his hearers—"is so cautious not to interrupt another . . . nobody holds so strongly as I do the necessity of ceremony, and the ill effects which follow the breach of it: yet people think me rude."[2] His hearers might well be amazed. Could he be unconscious of "the butt end of the pistol" which he used so frequently and so effectively? Could he have forgotten not the statement but what it implies when, speaking of his not being invited often to the houses of the great, he said, "great lords and great ladies don't love to have their mouths stopped."[3] "Sir, I am not used to be contradicted," he once said to Joseph Warton, to which Warton replied, "Better for your friends and for yourself, Sir, if you were; our admiration could not be increased, but our love might be."[4] And Dr. John Lettsom wrote: "he certainly was not polite, but he was not rude. He was

1 Bos. May 1778.   2 Pioz. Anec.
3 Bos. May 1781.   4 Lucas, p. 59.

sometimes jocular, but you felt as if you were playing with a lion's paw."[5]

Of course, Johnson talked for victory and was probably only half conscious of the wreckage he left behind him on the field. After one evening, he said to Boswell, "Well, we had a good talk." "Yes, Sir," answered Boswell; "you tossed and gored several persons."[6] Occasionally those so tossed and gored resented the operation, but Johnson was always ready to "make it up twenty different ways."[7] This is Johnson in talk. Yet few men knew more, or had more to say about, the art of living with one's fellow men. When he was unexpectedly confronted by the king, his manner was impeccable. He spoke still "in his firm manly manner, with a sonorous voice, and never in that subdued tone which is commonly used at the levee and in the drawing room."[8] To his friends he said, "I found his Majesty wished I should talk, and I made it my business to talk."[9]

Boswell cites an amusing example of Johnson on his best behavior. Beauclerk one morning had taken Mme. de Boufflers to call upon Johnson. "When our visit was over," Beauclerk relates, "she and I left him, and were got into the Inner Temple-lane, when all at once I heard a noise like thunder. This was occasioned by Johnson, who, upon a little recollection, had taken it into his head that he ought to have done the honours of his residence to a foreign lady of quality; and eager to show himself a man of gallantry, was hurrying down the staircase in violent agitation. He overtook us before we reached the Temple gate, and brushing in between me and Mme. de Boufflers, seized her hand and conducted her to her coach."[10] At Inverary, too, when he and Boswell had dinner with the Duke and Duchess of Argyll, he was politeness itself. "I never saw him so courtly," was Boswell's comment.[11]

---

5 Krutch.   6 Bos. 1768.   7 Bos. May 1778.
8 Bos. Feb. 1767.   9 Bos. Feb. 1767.   10 Bos. 1775.
11 Tour 25 October.

Johnson, in his social relations, reminds us of an acquaintance both of his and Beauclerk's, a man—Johnson insisted—of good principles. "Then, Sir," retorted Beauclerk, "he never wore out his principles in practice."[12] That, in matters social, was Samuel Johnson.

To profess what he does not mean, to promise what he cannot perform, to flatter ambition with prospects of promotion, and misery with hopes of relief, to soothe pride with appearances of submission, and appease enmity by blandishments and bribes, can surely imply nothing more or greater than a mind devoted wholly to its own purposes, a face that cannot blush, and a heart that cannot feel. [Ram. 79

Courage is a quality so necessary for maintaining virtue, that it is always respected, even when it is associated with vice. [Bos. 11 June 1784

. . . he whom every man thinks he can conquer, shall never be at peace. [Ram. 176

[Politeness is] fictitious benevolence. It supplies the place of it amongst those who see each other only in publick, or but little. Depend upon it, the want of it never fails to produce something disagreeable to one or other. [Tour 21 August

Honesty is not greater where elegance is less. [Journey, Glenshiel

The universal axiom in which all complaisance is included, and from which flow all the formalities which custom has established in civilized nations, is, *That no man shall give any*

12 Bos. April 1778.

preference to himself. A rule so comprehensive and certain, that, perhaps, it is not easy for the mind to image an incivility, without supposing it to be broken. [Ram. 98

Favourite: One chosen as a companion by his superiour; a mean wretch whose whole business is by any means to please. [Dict.

Depend upon it, Sir, vivacity is much an art, and depends greatly on habit. [Bos. 23 March 1776

Every man has at some time in his life an ambition to be a wag. [D'Arblay Diary

The task of every other slave [than the wit] has an end. The rower in time reaches the port; the lexicographer at last finds the conclusion of his alphabet; only the hapless wit has his labour always to begin, the call for novelty is never satisfied, and one jest only raises expectation of another. [Ram. 141

Boswell. I considered distinction of rank to be of so much importance in civilised society, that if I were asked on the same day to dine with the first Duke in England, and with the first man in Britain for genius, I should hesitate which to prefer. *Johnson.* To be sure, Sir, if you were to dine only once, and it were never to be known where you dined, you would choose rather to dine with the first man for genius; but to gain most respect, you should dine with the first Duke in England. For nine people in ten that you meet with, would have a higher opinion of you for having dined with a Duke; and the great genius himself would receive you better, because you had been with the great Duke. [Bos. 21 July 1763

Great qualities or uncommon accomplishments he did not

find necessary [for frequent dinner invitations]; for he had already seen that merit rather enforces respect than attracts fondness; and as he thought no folly greater than that of losing a dinner for any other gratification, he often congratulated himself, that he had none of that disgusting excellence which impresses awe upon greatness, and condemns its possessors to the society of those who are wise or brave, and indigent as themselves. [Ram. 206

[Gelaleddin] was sometimes admitted to their tables, where he exerted his wit and diffused his knowledge; but he observed, that where, by endeavour or accident, he had remarkably excelled, he was seldom invited a second time. [Idl. 75

No man likes to live under the eye of perpetual disapprobation. [Bos. 1777

Few spend their time with much satisfaction under the eye of uncontestable superiority; and, therefore, among those whose presence is courted at assemblies of jollity, there are seldom found men eminently distinguished for powers or acquisitions. The wit, whose vivacity condemns slower tongues to silence; the scholar, whose knowledge allows no man to fancy that he instructs him; the critic, who suffers no fallacy to pass undetected . . . are generally praised and feared, reverenced and avoided. [Ram. 188

Think as well and as kindly of me as you can, but do not flatter me. Cool reciprocations of esteem are the great comforts of life; hyperbolical praise only corrupts the tongue of the one and the ear of the other. [Letter to Mrs. T., June 1783

He that is much flattered, soon learns to flatter himself: we are commonly taught our duty by fear or shame, and how can

they act upon a man who hears nothing but his own praises?
[L.P., Swift

The mischief of flattery is, not that it persuades any man that
he is what he is not, but that it suppresses the influence of
honest ambition, by raising an opinion that honour may be
gained without the toil of merit. [Ram. 155

Kindness is generally reciprocal; we are desirous of pleasing
others, because we receive pleasure from them. [Ram. 166

Favours of every kind are doubled when they are speedily
conferred. [Ram. 195

He only confers favours generously, who appears, when they
are once conferred, to remember them no more. [Sermon XIX

No degree of knowledge attainable by man is able to set him
above the want of hourly assistance, or to extinguish the desire
of fond endearments and tender officiousness; and therefore no
one should think it unnecessary to learn those arts by which
friendship may be gained. Kindness is preserved by a constant
reciprocation of benefits or interchange of pleasures; but such
benefits only can be bestowed as others are capable to receive,
and such pleasures only imparted, as others are qualified to
enjoy. [Ram. 137

If we will have the kindness of others, we must endure their
follies. [Idl. 14

A man will please more upon the whole by negative qualities
than by positive; by never offending, than by giving a great deal
of delight. In the first place, men hate more steadily than they
love; and if I have said something to hurt a man once, I shall

not get the better of this by saying many things to please him. [Bos. 16 Sept. 1777

We always think ourselves better than we are, and are generally desirous that others should think us still better than we think ourselves. [Ram. 104

To receive and to communicate assistance, constitutes the happiness of human life: man may, indeed, preserve his existence in solitude, but can enjoy it only in society; the greatest understanding of an individual, doomed to procure food and clothing for himself, will barely supply him with expedients to keep off death from day to day; but as one of a large community performing only his share of the common business, he gains leisure for intellectual pleasures, and enjoys the happiness of reason and reflection. [Adv. 67

Common fame is to every man what he himself hears. [Deb. Walpole

He that is pleased with himself easily imagines that he shall please others. [L.P., Pope

He that lives in torpid insensibility, wants nothing of a carcase but putrefaction. It is the part of every inhabitant of the earth to partake the pains and pleasures of his fellow beings. [Idl. 24

He that could withstand conscience is frighted at infamy, and shame prevails when reason was defeated. [Ram. 155

No man can fall into contempt but those who deserve it. [Deb. Engl. Seamen

It is a maxim that no man ever was enslaved by influence while he was fit to be free. [Bos. 23 Sept. 1777

We are inclined to believe those whom we do not know, because they have never deceived us. [Idl. 80

It is apparent that men can be social beings no longer than they can believe each other. When speech is employed only as the vehicle of falsehood, every man must disunite himself from others, inhabit his own cave, and seek prey only for himself. [Idl. 20

. . . a dependent could not easily be made a friend. [Ram. 190

Friendship is seldom lasting but between equals, or where the superiority on one side is reduced by some equivalent advantage on the other. [Ram. 64

No man . . . can pay a more servile tribute to the great, than by suffering his liberty in their presence to aggrandize him in his own esteem. Between different ranks of the community there is necessarily some distance; he who is called by his superiour to pass the interval, may properly accept the invitation; but petulance and obtrusion are rarely produced by magnanimity; nor have often any nobler cause than the pride of importance, and the malice of inferiority. [L.P., Swift

Incommunicative taciturnity neither imparts nor invites friendship, but reposes on a stubborn sufficiency self-centred, and neglects the interchange of that social officiousness by which we are habitually endeared to one another. They that mean to make no use of friends will be at little trouble to gain them; and to be without friendship is to be without one of the first comforts of our present state. To have no assistance from other minds in resolving doubts, in appeasing scruples, in balancing deliberation is a very wretched destitution. [Letter to Mrs. T., Nov. 1783

Always, Sir, set a high value on spontaneous kindness. He whose inclination prompts him to cultivate your friendship of his own accord, will love you more than one whom you have been at pains to attach to you. [Bos. May 1781

I am now grown very solicitous about my old friends, with whom I passed the hours of my youth and cheerfulness, and am glad of any opportunity to revive the memory of past pleasures. I therefore tear open a letter with great eagerness when I know the hand in which it is superscribed. Your letters are always so welcome that you need not increase their value by making them scarce. [Letter to Edm. Hector, April 1757

A short letter to a distant friend is, in my opinion, an insult like that of a slight bow or cursory salutation. [Letter to Baretti (Bos. 1762)

Friendship is . . . one of those few states of which it is reasonable to wish the continuance through life, but the form and exercise of friendship varies, and we grow to be content to show kindness on important occasions without squandering our ardour on superfluities of empty civility. [Letter to Edm. Hector, Oct. 1756

. . . the worst way of being intimate, is by scribbling. [Tour 23 August

Many men would not be content to live [without a friend].

I hope I should not. They would wish to have an intimate friend, with whom they might compare minds, and cherish private virtues. [Bos. 24 April 1779

To have a friend, and a friend like you, may be numbered among the first felicities of life; at a time when weakness either of body or of mind loses the pride and confidence of self-sufficiency, and looks around for that help which perhaps human kindness cannot give, and which we yet are willing to expect from one another. [Letter to J. Ryland, Nov. 1784

How many friendships have you known formed upon principles of virtue? Most friendships are formed by caprice or by chance, mere confederacies in vice or leagues in folly. [Bos. 19 May 1784

It is discovered . . . that no man is much pleased with a companion, who does not increase, in some respect, his fondness of himself; and, therefore, he that wishes rather to be led forward to prosperity by the gentle hand of favour, than to force his way by labour and merit, must consider with more care how to display his patron's excellences than his own. [Ram. 104

Since you have written me with the attention and tenderness of ancient times, your letters give me a great part of the pleasure which a life of solitude admits. You will never bestow any share of your good will on one who deserves it better. Those who have loved longest love best. A sudden blaze of kindness may, by a single blast of coldness, be extinguished, but that fondness which length of time has connected with many circumstances and occasions, though it may for a while be suppressed by disgust or resentment with or without cause, is hourly revived by accidental recollection. To those who have lived long together everything seen and everything heard recalls some pleasure communicated, or some benefit conferred, some petty quarrel or some slight endearment. Esteem of great powers or amiable qualities may embroider a day or a week, but a friendship of twenty years is interwoven with the texture of life. A friend may be often found and lost, but an *old Friend* never can be found, and nature has provided that he cannot easily be lost. [Letter to Mrs. T., Nov. 1783

If a man does not make new acquaintance as he advances through life, he will soon find himself left alone. A man, Sir, should keep his friendship *in constant repair*. [Bos. 1755

Sir, I look upon every day to be lost, in which I do not make a new acquaintance. [Bos. 1784

. . . we must either outlive our friends you know, or our friends must outlive us; and I see no man that would hesitate about the choice. [Pioz. Anec.

The Irish are a FAIR PEOPLE;—they never speak well of one another. [Bos. 1775

. . . we sat silent for a long time, all employed in collecting importance into our faces, and endeavouring to strike reverence and submission into our companions. [Adv. 84

Self-love . . . does not hide our faults from ourselves, but persuades us that they escape the notice of others, and disposes us to resent censures lest we should confess them to be just. We are secretly conscious of defects and vices which we hope to conceal from the public eye, and please ourselves with innumerable impostures, by which, in reality, nobody is deceived. [Ram. 155

Nothing is little to him that feels it with great sensibility. [Bos. 1762

Sir, a man has no more right to *say* an uncivil thing, than to *act* one; no more right to say a rude thing to another than to knock him down. [Bos. 1780

It is commonly observed, that when two *Englishmen* meet, their first talk is of the weather. [Idl. 11

. . . two men of any other nation who are shewn into a room together, at a house where they are both visitors, will immediately find some conversation. But two Englishmen will probably go each to a different window, and remain in obstinate silence. Sir, we as yet do not enough understand the common rights of humanity. [Bos. 1783

Never speak of a man in his own presence. It is always indelicate, and may be offensive. [Bos. March 1776

. . . fewer have curiosity or benevolence to struggle long against the first impression; he therefore who fails to please in his salutation and address, is at once rejected and never obtains an opportunity of shewing his latent excellences, or essential qualities. [Ram. 166

Nothing therefore is more unjust than to judge of man by too short an acquaintance, and too slight inspection; for it often happens that, in the loose, and thoughtless, and dissipated, there is a secret radical worth which may shoot out by proper cultivation; that the spark of heaven, though dimmed and obstructed, is not yet extinguished, but may, by the breath of counsel and exhortation, be kindled into flame. [Ram. 70

Madam, before you flatter a man so grossly to his face, consider whether your flattery is worth having. [D'Arblay Diary

There are gradations in conduct; there is morality,—decency,
—propriety. None of these should be violated by a bishop. [Bos.
28 March 1781

A man should not let himself down, by speaking a language
which he speaks imperfectly. [Bos. 1775

But almost all absurdity of conduct arises from the imitation
of those whom we cannot resemble. [Ram. 135

. . . scarce any man becomes eminently disagreeable but by
a departure from his real character, and an attempt at something for which nature or education have left him unqualified.
[Ram. 179

Every man has a lurking wish to appear considerable in his
native place. [Letter to Reynolds, July 1771

We all live upon the hope of pleasing somebody; and the
pleasure of pleasing ought to be greatest, and at last always
will be greatest, when our endeavours are exerted in consequence of our duty. [Bos. 21 Aug. 1766

Fate never wounds more deep the gen'rous heart.
Than when a blockhead's insult points the dart.
["London"

A man should be careful never to tell tales of himself to his
own disadvantage. People may be amused and laugh at the
time, but they will be remembered, and brought out against
him upon some subsequent occasion. [Bos. March 1776

... insignificancy is always a shelter. [Ram. 135

Little people are apt to be jealous: but they should not be jealous; for they ought to consider, that superiour attention will necessarily be paid to superiour fortune or rank. Two persons may have equal merit, and on that account may have an equal claim to attention; but one of them may have also fortune and rank, and so may have a double claim. [Bos. May 1776

The modest man satisfies himself with peaceful silence, which all his companions are candid enough to consider as proceeding not from inability to speak, but willingness to hear. [Ram. 188

In the bottle discontent seeks for comfort, cowardice for courage, and bashfulness for confidence. [L.P., Addison

Delicacy does not surely consist . . . in impossibility to be pleased, and that is false dignity indeed which is content to depend upon others. [Pioz. Anec.

Women, by whatever fate, always judge absurdly of the intellect of boys. The vivacity and confidence that attract female admiration are seldom produced in the early part of life, but by ignorance at least, if not stupidity; for they proceed not from confidence of right but from fearlessness of wrong. Whoever has a clear apprehension must have quick sensibility, and where he has no sufficient reason to trust his judgement, will proceed with doubt and caution. [Ram. 194

He that hopes to be received as a wit in female assemblies should have a form neither so amiable as to strike with admiration, nor so coarse as to raise disgust, with an understanding too feeble to be dreaded, and too forcible to be despised. [Ram. 141

"Ought six people be kept waiting [at a dinner] for one?" "Why yes (answered Johnson, with a delicate humanity), if the one will suffer more by your sitting down, than the six will do by waiting." [Bos. 16 Oct. 1769

Every man has a right to utter what he thinks truth, and every other man has a right to knock him down for it. Martyrdom is the test. [Bos. 1780

... he, who accustoms himself to fraud in little things, wants only opportunity to practise it in greater; "he that has hardened himself by killing a sheep," says Pythagoras, "will with less reluctance shed the blood of a man." [Adv. 119

He that praises everybody praises nobody. [Bos. 1777(n)

Just praise is only a debt, but flattery is a present. The acknowledgement of those virtues on which conscience congratulates us, is a tribute that we can at any time exact with confidence; but the celebration of those which we only feign, or desire without any vigorous endeavours to attain them, is received as a confession of sovereignty over regions never conquered, as a favourable decision of disputable claims, and is more welcome as it is more gratuitous. [Ram. 155

Praise, like gold and diamonds, owes its value only to its scarcity. [Ram. 136

That praise is worth nothing of which the price is known. [L.P., Dryden

There is pride enough in the human heart to prevent much desire of acquaintance with a man, by whom we are sure to be neglected, however his reputation for science or virtue may ex-

cite our curiosity or esteem; so that the lover of retirement
needs not be afraid lest the respect of strangers should overwhelm him with visits. Even those to whom he has formerly
been known, will very patiently support his absence, when they
have tried a little to live without him, and found new diversions for those moments which his company contributed to
exhilarate. [Ram. 6

Few have abilities so much needed by the rest of the world
as to be caressed on their own terms; and he that will not con-
descend to recommend himself by external embellishments,
must submit to the fate of just sentiments meanly expressed,
and be ridiculed and forgotten before he is understood. [Ram.
168

*In answer to arguments urged by Puritans and Quakers against
showy dress:*

Let us all conform in outward customs, which are of no consequence, to the manners of those whom we live among, and
despise such paltry distinctions. Alas, Sir . . . a man who cannot
get to heaven in a green coat, will not find his way thither
the sooner in a grey one. [Pioz. Anec.

Whatever he did he seemed willing to do in a manner peculiar to himself, without sufficiently considering, that singularity, as it implies a contempt of the general practice, is a kind
of defiance which justly provokes the hostility of ridicule; he,
therefore, who indulges peculiar habits, is worse than others,
if he be not better. [L.P., Swift

Singularity is, I think, in its own nature universally and
invariably displeasing . . . To comply with the notions and prac-
tices of mankind, is in some degree the duty of a social being;
because by compliance only he can please, and by pleasing

only he can become useful: but as the end is not to be lost for the sake of the means, we are not to give up virtue to complaisance; for the end of complaisance is only to gain the kindness of our fellow-beings, whose kindness is desirable only as instrumental to happiness, and happiness must be always lost by departure from virtue. [Adv. 131

Perfect good breeding, he observed, consists in having no particular mark of any profession, but a general elegance of manners; whereas, in a military man, you can commonly distinguish the *brand* of a soldier, *l'homme d'épée*. [Bos. 16 Oct. 1769

It is seldom that the great or the wise suspect that they are despised or cheated. [L.P., Pope

Gentlemen of education, he observed, were pretty much the same in all countries; the condition of the lower orders, the poor especially, was the true mark of national discrimination. [Bos. 1770

The difference, he observed, between a well-bred and an ill-bred man is this:
One immediately attracts your liking, the other your aversion. You love the one till you find reason to hate him; you hate the other till you find reason to love him. [Bos. June 1784

A great mind disdains to hold any thing by courtesy, and therefore never usurps what a lawful claimant may take away. He that encroaches upon another's dignity, puts himself in his power; he is either repelled with helpless indignity, or endured by clemency and condescension. [L.P., Swift

. . . it frequently happens, that they who attempt this method of ingratiating themselves [by continual narration] please only at the first interview; and, for want of new supplies of intelligence, wear out their stories by continual repetition.

There would be, therefore, little hope of obtaining the praise of a good companion, were it not to be gained by more compendious methods; but such is the kindness of mankind to all, except those who aspire to real merit and rational dignity, that every understanding may find some way to excite benevolence; and whoever is not envied may learn the art of procuring love. We are willing to be pleased, but not willing to admire; we favour the mirth or officiousness that solicits our regard, but oppose the worth or spirit that enforces it. [Ram. 188

Great Kings have always been social. The King of Prussia, the only great King at present, is very social. Charles the Second, the last King of England who was a man of parts, was social; and our Henrys and Edwards were all social. [Bos. 20 July 1763

A man cannot with propriety speak of himself, except he relates facts . . . All censure of a man's self is oblique praise. It is in order to shew how much he can spare. It has all the invidiousness of self-praise, and all the reproach of falsehood. [Bos. 25 April 1778

Large offers and sturdy rejections are among the most common topicks of falsehood. [L.P., Milton

We are most inclined to love when we have nothing to fear, and he that encourages us to please ourselves, will not be long without preference in our affection to those whose learning holds us at the distance of pupils, or whose wit calls all attention from us, and leaves us without importance and without regard. [Ram. 72

[For bashfulness] I know not whether any remedies of much efficacy can be found. To advise a man unaccustomed to the eyes of multitudes to mount a tribunal without perturbation, to tell him whose life was passed in the shades of contemplation, that he must not be disconcerted or perplexed in receiving and returning the compliments of a splendid assembly, is to advise an inhabitant of Brazil or Sumatra not to shiver at an English winter, or him who has always lived upon a plain to look upon a precipice without emotion. It is to suppose custom instantaneously controllable by reason, and to endeavour to communicate, by precept, that which only time and habit can bestow. [Ram. 159

There is nothing more likely to betray a man into absurdity than *condescension;* when he seems to suppose his understanding too powerful for his company. [Bos. 1780

Never delight yourself with the dignity of silence or the superiority of inattention. [Letter to Mrs. T., July 1780

It generally happens that assurance keeps an even pace with ability; and the fear of miscarriage, which hinders our first attempts, is gradually dissipated as our skill advances towards certainty of success. That bashfulness, therefore, which prevents disgrace, that short and temporary shame which secures us from lasting reproach, cannot be properly counted among our misfortunes. . . . It may sometimes exclude pleasure, but seldom opens any avenue to sorrow or remorse. It is observed somewhere, that *few have repented of having forborne to speak.* [Ram. 159

To talk intentionally in a manner above the comprehension of those whom we address, is unquestionable pedantry; but surely complaisance requires, that no man should, without proof,

conclude his company incapable of following him to the highest
elevation of his fancy, or the utmost extent of his knowledge.
It is always safer to err in favour of others than ourselves, and
therefore we seldom hazard much by endeavouring to excel.
[Ram. 173

The prejudices of mankind seem to favour him who errs by
under-rating his own powers: he is considered as a modest and
harmless member of society, not likely to break the peace by
competition, to endeavour after such splendour of reputation
as may dim the lustre of others, or to interrupt any in the enjoyment of themselves; he is no man's rival, and, therefore, may
be every man's friend. [Adv. 81

Softness, diffidence, and moderation will often be mistaken
for imbecility and defection; they lure cowardice to the attack
by the hopes of easy victory, and it will soon be seen that he
whom every man thinks he can conquer, shall never be at peace.
[Ram. 176

It is well known that the most certain way to give any man
pleasure, is to persuade him that you receive pleasure from him,
to encourage him to freedom and confidence, and to avoid any
such appearance of superiority as may overbear and depress
him. We see many that by this art only spend their days in
the midst of caresses, invitations, and civilities; and without
any extraordinary qualities or attainments, are the universal
favourites of both sexes, and certainly find a friend in every
place. [Ram. 72

He that would please must rarely aim at such excellence as
depresses his hearers in their own opinion, or debars them
from the hope of contributing reciprocally to the entertainment
of the company. Merriment, extorted by sallies of imagination,

sprightliness of remarks, or quickness of reply, is too often what the Latins call the Sardinian laughter, a distortion of the face without gladness of heart. [Ram. 188

She smiles not by sensation, but by practice. [Idl. 100

As I know more of mankind I expect less of them, and am ready now to call a man *a good man,* upon easier terms than I was formerly. [Bos. Sept. 1783

Heroic virtues (said he) are the *bons mots* of life; they do not appear often, and when they do appear are too much prized I think; like the aloe-tree, which shoots and flowers once in a hundred years. But life is made up of little things; and that character is the best which does little but repeated acts of beneficence; as that conversation is the best which consists in elegant and pleasing thoughts expressed in natural and pleasing terms. [Pioz. Anec.

Politeness obliges us to appear pleased with a man's works when he is present. No man will be so ill bred as to question you. You may therefore pay compliments without saying what is not true. I should say to Lord Scarsdale of his large room, "My Lord, this is the most *costly* room that I ever saw;" which is true. [Bos. 19 Sept. 1777

Bounty always receives part of its value from the manner in which it is bestowed. [Letter to Bute, 1762

What is nearest us touches us most. The passions rise higher at domestic than at imperial tragedies. [Piozzi, Johnsoniana

When we describe our sensations of another's sorrows, either in friendly or ceremonious condolence, the customs of the world scarcely admit of rigid veracity. [Idl. 50

In lapidary inscriptions a man is not upon oath. [Bos. 1775

While grief is fresh, every attempt to divert only irritates. You must wait till grief be *digested*, and then amusement will dissipate the remains of it. [Bos. 10 April 1776

People in distress never think that you feel enough . . . it is affectation to pretend to feel the distress of others, as much as they do themselves. It is equally so, as if one should pretend to feel as much pain while a friend's leg is cutting off, as he does. [Bos. 25 March 1776

Every class of society has its cant of lamentation, which is understood or regarded by none but themselves; and every part of life has its uneasiness, which those who do not feel them will not commiserate. [Ram. 128

I deny the lawfulness of telling a lie to a sick man for fear of alarming him. You have no business with consequences; you are to tell the truth. Besides, you are not sure what effect your telling him that he is in danger may have. It may bring his distemper to a crisis, and that may cure him. Of all lying, I have the greatest abhorrence of this, because I believe it has been frequently practised on myself. [Bos. 13 June 1784

It may be laid down as a position which will seldom deceive, that when a man cannot bear his own company, there is something wrong. [Ram. 5

All quarrels ought to be avoided studiously, particularly conjugal ones, as no one can possibly tell where they may end . . . the cup of life is surely bitter enough, without squeezing in the hateful rind of resentment. [Pioz. Anec.

To be obliged, is to be in some respect inferior to another; and few willingly indulge the memory of an action which raises one whom they have always been accustomed to think below them. [Ram. 166

. . . whoever pays a visit that is not desired, or talks longer than the hearer is willing to attend, is guilty of an injury which he cannot repair, and takes away that [time] which he cannot give. [Idl. 14

Tediousness is the most fatal of all faults; negligences or errours are single and local, but tediousness pervades the whole; other faults are censured and forgotten, but the power of tediousness propagates itself. He that is weary the first hour, is more weary the second; as bodies forced into motion contrary to their tendency, pass more and more slowly through every successive interval of space. [L.P., Prior

There is in Beauclerk a predominance over his company, that one does not like. But he is a man who has lived so much in the world, that he has a short story on every occasion; he is always ready to talk and is never exhausted. [Bos. 24 April 1779

To let friendship die away by negligence and silence, is certainly not wise. It is voluntarily to throw away one of the greatest comforts of this weary pilgrimage. [Bos. 20 March 1782

[There are petty] arts by which cheerfulness is promoted, and sometimes friendship established; arts which those who despise them should not rigorously blame, except when they are practised at the expense of innocence; for it is always necessary to be loved, but not always necessary to be reverenced. [Ram. 188

Dr. Taylor [speaking of a physician] said, "I fight many

battles for him, as many people in the country dislike him."
Johnson. "But you should consider, Sir, that by every one of
your victories he is a loser; for every man of whom you get
the better, will be very angry and will resolve not to employ
him; whereas if people get the better of you in argument about
him, they'll think, 'We'll send for Dr. —— nevertheless.' " [Bos.
26 March 1776

He that overvalues himself will undervalue others, and he
that undervalues others will oppress them. [Sermon VI

That every man is important in his own eyes, is a position of
which we all . . . once an hour confess the truth. [Idl. 12

. . . every man believes himself important to the public . . .
[But] to get a name, can happen but to few. A name, even in
the most commercial nation, is one of the few things which
cannot be bought. It is the free gift of mankind, which must
be deserved before it will be granted, and is at last unwillingly
bestowed. But this unwillingness only increases desire in him
who believes his merit sufficient to overcome it. [Idl. 12

A man may be so much of every thing, that he is nothing of
any thing. [Bos. 30 March 1783

A man should pass a part of his time with *the laughers,* by
which means any thing ridiculous or particular about him might
be presented to his view, and corrected. [Bos. 1783

*A man once quoted to Johnson this reflection on the happiness
of a savage life:*

"Here am I, free and unrestrained, amidst the rude magnificence of Nature, with this Indian woman by my side, and this
gun, with which I can procure food when I want it: what more

can be desired for human happiness?" . . . *Johnson*. "Do not allow yourself, Sir, to be imposed upon by such gross absurdity. It is sad stuff; it is brutish. If a bull could speak, he might as well exclaim,—Here am I with this cow and this grass; what being can enjoy greater felicity?" [Bos. 21 April 1773

The savages have no bodily advantages beyond those of civilised men. They have not better health; and as to care or mental uneasiness, they are not above it, but below it, like bears. [Bos. 30 Sept. 1769

The traveller wanders through a naked desert, gratified sometimes, but rarely, with the sight of cows; and now and then finds a heap of loose stones and turf in a cavity between rocks, where a Being born with all those powers which education expands, and all those sensations which culture refines, is condemned to shelter itself from the wind and the rain. Philosophers there are who try to make themselves believe that this life is happy, but they believe it only while they are saying it, and never yet produced conviction in a single mind. [Letter to Mrs. T. from Syke, September 1773

A tavern chair [is] the throne of human felicity. [Bos. 21 March 1776

A man who exposes himself when he is intoxicated, has not the art of getting drunk. [Bos. 24 April 1779

The full tide of human existence is at Charing-cross. [Bos. 2 April 1775

Quoting Foote:
He is not only dull himself, but the cause of dullness in others. [Bos. 1783

. . . such is the unwillingness of mankind to admit transcend-
ant merit, that, though it be difficult to obliterate the reproach
of miscarriages by any subsequent achievement, however illustrious, yet the reputation raised by a long train of success may
be finally ruined by a single failure; for weakness or errour will
be always remembered by that malice and envy which it gratifies.

[Let us not therefore] expect from the world the indulgence
with which most are disposed to treat themselves; and in the
hour of listlessness imagine, that the diligence of one day will
atone for the idleness of another, and that applause begun by
approbation will be continued by habit.

He that is himself weary will soon weary the public . . . let
him not endeavour to struggle with censure, or obstinately
infest the stage till a general hiss commands him to depart.
[Ram. 207

It is always observable that silence propagates itself, and that
the longer talk has been suspended, the more difficult it is to
find any thing to say. [Adv. 84

He must mingle with the world who desires to be useful.
[Pioz. Anec.

. . . the solitary mortal is certainly luxurious, probably superstitious, possibly mad; the mind stagnates for want of employment, grows morbid, and is extinguished like a candle in foul
air. [Pioz. Anec.

[Newton] stood alone, merely because he had left the rest of
mankind behind him, not because he deviated from the beaten
track . . . Singularity [peculiarity] is, I think, in its own nature

universally and invariably displeasing . . . In moral and religious questions only . . . the external mode is to be in some measure regulated by the prevailing taste of the age in which we live; for he is certainly no friend to virtue, who neglects to give it any lawful attraction, or suffers it to deceive the eye or alienate the affections for want of innocent compliance with fashionable decorations. [Adv. 131

. . . gratitude is a fruit of great cultivation; you do not find it among gross people. [Tour 20 September

Johnson. "Don't set up for what is called hospitality; it is a waste of time, and a waste of money; you are eaten up, and not the more respected for your liberality. If your house be like an inn, nobody cares for you. A man who stays a week with another, makes him a slave for a week." *Boswell.* "But there are people, Sir, who make their houses a home to their guests, and are themselves quite easy." *Johnson.* "Then, Sir, home must be the same to the guests, and they need not come." [Bos. 15 May 1783

You may be prudently attached to great men, and yet independent. You are not to do what you think wrong; and, Sir, you are to calculate, and not pay too dear for what you get. You must not give a shilling's worth of court for six-pence worth of good. But if you can get a shilling's worth of good for six-pence worth of court, you are a fool if you do not pay court. [Bos. Feb. 1766

To Mrs. Garrick upon her husband's death:

Dr. Johnson sends most respectful condolence to Mrs. Garrick, and wishes that any endeavour of his could enable her to support a loss which the world cannot repair. [Letter, Feb. 1779

To Sir Joshua Reynolds, acknowledging a gift for some poor person:

It was not before yesterday that I received your splendid benefaction. To a hand so liberal in distributing, I hope nobody will envy the power of acquiring. [Bos. 23 June 1781

To Miss Adams who remarked that the little coffeepot in which she made his coffee was the only thing she could call her own:

Don't say so, my dear; I hope you don't reckon my heart as nothing. [Bos. 10 June 1784

To Miss Williams, who visited Dr. Johnson in his illness:

I am very ill indeed, Madam. I am very ill even when you are near me; what should I be were you at a distance? [Bos. 30 May 1784

To Mrs. Siddons, the famous actress, who came into the room where there was no chair ready for her:

Madam, you who so often occasion a want of seats to other people, will the more easily excuse the want of one yourself. [Bos. Oct. 1783

To Mr. Thrale, who was pointing out what he thought beautiful vistas in France:

Never heed such nonsense. A blade of grass is always a blade of grass, whether in one country or another. Let us, if we *do* talk, talk of something; men and women are my subjects of enquiry. Let us see how these differ from those we have left behind. [Pioz. Anec.

On Wooing and Wedding

Every man is a worse man in proportion as he is
unfit for the married state.

Bos. 1776

Some time in 1770 Johnson remarked that "even ill-assorted marriages were preferable to cheerless celibacy." Presumably he knew what he was talking about, for he had seen such marriages at close range and at the time had been a widower for eighteen years.

He was himself the product of an ill-assorted marriage. His father, Michael Johnson, though a considerable figure in Lichfield, seems to have thought his wife—a petty squire's daughter —better born than he was. She had no doubt that she was. He was forty-nine when they married, she thirty-seven. The match, if such it can be called, was probably a prosaic enough arrangement between two eldering persons who preferred marriage on any terms to "cheerless celibacy"; and as time went on, it became more and more cheerless. In spite of all, the two made a home, reared two sons, managed to get Sam at least adequately schooled, sent him to Oxford; and when his funds and hopes there ran out, they could provide him asylum while he wrestled with his future. An ill-assorted marriage to be sure, but not an altogether unsuccessful one.

Johnson's own marriage seemed on the surface little less than grotesque. He had left college without a degree, had tried in vain to earn a living in various ways, and, at the age of twenty-

five—without profession or prospects—married the widow of
his late friend Henry Porter. She was twenty years older than
he, the mother of three children—the eldest a young lady of
eighteen. For two centuries people have asked why. He had
little to gain from the match; she nothing. It is reasonable, then,
to accept Johnson's own explanation, "Sir, it was a love match
on both sides."[1] One is irresistibly reminded, however, of the
statement Johnson was to make years later: "A man is poor; he
thinks, 'I cannot be worse, and so I'll e'en take Peggy.'"[2] But
the marriage worked. It survived the failure of a school at
Edial, the desperate poverty of the Grub Street days. Johnson,
never a domestic animal, could not have been easy for his wife
to live with. His wife, with her passion for clean floors, was
equally difficult for Johnson. Of course they bickered. Yet
Johnson not only loved her; he could admire her and say of
her that she could read comedy better than anyone he ever
heard.[3] She could admire him and say of him, "This is the
most sensible man I ever saw in my life";[4] and after a few
numbers of The Rambler had appeared, she told him: "I
thought very well of you before; but I did not imagine you
could have written anything equal to this."[5]

After her death in 1752, he was to grieve for her as long as
he lived; and the depth of his bereavement can perhaps be
measured by his words in the preface to the Dictionary, which
came out three years later. "I may surely be contented without
the praise of perfection, which, if I could obtain, in this gloom
of solitude what would it avail me? I have protracted my work
till most of those whom I wished to please are sunk into the
grave, and success and miscarriage are empty sounds."

An ill-assorted marriage, yet for seventeen years it did much
to make tolerable the life of a man who even in his late forties
was still struggling to emerge from obscurity. Small wonder,

---

[1] Bos. 1735.   [2] Bos. 26 Oct. 1769.   [3] Pioz. Anec.
[4] Bos. 1734.   [5] Bos. 1750.

then, if Johnson said that marriages could be happy if they were arranged by the Lord Chancellor without the parties having any choice in the matter.

Love is the wisdom of a fool and the folly of the wise. [Cooke, John. Misc.

Love is only one of many passions, and . . . has no great influence upon the sum of life. [Pref. Shakespeare

. . . many fancied that they were in love when in truth they were only idle. [Ras. 25

Of the passion of love, he remarked, that its violence and ill effects were much exaggerated, for who knows any real sufferings on that head more than from the exorbitancy of any other passion? [Bos. 1770

[A lady was] deriding the novels of the day because they treated about love. "It is not (replied our philosopher) because they treat, as you call it, about love, but because they treat of nothing, that they are despicable: we must not ridicule a passion which he who never felt never was happy, and he who laughs at never deserves to feel—a passion which has caused the change of empires and the loss of worlds—a passion which has inspired heroism and subdued avarice." [Pioz. Anec.

It is commonly a weak man who marries for love. [Bos. 28 March 1776

. . . that which is to be loved long must be loved with reason rather than with passion. [Idl. 59

Marriage has many pains, but celibacy has no pleasures. [Ras. 26

Good wives make good husbands. [Bos. 9 Jan. 1758

Speaking of late marriages, Johnson said:

. . . more was lost in point of time, than compensated for by any possible advantages. Even ill assorted marriages were preferable to cheerless celibacy. [Bos. 1770

A man in London was in less danger of falling in love indiscreetly, than any where else; for there the difficulty of deciding between the conflicting pretensions of a vast variety of objects, kept him safe. [Bos. 1770

To Boswell, who was about to marry:

Now . . . that you are going to marry, do not expect more from life, than life will afford. You may often find yourself out of humour, and you may often think your wife not studious enough to please you; and yet you may have reason to consider yourself as upon the whole very happily married. [Bos. 10 Nov. 1770

But in love, as in every other passion, of which hope is the essence, we ought always to remember the uncertainty of events. There is, indeed, nothing that so much seduces reason from vigilance, as the thought of passing life with an amiable woman; and if all would happen that a lover fancies, I know not what other terrestrial happiness would deserve pursuit. But love and marriage are different states. Those who are to suffer the evils together, and to suffer often for the sake of one another, soon lose that tenderness of look, and that benevolence of mind, which arose from the participation of unmingled pleasure and successive amusement. A woman, we are sure, will not always be fair; we are not sure she will always be virtuous: and man cannot retain through life that respect and assiduity by which he pleases for a day or for a month. I do

not, however, pretend to have discovered that life has any thing
more to be desired than a prudent and virtuous marriage. [To
Baretti, Bos. 21 Dec. 1762

. . . if you shut up any man with any woman, so as to make
them derive their whole pleasure from each other, they would
inevitably fall in love, as it is called, with each other. [Pioz.
Anec.

My mother and father had not much happiness from each
other. They seldom conversed; for my father could not bear
to talk of his affairs, and my mother, being unacquainted with
books, cared not to talk of anything else. She concluded we were
poor because we lost by some of our trades . . . Of business she
had no distinct conception, and therefore her discourse was
composed of complaint, fear, and suspicion. [Miss Boothby

A man of sense and education should meet a suitable companion in a wife. It was a miserable thing when the conversation could only be such as, whether the mutton should be
boiled or roasted, and probably a dispute about that. [Bos. 1770

Marriage, Sir, is much more necessary to a man than to a
woman; for he is much less able to supply himself with domestick comforts . . . I had often wondered why young women
should marry, as they have so much more freedom, and so much
more attention paid to them while unmarried. [Bos. 25 March
1776

Boswell remarked that the great defect of Othello was that it
had no moral:

Sir, we learn from Othello this very useful moral, not to make
an unequal match. [Bos. 12 April 1776

. . . prudence and benevolence will make marriage happy.
The general folly of mankind is the cause of general complaint.
What can be expected but disappointment and repentance
from a choice made in the immaturity of youth, in the ardour
of desire, without judgement, without foresight, without inquiry
after conformity of opinions, similarity of manners, rectitude of
judgment, or purity of sentiment? [Ras. 29

Sir, it is so far from being natural for a man and woman to
live in a state of marriage, that we find all the motives which
they have for remaining in that connection, and the restraints
which civilised society imposes to prevent separation, are hardly
sufficient to keep them together. [Bos. 31 March 1772

[Johnson despised none more] than the man who marries for
a maintenance: and of a friend who made his alliance on no
higher principles, he said once, "Now has that fellow . . . obtained a certainty of three meals a day, and for that certainty,
like his brother dog in the fable, he will get his neck galled for
life with a collar." [Pioz. Anec.

[A man should marry] first, for virtue; secondly, for wit;
thirdly, for beauty; and fourthly, for money. [Hawkins, Johnsoniana

Were it not for imagination, Sir . . . a man would be as
happy in the arms of a chambermaid as of a Duchess. But such
is the adventitious charm of fancy, that we find men who have
violated the best principles of society . . . that they might
possess a woman of rank. [Bos. 9 May 1778

. . . the married praise the ease and freedom of a single state,
and the single fly to marriage from the weariness of solitude.
[Ram. 45

She has some softness indeed, but so has a pillow . . . being married to those sleepy-souled women, is just like playing cards for nothing: no passion is excited, and the time is filled up. I do not envy a fellow one of those honey-suckle wives for my part, as they are but *creepers* at best, and commonly destroy the tree they so tenderly cling about. [Pioz. Anec.

Of the poet Waller:

He doubtless praised some whom he would have been afraid to marry; and perhaps married one whom he would have been ashamed to praise. Many qualities contribute to domestic happiness, upon which poetry has no colours to bestow; and many airs and sallies may delight imagination which he who flatters them can never approve. [L.P., Waller

To a gentleman who wished to marry a lady but was afraid of her superiority of talents:

Sir . . . you need not be afraid; marry her. Before a year goes about, you'll find that reason much weaker, and that wit not so bright. [Bos. Spring 1768

There wanders about the world a wild notion that extends over marriage more than over any other transaction. If Miss (Plumbe) followed a trade, would it be said that she was bound in conscience to give or refuse credit at her Father's choice? And is not marriage a thing in which she is more interested and has therefore more right of choice? When I may suffer for my own crimes, when I may be sued for my own debts, I may judge by parity of choice for my own happiness. A Parent's moral right can arise only from his kindness, and his civil right only from his money. [Letter to Mrs. T., May 1773

A young woman married a man much her inferior in rank. Mrs. Thrale was all for forgiveness. Johnson said:

Were I a man of rank, I would not let a daughter starve who

had made a mean marriage; but . . . I would support her only in that which she herself had chosen . . . You are to consider, Madam, that it is our duty to maintain the subordination [that obtains in] civilised society; and when there is a gross and shameful deviation from rank, it should be punished so as to deter others from the same perversion. [Bos. 28 March 1775

To Boswell, who asked whether certain men and women are "made for each other" and cannot be happy unless they marry:

To be sure not, Sir. I believe marriages would in general be as happy, and often more so, if they were all made by the Lord Chancellor, upon a due consideration of characters and circumstances, without the parties having any choice in the matter. [Bos. 22 March 1776

We then talked of marrying women of fortune; and I mentioned a common remark, that a man may be, upon the whole, richer by marrying a woman with a very small portion, because a woman of fortune will be proportionally expensive; whereas a woman who brings none will be very moderate in expenses. "Depend upon it, Sir [said Johnson], this is not true. A woman of fortune being used to the handling of money, spends it judiciously; but a woman who gets the command of money for the first time upon her marriage, has such a gust in spending it that she throws it away with great profusion." [Bos. 28 March 1776

When any disputes arose between our married acquaintance, Mr. Johnson always sided with the husband, "whom," he said, "the woman had probably provoked so often, she scarce knew when or how she had disobliged him first." "Women," says Dr. Johnson, "give great offence by a contemptuous spirit of noncompliance on petty occasions. The man who calls his wife to walk with him in the shade, and she feels a strange desire just at that moment to sit in the sun: he offers to read her a play, or sing her a song, and she calls the children in to disturb them, or advises him to seize that opportunity of settling the family accounts. Twenty such tricks will the faithfulest wife in the world not refuse to play, and then look astonished when the fellow fetches in a mistress." [Pioz. Anec.

I pitied a friend . . . who had a whining wife . . . "He does not know that she whimpers (says Johnson); when a door has creaked for a fortnight together, you may observe—the master will scarcely give sixpence to get it oiled." [Pioz. Anec.

A country gentleman should bring his lady to visit London as soon as he can, that they may have agreeable topics for conversation when they are by themselves. [Bos. 1777

No money is better spent than what is laid out for domestick satisfaction. A man is pleased that his wife is drest as well as other people; and a wife is pleased that she is drest. [Bos. 14 April 1775

A gentleman who had been very unhappy in marriage, married immediately after his wife died: Johnson said, it was the triumph of hope over experience. [Bos. 20 Sept. 1770

Of a man who married early after the death of his first wife:

Were he not to marry again, it might be concluded that his first wife had given him a disgust to marriage; but by taking a second wife, he pays the highest compliment to the first, by shewing that she made him so happy as a married man, that he wishes to be so a second time. [Bos. 1769

When told that a lady maintained that her husband's number-less infidelities released her from conjugal obligations:

This is miserable stuff, Sir. To the contract of marriage, be-sides the man and wife, there is a third party—Society; and, if it be considered as a vow—God; and, therefore, it cannot be dissolved by their consent alone. Laws are not made for par-ticular cases . . . A woman may be unhappy with her husband; but she cannot be freed from him without the approbation of the civil and ecclesiastical power. [Bos. 7 April 1776

He that outlives a wife whom he has long loved, sees himself disjoined from the only mind that has the same hopes, and fears, and interest; from the only companion with whom he has shared much good or evil; and with whom he could set his mind at liberty to retrace the past, or anticipate the future. The continuity of being is lacerated; the settled course of senti-ment and action is stopped; and life stands suspended and motionless, till it is driven by external causes into a new chan-nel. But the time of suspense is dreadful. [Letter to Lawrence, Bos. Jan. 1780

I believe it will be found that those who marry late are best pleased with their children, and those who marry early with their partners. [Ras. 29

That woman (said he) loved her husband as we hope and desire to be loved by our guardian angel. Fitzherbert was a gay good-humoured fellow, generous of his money and of his meat, and desirous of nothing but cheerful society among people dis-tinguished in *some* way, in *any way,* I think; for Rousseau and St. Austin would have been equally welcome to his table and to his kindness: the lady, however, was of another way of think-ing; her first care was to preserve her husband's soul from cor-ruption; her second, to keep his estate entire for their children

... [Her husband] felt her influence too powerfully ... no man will be fond of what forces him daily to feel himself inferiour. She stood at the door of her Paradise in Derbyshire, like the angel with the flaming sword, to keep the devil at a distance. But she was not immortal, poor dear! She died, and her husband felt at once afflicted and released. [Pioz. Anec.

On Law and Government

. . . the more numerous men are, the more difficult it is for them to agree in any thing; and so they are governed.

Bos. Oct. 1769

Although Johnson could express considerable indignation at the methods of suppression used by the government in Scotland after 1745, he was speaking more as a sentimental Jacobite than as a dispassionate observer. Indeed, for some of the results of the English penetration into the Highlands he had tempered words of praise. On the whole, however, nowhere is his natural skepticism more clearly expressed than in his discussion of government as a whole. For law as an instrument of government he had a lively interest and, indeed, considerable respect.

Of course, he was looking out on the eighteenth-century world, which meant Europe, a world in which a recognized degree of law and order obtained, and of which the phrase "one world" could properly be used as we have been unable to use it since. Kings and princes ruled in a more or less absolute way; wars were fought in a more or less limited way. The gap between rulers and ruled was as wide as the Grand Canyon. There was little nonsense about "getting on"; everyone had his place. A proper scheme of subordination—tolerable because, in Johnson's phrase, it was accidental[1]—made for general contentment. Property was still the great principle of society.[2] In short, the

---

[1] Bos. 21 July 1763.   [2] 7 May 1773.

ferment stemming from Rousseau and from the success of the American Revolution were not yet affecting government, at least. Johnson and his friends could think their century the most civilized time in history. It probably was.

"Public affairs," Johnson once said in a grand sweeping gesture, "vex no man."[3] And for popular liberty he had only "rough contempt." In 1772, when the revolt in America was blowing up to gale force, he said to Sir Adam Fergusson, "I would not give half a guinea to live under one form of government rather than another. It is of no moment to the happiness of the individual. Sir, the danger of the abuse of power is nothing to a private man. What Frenchman is prevented from passing his life as he pleases?"[4] Johnson thought as his century thought. Shrewd as he was in so many things, he could not imagine that in only a short while the egalitarianism of Mrs. Knowles, of which he made such rough sport, was to sweep the world about him; and that even ownership of property— the "great principle"—would be called into question.

. . . the law is the last result of human wisdom acting upon human experience for the benefit of the public. [Pioz. Anec.

As manners make laws, manners likewise repeal them. [Letter to Bos., Feb. 1776

. . . all rebellion is natural to man. [Tour 30 November

Nature has given women so much power that the law has very wisely given them little. [Letter to Taylor, Aug. 1763

Politicians remark, that no oppression is so heavy or lasting as that which is inflicted by the perversion and exorbitance of

3 Bos. 15 May 1783. 4 Bos. 31 March 1772.

legal authority. The robber may be seized, and the invader repelled, whenever they are found; they who pretend no right but that of force, may by force be punished or suppressed. But when plunder bears the name of impost, and murder is perpetrated by a judicial sentence, fortitude is intimidated, and wisdom confounded; resistance shrinks from an alliance with rebellion, and the villain remains secure in the robes of the magistrate. [Ram. 148

Natural right [avails] little without the protection of law; and the primary notion of law is restraint in the exercise of natural right. A man is therefore, in society, not fully master of what he calls his own, but he still retains all the power which law does not take from him. [Bos. 3 Feb. 1776

Man is, for the most part, equally unhappy when subjected, without redress, to the passions of another, or left without control, to the dominion of his own. This every man, however unwilling he may be to own it of himself, will very readily acknowledge of his neighbour. No man knows any one, except himself, whom he judges fit to be set free from the coercion of laws, and to be abandoned to his own choice. . . . Government is, therefore, necessary, in the opinion of every one, to the safety of particular men, and the happiness of society. [Sermon XXIV

All government supposes subjects, all authority implies obedience; to suppose in one the right to command what the other has a right to refuse, is absurd and contradictory. A state so constituted must rest forever in motionless equipoise, with equal attractions of contrary tendency. [False Alarm

[To the statement that] liberty is the birthright of man, and where obedience is compelled, there is no liberty, the answer is

. . . simple. Government is necessary to man, and where obedience is not compelled, there is no government. If the subject refuses to obey, it is the duty of authority to use compulsion. Society cannot subsist but by the power, first of making laws, and then of enforcing them. [Taxation

Law is nothing without power; and in the Highlands the sentence of a distant court could not be easily executed, nor perhaps very safely promulgated, among men ignorantly proud and habitually violent, unconnected with the general system, and accustomed to reverence only their own lords. [Journey, Highlands

. . . in political regulations, good cannot be complete, it can only be predominant. [Journey, Ostig

No scheme of policy has, in any country, yet brought the rich and poor on equal terms into courts of judicature. Perhaps experience, improving on experience, may in time effect it. [Journey, Ostig

It has been asserted, that for the law to be known is of more importance than to be right. [Pref. Dict.

It is one of the maxims of the civil law, that *definitions are hazardous*. [Ram. 125

Tradition is but a meteor which, if once it falls, cannot be rekindled. [Journey, Ostig

The power of punishment is to silence, not to confute. [Sermon XXIII

To revenge reasonable incredulity, by refusing evidence, is

a degree of insolence with which the world is not yet acquainted; and stubborn audacity is the last refuge of guilt.
[Journey, Ostig

It is vain to continue an institution, which experience shews
to be ineffectual. We have now imprisoned one generation of
debtors after another, but we do not find that their numbers
lessen. We have now learned, that rashness and imprudence
will not be deterred from taking credit; let us try whether fraud
and avarice may be more easily restrained from giving it. [Idl.
22

They who would rejoice at the correction of a thief, are yet
shocked at the thought of destroying him. His crime shrinks to
nothing, compared with his misery; and severity defeats itself
by exciting pity....
He who knows not how often rigorous laws produce total
impunity, and how many crimes are concealed and forgotten
for fear of hurrying the offender to that state in which there is
no repentance, has conversed very little with mankind. And
whatever epithet of reproach or contempt this comparison may
incur from those who confound cruelty with firmness, I know
not whether any wise man would wish it less powerful, or less
extensive. [Ram. 114

... mutual cowardice keeps us in peace. Were one half of
mankind brave, and one half cowards, the brave would be always beating the cowards. Were all brave, they would lead a
very uneasy life; all would be continually fighting: but being
all cowards, we go on very well. [Bos. 28 April 1778

A lawyer has no business with the justice or injustice of the
cause which he undertakes, unless his client asks for his opinion;

and then he is bound to give it honestly. The justice or injustice of the cause is to be decided by the judge. [Tour 15 August

Boswell asked Johnson what he thought of a lawyer's supporting a cause which he knew to be bad:

Sir, you do not know it to be good or bad till the Judge determines it . . . You are to state facts fairly; so that your thinking . . . a cause to be bad must be from reasoning, must be from your supposing your arguments to be weak and inconclusive. But, Sir, that is not enough. An argument which does not convince yourself, may convince the Judge to whom you urge it: and if it does convince him, why, then, Sir, you are wrong, and he is right. It is his business to judge; [you are] to say all you can for your client, and then hear the Judge's opinion. [Bos. Spring 1768

In a prison the awe of the publick eye is lost, and the power of the law is spent; there are few fears, there are no blushes. [Idl. 38

As government advances towards perfection, provincial judicature is perhaps in every empire gradually abolished. [Journey, Highlands

There must always be a struggle between a father and son, while one aims at power and the other at independence. [Bos. 14 July 1763

All *boys* love liberty, till experience convinces them they are not so fit to govern themselves as they imagined. [Bos. 16 April 1779

We are all agreed as to our own liberty; we would have as much of it as we can get; but we are not agreed as to the liberty of others: for in proportion as we take, others must lose. [Bos. 16 April 1779

. . . if by liberty nothing else is meant, than security from the persecutions of power, it is so fully possessed by us, that little more is to be desired, except that one should talk of it less, and use it better. [Review, *Evidence against Queen of Scots*

They make a rout about *universal* liberty, without considering that all that is to be valued . . . is *private* liberty. Political liberty is good only so far as it produces private liberty. Now, Sir, there is the liberty of the press, which you know is a constant topick. Suppose you and I and two hundred more were restrained from printing our thoughts: what then? What proportion would that restraint upon us bear to the private happiness of the nation? [Bos. May 1768

Liberty is, to the lowest rank of every nation, little more than a choice of working or starving; and this choice is, I suppose, equally allowed in every country. [Brav. Engl. Soldier

Why all this childish jealousy of the power of the crown? The crown has not power enough. When I say that all governments are alike, I consider that in no government power can be abused long. Mankind will not bear it. If a sovereign oppresses his people to a great degree, they will rise and cut off his head. There is a remedy in human nature against tyranny, that will keep us safe under every form of government. Had not the people of France thought themselves honoured as sharing in the brilliant actions of Louis XIV, they would not have endured him; and we may say the same of the King of Prussia's people. [Bos. 31 March 1772

He that changes his party by his humour is not more virtuous than he who changes it by interest. He loves himself rather than truth. [L.P., Milton

. . . as any man acts in a wider compass, he must be more exposed to opposition from enmity, or miscarriage from chance; whoever has many to please or to govern, must use the ministry of many agents, some of whom will be wicked, and some ignorant; by some he will be misled, and by others betrayed. If he gratifies one, he will offend another; those that are not favoured will think themselves injured; and since favours can be conferred but upon few, the greater number will be always discontented. . . .

Discontent . . . will not always be without reason under the most just and vigilant administration of public affairs. [Ras. 27

Every society has a right to preserve publick peace and order, and therefore has a good right to prohibit the propagation of opinions which have a dangerous tendency. To say the *magistrate* has this right, is using an inadequate word: it is the *society* for which the magistrate is agent. He may be morally or theologically wrong in restraining the propagation of opinions which he thinks dangerous, but he is politically right. [Bos. 7 May 1773

Mayo. Sir, is it not very hard that I should not be allowed to teach my children what I really believe to be the truth? *Johnson.* . . . Suppose you teach your children to be thieves? *Mayo.* This is making a joke of the subject. *Johnson.* Nay, Sir, take it thus: that you teach them the community of goods, for which there are as many plausible arguments as for most erroneous doctrines. You teach them that all things at first were in common, and that no man had a right to any thing but as he laid his hands upon it; and that this still is, or ought to be, the rule amongst mankind. Here, Sir, you sap a great principle in society,—property. And don't you think the magistrate would have a right to prevent you? . . . *Mayo.* I think the magistrate has no right to interfere till there is some overt act. *Boswell.* So, Sir, though he sees an enemy to the state charging a blunderbuss, he is not to interfere till it is fired off? *Mayo.* He must be sure of its direction against the state. *Johnson.* The magistrate is to judge of that. [Bos. 7 May 1773

A country governed by a despot is an inverted cone. [Bos. 14 April 1778

From the impossibility of confining numbers to the constant and uniform prosecution of a common interest, arises the difficulty of securing subjects against the encroachments of governours. Power is always gradually stealing away from the many to the few, because the few are more vigilant and more consistent; it still contracts to a smaller number, till in time it centres in a single person.

Thus all the forms of governments instituted among mankind, perpetually tend towards monarchy; and power, however diffused through the whole community, is, by negligence or corruption, commotion or distress, reposed at last in the chief magistrate. [Adv. 45

As the great end of government is to give every man his own, no inconvenience is greater than that of making right uncertain. [Bos. 1 May 1773

Political truth is equally in danger from the praise of courtiers and the exclamations of Patriots. [L.P., Waller

The objection, in which is urged the injustice of making the innocent suffer with the guilty, is an objection not only against society, but against the possibility of society. All societies, great

and small, subsist upon this condition; that as the individuals
derive advantages from union, they may likewise suffer inconveniences. [Bos. May 1775

Political institutions are formed upon the consideration of
what will most frequently tend to the good of the whole. Thus
it is better . . . that a nation should have a supreme legislative
power, although it may at times be abused . . . If the abuse be
enormous, Nature will rise up, and claiming her original rights,
overturn a corrupt political system. [Bos. 6 July 1763

The general story of mankind will evince, that lawful and
settled authority is very seldom resisted when it is well employed. [Ram. 50

Whiggism is a negation of all principle. [Bos. 14 July 1763

Of all kinds of credulity, the most obstinate and wonderful
is that of political zealots; of men, who being numbered, they
know not how or why, in any of the parties that divide state,
resign the use of their own eyes and ears, and resolve to believe
nothing that does not favour those whom they profess to follow. [Idl. 10

[No man is] more an enemy to publick peace, than he who
fills weak heads with imaginary claims, and breaks the series of
civil subordination, by inciting the lower classes of mankind to
encroach upon the higher. [Bos. 1 May 1773

Patriotism is the last refuge of a scoundrel . . . that pretended
patriotism which so many, in all ages and countries, have made
a cloak for self-interest. [Bos. 7 April 1775

He that has once concluded it lawful to resist power, when

it wants merit, will soon find a want of merit, to justify his resistance of power. [Sermon XXIII

. . . the onset of the Highlanders was very formidable. As an army cannot consist of philosophers, a panic is easily excited by any unwonted mode of annoyance. New dangers are naturally magnified; and men accustomed only to exchange bullets at a distance, and rather to hear their enemies than see them, are discouraged and amazed when they find themselves encountered hand to hand, and catch the gleam of steel flashing in their faces. [Journey, Ostig

The prejudice of the Tory is for establishment; the prejudice of the Whig is for innovation. [Bos. May 1781

The great differences that disturb mankind are not about ends, but means. [Idl. 36

A wise Tory and a wise Whig, I believe, will agree. Their principles are the same, though their modes of thinking are different. [Bos. May 1781

I remember being present when [an eminent public figure] shewed himself to be so corrupted, or at least so different from what I think right, as to maintain, that a member of parliament should go along with his party right or wrong. Now, Sir, this is so remote from native virtue, from scholastick virtue, that a good man must have undergone a great change before he can reconcile himself to such a doctrine. It is maintaining that you may lie to the publick; for you lie when you call that right which you think wrong, or the reverse. [Bos. 15 April 1773

To be out of place [office] is not necessarily to be out of power. [Deb. Indem. Evidence

Tory: One who adheres to the ancient constitution of the state and the apostolical hierarchy of the Church of England. [Dict.

Whig: The name of a faction. [Dict.

Speaking in praise of a friend of his and Boswell's:

Sir, he is a cursed Whig, a *bottomless* Whig, as they all are now. [Bos. 26 May 1783

To Mr. Arnold, tutor in St. John's College:

Sir, you are a young man, but I have seen a great deal of the world, and take it upon my word and experience, that where you see a Whig, you see a rascal. [Cole, John. Misc.

Boswell. "Eld said a Tory was a creature generated between a non-juring parson and one's grandmother." *Johnson.* "And I have always said, the first Whig was the Devil." [Bos. 28 April 1778

. . . the two lowest of all human beings [are] a scribbler for a party and a commissioner of excise. [Idl. 65

Excise: A hateful tax levied upon commodities, and adjudged not by the common judges of property, but wretches hired by those to whom the excise is paid. [Dict.

Pension: An allowance made to anyone without an equivalent. In England it is generally understood to mean pay given to a state hireling for treason to his country. [Dict.

About things which the public thinks long, it commonly manages to think right. [L.P., Addison

I have found reason to pay great regard to the voice of the people, in cases where knowledge has been forced upon them by experience, without long deductions, or deep researches. [Ram. 25

Boswell once remarked that there was no civilized country in the world where the misery of want in the lower classes was prevented.

I believe, Sir, there is not; but it is better that some should be unhappy, than that none should be happy, which would be the case in a general state of equality. [Bos. 7 April 1776

It is difficult for a farmer in England to find day-labourers, because the lowest manufacturers can always get more than a day-labourer. It is of no consequence how high the wages of manufacturers are; but it would be of very bad consequence to raise the wages of those who procure the immediate necessaries of life, for that would raise the price of provisions. Here then is a problem for politicians. It is not reasonable that the most useful body of men should be the worst paid; yet it does not appear how it can be ordered otherwise . . . In the mean time, it is better to give temporary assistance to poor labourers, at times when provisions are high, than to raise wages; because, if wages are once raised, they will never get down again. [Tour 28 September

I am not certain that it is equally impossible to exempt the lower classes of mankind from poverty; because, though whatever be the wealth of the community, some will always have least, and he that has less than any other is comparatively poor; yet I do not see any coactive necessity that many should be without the indispensable conveniences of life; but am sometimes inclined to imagine, that, casual calamities excepted, there might, by universal prudence, be procured an universal exemption from want; and that he who should happen to have least, might notwithstanding have enough. [Ram. 57

Poverty is very gently paraphrased by *want of riches.* In that sense almost every man may in his own opinion be poor. But there is another poverty which is *want of competence* of all that can soften the miseries of life, of all that can diversify attention, or delight imagination. There is yet another poverty which is want *of necessaries,* a species of poverty which no care of the publick, no charity of particulars, can preserve many from feeling openly, and many secretly. . . . The milder degrees of poverty are sometimes supported by hope, but the more severe often sink down in motionless despondence. [Review, A *Free Inquiry*

The true state of every nation is the state of common life. The manners of a people are not to be found in the schools of learning, or the palaces of greatness, where the national character is obscured by philosophy or vanity; nor is public happiness to be estimated by the assemblies of the gay, or the banquets of the rich. The great mass of nations is neither rich nor gay. They whose aggregate constitutes the people are found in the streets and the villages, in the shops and farms; and from them collectively considered must the measure of general prosperity be taken. As they approach to delicacy a nation is refined; as their conveniences are multiplied, a nation, at least a commercial nation, must be denominated wealthy. [Journey, Banff

The prosperity of a people is proportionate to the number of hands and minds usefully employed. To the community . . . idleness [is] an atrophy. Whatever body, and whatever society, wastes more than it acquires, must gradually decay; and every being that continues to be fed, and ceases to labour, takes away something from the publick stock. [Idl. 22

Speaking of the national debt, he said, it was an idle dream to suppose that the country could sink under it. Let the publick creditors be ever so clamorous, the interest of millions must ever prevail over that of thousands. [Bos. 1770

Decent provision for the poor, is the true test of civilisation. [Bos. 1770

To fix the price of any commodity of which the quantity and the use may vary their proportions is the most excessive degree of ignorance. No man can determine the price of corn, unless he can regulate the harvest, and keep the number of people ever at a stand. [Deb. Engl. Seamen

If the changes that we fear be thus irresistible, what remains but to acquiesce with silence, as in the other insurmountable distresses of humanity? It remains that we retard what we cannot repel, that we palliate what we cannot cure. Life may be lengthened by care, though death cannot be ultimately defeated: tongues, like governments, have a natural tendency to degeneration; we have long preserved our constitution, let us make some struggles for our language. [Pref. Dict.

Let fanciful men do as they will, depend upon it, it is difficult to disturb the system of life. [Bos. 26 Oct. 1769

Sir, most schemes of political improvement are very laughable things. [Bos. 26 Oct. 1769

Sir, your levellers wish to level *down* as far as themselves; but they cannot bear levelling *up* to themselves. [Bos. 21 July 1763

Community of possession must include spontaneity of production; for what is obtained by labour will be of right the property of him by whose labour it is gained. And while a rightful claim to pleasure or to affluence must be procured either by slow industry or uncertain hazard, there will always be multitudes whom cowardice or impatience incite to more safe and more speedy methods, who strive to pluck the fruit without cultivating the tree, and to share the advantages of victory without partaking the danger of the battle. [Ram. 131

. . . in every society the man of intelligence must direct the man of labor. [Journey, Ostig

So far is it from being true that men are naturally equal, that no ι ᒧ people can be half an hour together, but one shall acquire an evident superiority over the other. [Bos. 15 Feb. 1766

I am a friend to subordination, as most conducive to the happiness of society. There is a reciprocal pleasure in governing and being governed. [Bos. 25 June 1763

Money confounds subordination by overpowering the distinctions of rank and birth, and weakens authority by supplying power of resistance or expedients for escape. [Journey, Ostig

Mankind are happier in a state of inequality and subordination. Were they to be in this pretty state of equality, they would soon degenerate into brutes . . . Sir, all would be losers, were all to work for all: they would have no intellectual improvement. All intellectual improvement arises from leisure; all leisure arises from one working for another. [Bos. 13 April 1773

Mr. Dempster said that men should be judged only according to their intrinsic merit:

Why, Sir, mankind have found that this cannot be. How shall we determine the proportion of intrinsick merit? Were that to be the only distinction amongst mankind, we should soon quarrel about the degrees of it. Were all distinctions abolished, the strongest would not long acquiesce, but would endeavour to obtain a superiority by their bodily strength. But, Sir, as subordination is very necessary for society . . . all civilised nations have settled it upon a plain invariable principle. A man is born to hereditary rank; or his being appointed to certain offices, gives him a certain rank. Subordination tends greatly to human happiness. Were we all upon an equality, we should have no other enjoyment than mere animal pleasure. [Bos. 20 July 1763

[In an egalitarian society] there would be a perpetual struggle for precedence, were there no fixed invariable rules for the distinction of rank, which creates no jealousy, as it is allowed to be accidental. [Bos. 21 July 1763

Sir, I would no more deprive a nobleman of his respect, than of his money. I consider myself as acting a part in the great system of society; and I do to others as I would have them to do to me. I would behave to a nobleman as I should expect he would behave to me, were I a nobleman and he Sam. Johnson. [Bos. 21 July 1763

Subordination supposes power on one part and subjection on the other; and if power be in the hands of men, it will sometimes be abused. [Ras. 8

In answer to Boswell, who thought men happier in the ancient feudal state of subordination than in the modern state of independence:

To be sure, the *Chief* was: but we must think of the number of individuals. That *they* were less happy, seems plain; for that state from which all escape as soon as they can, and to which none return after they have left it, must be less happy; and this is the case with the state of dependence on a chief or great man. [Tour 25 August

Subordination in human affairs is well understood; but when it is attributed to the universal system, its meaning grows less certain—like the petty distinctions of locality, which are of good use upon our own globe, but have no meaning with regard to infinite space, in which nothing is *high* or *low*. [Review, A *Free Inquiry*

While every man is fed by his own hands, he has no need of any servile arts: he may always have wages for his labour; and is no less necessary to his employer, than his employer is to him. . . . From this neglect of subordination I do not deny that some inconveniences may from time to time proceed: the power of the law does not always sufficiently supply the want of reverence or maintain proper distinction between different ranks. But good and evil will grow up in the world together; and they who complain, in peace, of the insolence of the populace, must remember, that their insolence in peace is bravery in war. [Brav. Engl. Soldier

The history of mankind informs us that a single power is seldom broken by a confederacy. States of different interests and aspects malevolent to each other, may be united for a time by common distress; and in the ardour of self-preservation fall unanimously upon an enemy, by whom they are all equally endangered. But . . . after the conquest of a province, they will quarrel in the division; after the loss of a battle, all will be endeavouring to secure themselves by abandoning the rest. [Adv. 45

What mankind has lost and gained by the genius and designs of this prince [Henry the Navigator] it would be long to compare and very difficult to estimate. Much knowledge has been acquired, and much cruelty has been committed; the belief of religion has been very little propagated, and its laws have been outrageously and enormously violated. The Europeans have scarcely visited any coast, but to gratify avarice, and extend corruption; to arrogate dominion without right, and practice cruelty without incentive. Happy had it been for the oppressed, if the designs of Henry had slept in his bosom, and surely more happy for the oppressers. [Introd. World Displayed

To hinder insurrection [in Scotland] by driving away the people, and to govern peaceably by having no subjects, is an expedient that argues no great profundity of politics. To soften the obdurate, to convince the mistaken, to mollify the resentful, are worthy of a statesman; but it affords a legislator little self-applause to consider that, where there was formerly an insurrection, there is now a wilderness. [Journey, Ostig

[The Highlanders'] pride has been crushed by the heavy hand of a vindictive conqueror whose severities have been followed by laws which, though they cannot be called cruel, have produced much discontent, because they operate upon the surface of life, and make every eye bear witness to subjection. [Journey, Ostig

The Irish are in a most unnatural state; for we see there the minority prevailing over the majority. There is no instance, even in the ten persecutions, of such severity as that which the Protestants of Ireland have exercised against the Catholicks. Did we tell them we have conquered them, it would be above board: to punish them by confiscation and other penalties, as rebels, was monstrous injustice. King William was not their lawful sovereign; he had not been acknowledged by the Parliament of Ireland, when they appeared in arms against him. [Bos. 7 May 1773

Let the authority of the English government [over the Irish] perish, rather than be maintained by iniquity. Better would it be to restrain the turbulence of the natives by the authority of the sword, and to make them amenable to law and justice by an effectual and vigorous police, than to grind them to powder by all manner of disabilities and incapacities. Better (said he) to hang or drown people at once, than by an unrelenting persecution to beggar and starve them. [Bos. 1770

To find a new country and to invade it have always been the same. [Intro. World Displayed

Some colonies indeed have been established more peaceably than others. The utmost extremity of wrong has not always been practiced; but those that have settled in the new world on the fairest terms have no other merit than that of a scrivener who ruins in silence, over a plunderer who ruins by force; all have taken what had other owners, and all have had recourse to arms rather than quit the prey on which they had fastened. [State of Affairs

Yet what the Romans did to other nations was in a great degree done by Cromwell to the Scots; he civilised them by conquest, and introduced by useful violence the arts of peace ... Till the Union ... the culture of their lands was unskilful, and their domestic life unformed; their tables were coarse as the feasts of Esquimaux, and their houses filthy as the cottages of Hottentots. [Journey, Inverness

> Yet Reason frowns on War's unequal game,
> Where wasted nations raise a single name;
> And mortgag'd states their grandsires' wreaths regret,
> From age to age in everlasting debt;
> Wreaths which at last the dear-bought right convey
> To rust on medals, or on stones decay.
> [Van. H. Wishes

On the Pursuit of Pleasure

A great deal of our industry, and all our ingenuity,
is exercised in procuring pleasure.

Bos. 14 April 1778

Young Boswell, in seeking out Johnson, was seeking the
author of The Rambler, the thinker whose essays were designed
"to inculcate wisdom or piety."[1] In his Life he rarely shows
Johnson in the gay, even frolicsome, moods that so endeared
him to his closest friends. Boswell's Johnson was the philosopher on whom cheerfulness but rarely broke in,[2] the tremen-
dous companion who talked for victory, who tossed and gored
his opponents in argument, and who—when all else failed—
overwhelmed them with abuse or ridicule.

The fact is that there was another Johnson, one who found
pleasure and even cheerfulness in mundane things. He was the
Johnson who got out of bed at three in the morning to "have
a frisk" with Langton and Beauclerk, his juniors by twenty
years. Ten years later, at one in the morning, Boswell asked
him to go to the Mitre. Johnson refused, but only because it
"was too late; they won't let us in."[3] Hawkins relates that one
morning, after an all-night celebration of Mrs. Lenox's first
book, Johnson's face "glowed with meridian splendour."[4]

Out in the country, he could roll down the long, grassy slope
of a meadow;[5] could remove his hat, coat, and wig to jump over

[1] Ram. 208. [2] Bos. April 1778. [3] Bos. 1769.
[4] Hawkins. [5] Best, John. Misc.

a rail;[6] could labor into breathlessness, trying with a long pole to push a dead cat over the brink of a tiny waterfall;[7] could kick off his shoes and run a footrace with a young lady (he won).[8] He even went hunting and rode so boldly as to fly most of the hedges—this, he explained later, to save himself the trouble of alighting and remounting.[9] And in Scotland he amazed and amused a company by pulling his coat-tails around to make the pouch, and imitating the gait, of a kangaroo.[10]

But in all this, as in so much of his search for company, he was trying to get away from himself. He seemed in his spiritual moods to exemplify the physical law that action and reaction are equal and opposite in direction. His gayest moments would sometimes, within a matter of minutes, give way to silence and black melancholy. Hence, people, he probably reasoned, should enjoy themselves in any way they could; but all enjoyment— like most human effort—was vain.

In a word, Johnson, in spite of what Boswell calls his "gust of life," felt the tepid air of futility and the cold breath of mortality during all his days. But somehow in him the gale of life blew so high that, although he could feel that all was vanity, he could not live as though he believed it.

Pleasure of itself is not a vice. [Bos. April 1778

The distrust which intrudes so often on your mind is a mode of melancholy, which, if it be the business of a wise man to be happy, it is foolish to indulge. [Bos. 14 Sept. 1777

The liberty of . . . harmless pleasures . . . will not be disputed; but it is still to be examined what pleasures are harmless. The evil of any pleasure . . . is not in the act itself, but

---

[6] Reed, Johnsoniana.   [7] Bos. April 1777.   [8] Miss Reynolds.
[9] Hawkins.   [10] Bos. (Hill-Powell, V, App. D).

in its consequences. Pleasure, in itself harmless, may become mischievous, by endearing us to a state which we know to be transitory . . . and withdrawing our thoughts from that, of which every hour brings us nearer to the beginning, and of which no length of time will bring us to the end. Mortification is not virtuous in itself, nor has any other use, but that it disengages us from the allurements of sense. [Ras. 47

Life is short. The sooner that a man begins to enjoy his wealth the better. [Bos. 19 April 1773

. . . pleasures of some sort are necessary to the intellectual as to the corporeal health; and those who resist gaiety, will be likely for the most part to fall a sacrifice to appetite; for the solicitations of sense are always at hand, and a dram to a vacant and solitary person is a speedy and seducing relief. [Pioz. Anec.

Boswell thought that a country gentleman might contrive to pass his life very agreeably:

Why, Sir, you cannot give me an instance of any man who is left to lay out his own time contriving not to have tedious hours. [For the Defense, p. 128

I told him, that [music] affected me to such a degree, as often to agitate my nerves painfully, producing in my mind alternate sensations of pathetick dejection, so that I was ready to shed tears; and of daring resolution so that I was inclined to rush into the thickest part of the battle. "Sir (said he), I should never hear it, if it made me such a fool." [Bos. 23 Sept. 1777

[Music] excites in my mind no ideas, and hinders me from contemplating my own. [Hawkins

Music is the only sensual pleasure without vice. [Seward, John. Misc.

I am sorry I have not learnt to play at cards. It is very useful in life: it generates kindness, and consolidates society. [Tour 21 November

In the presence of a very talkative woman, who remarked that Johnson preferred the company of men to that of ladies:

I am very fond of the company of ladies; I like their beauty, I like their delicacy. I like their vivacity, and I like their *silence.* [Seward, John. Misc.

. . . no mind is much employed upon the present; recollection and anticipation fill up almost all our moments. [Ras. 30

There is nothing, Sir, too little for so little a creature as man. It is by studying little things that we attain the great art of having as little misery and as much happiness as possible. [Bos. 14 July 1763

Every man . . . may, by examining his own mind, guess what passes in the minds of others: when you feel that your own gaiety is counterfeit, it may justly lead you to suspect that of your companions not to be sincere. Envy is commonly reciprocal. We are long before we are convinced that happiness is never to be found, and each believes it possessed by others, to keep alive the hope of obtaining it for himself. [Ras. 16

. . . for the pyramids no reason has ever been given, adequate to the cost and labour of the work . . . [They seem] to have been erected only in compliance with that hunger of imagination which preys incessantly upon life, and must be always appeased by some employment. Those who have already all that they can enjoy, must enlarge their desires. He that has built for use till use is supplied, must begin to build for vanity, and extend his plan to the utmost power of human performance, that he may not be soon reduced to form another wish.

I consider [the Great Pyramid] as a monument to the insufficiency of human enjoyments. A king whose power is unlimited, and whose treasures surmount all real and imaginary wants is compelled to solace, by the erection of a pyramid, the satiety of dominion and tastelessness of pleasures, and to amuse the tediousness of declining life, by seeing thousands labouring without end, and one stone, for no purpose, laid upon another. Whoever thou art, that, not content with a moderate condition, imaginest happiness in royal magnificence, and dreamest that command or riches can feed the appetite of novelty with perpetual gratifications, survey the pyramids, and confess thy folly! [Ras. 32

Such is the emptiness of human enjoyment, that we are always impatient of the present. Attainment is followed by neglect, and possession by disgust; and the malicious remark of the Greek epigrammatist on marriage may be applied to every other course of life, that its two days of happiness are the first and the last. [Ram. 207

Pride . . . is seldom delicate; it will please itself with very mean advantages; and envy feels not its own happiness but when it may be compared with the misery of others. [Ras. 9

Nothing is more hopeless than a scheme of merriment. . . . Merriment is always the effect of a sudden impression. The jest which is expected is already destroyed. [Idl. 58

. . . quiet is not the daughter of grandeur, or of power . . .

her presence is not to be bought by wealth, nor enforced by conquest. [Ras. 27

I should think it cruelty to crush an insect who had provoked me only by buzzing in my ear; and would not willingly interrupt the dream of harmless stupidity, or destroy the jest which makes its author laugh. [Ram. 93

To every place of entertainment we go with expectation and desire of being pleased; we meet others who are brought by the same motives; no one will be the first to own the disappointment; one face reflects the smile of another, till each believes the rest delighted and endeavours to catch and transmit the circulating rapture. In time all are deceived by the cheat to which all contribute. The fiction of happiness is propagated by every tongue, and confirmed by every look, till at last all profess the joy which they do not feel, content to yield to the general delusion; and when the voluntary dream is at an end, lament that bliss is of so short a duration. [Idl. 18

A publick performer is so much in the power of spectators, that all unnecessary severity is restrained by that general law of humanity which forbids us to be cruel where there is nothing to be feared. [Idl. 25

Hope is an amusement rather than a good. [Pioz. Anec.

I am a great friend to publick amusements; for they keep people from vice. [Bos. 31 March 1772

The publick pleasures of far the greater part of mankind are counterfeit. Very few carry their philosophy to places of diversion, or are very careful to analyse their enjoyments. The general condition of life is so full of misery, that we are glad to catch delight without enquiring whence it comes, or by what power it is bestowed. [Idl. 18

No man is a hypocrite in his pleasures. [Bos. June 1784

The noblest prospect which a Scotchman ever sees, is the high road that leads him to England! [Bos. 6 July 1763

Human life is every where a state in which much is to be endured, and little to be enjoyed. [Ras. 11

The joy of life is variety; the tenderest love requires to be renewed by intervals of absence. [Idl. 39

There are goods so opposed that we cannot seize both, but, by too much prudence, may pass between them at too great a distance to reach either. This is often the fate of long consideration; he does nothing who endeavours to do more than is allowed to humanity. Of the blessings set before you make your choice, and be content. No man can taste the fruits of autumn, while he is delighting his scent with the flowers of the spring: no man can at the same time fill his cup from the source and from the mouth of the Nile. [Ras. 29

Johnson's Mercator, retired and weary of the emptiness of his new life, says:

Such . . . is the life to which I am condemned by a foolish endeavour to be happy by imitation . . . I toiled . . . with cheerfulness, in expectation of the happy hour in which I might be idle: the privilege of idleness is attained, but has not brought with it the blessing of tranquillity. [Adv. 102

Terrestrial happiness is of short continuance. The brightness of the flame is wasting its fuel; the fragrant flower is passing away in its own odours. [Idl. 101

Gaiety is a duty when health requires it [Letter to Eliz. Aston, March 1777

One of the amusements of idleness is reading without the fatigue of close attention, and the world therefore swarms with writers whose wish is not to be studied, but to be read. [Idl. 30

The drone of timidity presumes likewise to hope, but without ground and without consequence . . . he . . . dozes away the day in musing upon the morrow; and at the end of life is roused from his dream only to discover that the time of action is past, and that he can now shew his wisdom only by repentance. [Adv. 69

You hunt in the morning (says he), and crowd to the public rooms at night, and call it *diversion*; when your heart knows it is perishing with poverty of pleasures, and your wits get blunted for want of some other mind to sharpen them upon. There is in this world no real delight (excepting those of sensuality), but exchange of ideas in conversation; and whoever has once experienced the full flow of London talk, when he retires to country friendships and rural sports, must either be contented to turn baby again and play with a rattle, or he will pine away like a great fish in a little pond, and die for want of his usual food. [Pioz. Anec.

. . . we do not always find visible happiness in proportion to visible virtue. All natural, and almost all political evils, are incident alike to the bad and good: they are confounded in the misery of a famine, and not much distinguished in the fury of a faction . . . All that virtue can afford, is quietness of conscience, and a steady prospect of a happier state; this may enable us to endure calamity with patience; but, remember that patience must suppose pain. [Ras. 27

I live in the crowds of jollity, not so much to enjoy company as to shun myself, and am only loud and merry to conceal my sadness. [Ras. 16

Whoever thinks of going to bed before twelve o'clock . . . is a scoundrel. [Hawkins, John. Misc.

I take the true definition of exercise to be labour without weariness. [Bos. 3 June 1782

[Hunting] was the labour of the savages of North America, but the amusement of the gentlemen of England. [Kearsley, John. Misc.

I could have set them right upon several subjects, Sir; for instance, the gentleman who said he could not imagine how pleasure could be derived from hunting—the reason is, because man feels his own vacuity less in action than when at rest. [Croker, John. Misc.

I have now learned (said he), by hunting, to perceive that it is no diversion at all, nor ever takes a man out of himself for a moment: the dogs have less sagacity than I could have prevailed on myself to suppose; and the gentlemen often call to me not to ride over them. It is strange, and very melancholy, that the paucity of human pleasures should persuade us ever to call hunting one of them. [Pioz. Anec.

Such . . . is the state of life that none are happy but by the anticipation of change: the change itself is nothing; when we have made it, the next wish is to change again. [Ras. 47

Yet, as much of life must be passed in affairs considerable only by their frequent occurrence, and much of the pleasure which our condition allows, must be produced by giving elegance to trifles, it is necessary to learn how to become little without becoming mean, to maintain the necessary intercourse of civility, and to fill up the vacuities of actions by agreeable appearances. [Ram. 152

[Allow children] to be happy in their own way, for what better way will they ever find? [Letter to Mrs. T., July 1780

Let him that desires to see others happy make haste to give while his gift can be enjoyed, and remember that every moment of delay takes away something from the value of his benefaction . . . while he forms his purpose the day rolls on, and *the night cometh when no man can work.* [Idl. 43

What signifies, says some one, giving halfpence to beggars? They only lay it out in gin and tobacco. "And why should they be denied such sweeteners of existence (says Johnson)? It is surely very savage to refuse them every possible avenue to pleasure, reckoned too coarse for our acceptance. Life is a pill which none of us can bear to swallow without gilding; yet for the poor we delight in stripping it still barer, and are not ashamed to shew even visible displeasure if ever the bitter taste is taken from their mouths." [Pioz. Anec.

Much of the pleasure which the first survey of the world affords, is exhausted before we are conscious of our felicity, or able to compare our condition with some other possible state. We have therefore few traces of the joy of our earliest discoveries; yet we all remember a time when nature had so many untasted gratifications, that every excursion gave delight which can now be found no longer, when the noise of a torrent, the rustle of a wood, the song of birds, or the play of lambs had power to fill the attention, and suspend all perception of the course of time.

But these early pleasures are soon at an end; we have seen in a very little time so much, that we call out for new objects of observation, and endeavour to find variety in books and life. But study is laborious, and not always satisfactory; and conversation has its pains as well as pleasures; we are willing to learn, but not to be taught; we are pained by ignorance, but pained yet more by another's knowledge. [Idl. 44

It is seldom that [in returning to old scenes] we find either men or places such as we expect them. He that has pictured a prospect upon his fancy, will receive little pleasure from his eyes; he that has anticipated the conversation of a wit, will wonder to what prejudice he owes his reputation. Yet it is necessary to hope, though hope should always be deluded; for hope itself is happiness, and its frustrations, however frequent, are yet less dreadful than its extinction. [Idl. 58

Such is the condition of life, that something is always wanting to happiness. In youth, we have warm hopes which are soon blasted by rashness and negligence, and great designs which are defeated by inexperience. In age, we have knowledge and prudence without spirit to exert, or motives to prompt them; we are able to plan schemes, and regulate measures; but have not time remaining to bring them to completion. [Ram. 196

. . . so scanty is our present allowance of happiness, that in many situations life could scarcely be supported, if hopes were not allowed to relieve the present hour by pleasures borrowed from futurity. [Adv. 69

When Socrates passed through shops of toys and ornaments [at the fair in Athens], he cried out, *How many things are here which I do not need!* And the same exclamation may every man make who surveys the common accommodations of life. [Idl. 37

Before dinner men meet with great equality of understanding; and those who are conscious of their inferiority, have the modesty not to talk. When they have drunk wine, every man feels himself happy, and loses that modesty, and grows impudent and vociferous: but he is not improved; he is only not sensible of his defects. [Bos. 12 April 1776

Wine makes a man better pleased with himself. I do not say that it makes him more pleasing to others. Sometimes it does. But the danger is, that while a man grows better pleased with himself, he may be growing less pleasing to others. Wine gives a man nothing. It neither gives him knowledge nor wit; it only animates a man, and enables him to bring out what a dread of company has repressed. It only puts in motion what has been locked up in frost. [Bos. 28 April 1778

Sir, claret is the liquor for boys; port, for men; but he who aspires to be a hero (smiling) must drink brandy. [Bos. 7 April 1779

[Claret] neither makes boys men, nor men boys. You'll be drowned by it, before it has any effect upon you. [Bos. 30 March 1781

Mrs. Williams once remarked about drinking:
"I wonder what pleasure men can take in making beasts of themselves." "I wonder, Madam," replied the Doctor, "that you have not penetration enough to see the strong inducement to

this excess; for he who makes a *beast* of himself gets rid of the pain of being a man." [Stockdale, John. Misc.

In that article [tea] I am a hardened sinner who has for years diluted his meals with the infusion of that fascinating plant; whose tea-kettle has no time to cool; who with tea solaced the midnight hour, and with tea welcomed the morning. [Review, *Eight Days' Journey*

Of a plain dinner in which nothing special had been prepared for him as a guest:

This was a good dinner enough, to be sure; but it was not a dinner to *ask* a man to. [Bos. 5 Aug 1763

There is no private house (said he), in which people can enjoy themselves so well, as at a capital tavern. Let there be ever so great a plenty of good things, ever so much grandeur, ever so much elegance, ever so much desire that every body should be easy . . . there must always be some degree of care and anxiety . . . There is nothing which has yet been contrived by man, by which so much happiness is produced as by a good tavern or inn. [Bos. 21 March 1776

As soon as I enter the door of a tavern, I experience an oblivion of care, and a freedom from solicitude: when I am seated, I find the master courteous, and the servants obsequious to my call; anxious to know and ready to supply my wants. Wine there exhilarates my spirits, and prompts me to free conversation and an interchange of discourse with those whom I most love: I dogmatize and am contradicted, and in this conflict of opinions and sentiments I find delight. [Hawkins

. . . that which is not best may be yet very free from bad, and he that shall complain of his fare in the Hebrides has improved his delicacy more than his manhood. [Journey, Corrichatachan

Johnson, resenting the bad mutton served at an inn during a trip to Oxford:

It is as bad as bad can be: it is ill-fed, ill-killed, ill-kept, and ill-drest. [Bos. 3 June 1784

This is one of the disadvantages of wine. It makes a man mistake words for thoughts. [Bos. 28 April 1778

Some people (said he) have a foolish way of not minding, or pretending not to mind, what they eat. For my part, I mind my belly very studiously, and very carefully; for I look upon it, that he who does not mind his belly will hardly mind any thing else. [Bos. 5 Aug. 1763

Depend upon it, Sir, every state of society is as luxurious as it can be. Men always take the best they can get . . . to be merely satisfied is not enough. It is in refinement and elegance that the civilised man differs from the savage. [Bos. 14 April 1778

The sad complaint of a retired man of business:

I eat not because I am hungry, but because I am idle. Adv. 102

Gluttony is, I think, less common among women than among men. Women commonly eat more sparingly and are less curious in the choice of meat; but if once you find a woman gluttonous, expect from her very little virtue. Her mind is enslaved to the lowest and grossest temptation. [Letter to Susanna Thrale, July 1783

Johnson, quoting a Dr. Barrowby:

I wish I was a Jew . . . I should then have the gust of eating [pork], with the pleasure of sinning. [Bos. 1784

[We were] entertained by Sir Eyre Coote . . . with such elegance of conversation as left us no attention to the delicacies of his table. [Journey, Fort George

Speaking to Boswell about "in vino veritas":

I would not keep company with a fellow who lyes as long as he is sober, and whom you must make drunk before you can get a word of truth out of him. [Bos. 15 April 1772

To Johnson, about to say grace before dinner, Mrs. Johnson had once said:

Nay, hold, Mr. Johnson, and do not make a farce of thanking God for a dinner which in a few minutes you will protest not eatable. [Pioz. Anec.

All the pleasure that is received [from travel] ends in an opportunity of splendid falsehood, in the power of gaining notice by the display of beauties which the eye was weary of beholding, and a history of happy moments, of which, in reality, the most happy was the last. [Idl. 50

[We missed] the pleasure of alarming villages with the tumult of our passage, and of disguising our insignificancy by the dignity of hurry. [Ram. 142

If (said he) I had no duties, and no reference to futurity, I would spend my life in driving briskly in a post-chaise with a pretty woman. [Bos. 19 Sept. 1777

What I gained by being in France was, learning to be better satisfied with my own country. [Bos. 13 May 1778

Sir, that all who are happy, are equally happy, is not true. A peasant and a philosopher may be equally *satisfied*, but not equally *happy*. Happiness consists in the multiplicity of agreeable consciousness. A peasant has not capacity for having equal happiness with a philosopher. [Bos. Feb. 1766

Boswell observed that things were done upon the supposition of happiness—grand houses built, fine gardens made, splendid places of public entertainment contrived:

Alas, Sir, these are only struggles for happiness. When I first entered Ranelagh, it gave an expansion and gay sensation to my mind, such as I never experienced any where else. But, as Xerxes wept when he viewed his immense army, and considered that not one of that great multitude would be alive a hundred years afterwards, so it went to my heart to consider that there was not one in all that brilliant circle, that was not afraid to go home and think; but that the thoughts of each individual there, would be distressing when alone." [Bos. 23 Sept. 1777

The Johnson who could ride madly after the hounds, who could send forth peals of laughter so loud that in the silence of the night his voice seemed to resound from Temple Bar to Fleetditch, rarely appears in his writing. Once, at least, he wrote a letter to Mrs. Thrale which showed the same kind of elephantine playfulness that amazed the Covent Garden costermongers in the morning after his all-night frisk with Langton and Beauclerk. It was written in January 1773.

MADAM:

The inequalities of human life have always employed the meditation of deep thinkers, and I cannot forbear to reflect on the difference between your condition and my own. You live upon mock-turtle and stewed rumps of beef; I dined yesterday on crumpets. You sit with parish officers, caressing and caressed, the idol of the table and the wonder of the day. I pine in the solitude of sickness, not bad enough to be pitied, and not well enough to be endured. You sleep away the night, and laugh or scold away the day. I cough and grumble, grumble and cough. Last night was very tedious, and this day makes no promises of much ease. However, I have this day put on my shoes and hope that gout is gone. I shall have only the cough to contend with, and I doubt whether I shall get rid of that without change of place. I caught cold in the coach as I went away and am disordered by very little things. Is it accident or age?

I am, dearest madam,

SAM. JOHNSON

On Youth and Age

*There are many who . . . talk of the ingratitude of
the age, curse their heirs for impatience, and wonder
that young men cannot take pleasure in their father's
company.*

Ram. 50

The casual reader of Johnson may be surprised at the frequency with which a contrast is made, one way or another, between youth and age. The reason is not hard to find. Johnson loved the young; he hated to think of himself as growing old. Boswell, Beauclerk, Langton, Mrs. Thrale—to mention only a few of those who were so important in Johnson's life—were all in their twenties when they first met Johnson, then at least in his forties. Hector and Taylor, his contemporaries, were not so conspicuous in his life; and when Mr. Edwards—a college acquaintance—quoted, in the course of their meeting, "O my coevals! remnants of yourselves," Johnson shook his head with impatience. He was "putting in for a hundred."[1]

Nor in Johnson's mind was the contrast between youth and age one of years alone. The adjectives which Johnson uses show the way he thinks. Youth is glad, sprightly, generous; age is gloomy, torpid, malignant. Youth rushes out with the vigor and valor of ignorance; age inches along with the circumspection and weariness of experience. At bottom Johnson sees youth as ex-

[1] Bos. 17 April 1778.

pending life rashly, and perhaps unwisely, and age as hoarding life ungenerously and probably just as unwisely.

Johnson's own vitality and mental alertness were remarkable. He was sixty-two when he went off on the arduous trip through the Highlands and the inner Hebrides, a trip that seemed less hard on him than on the much younger Boswell. From the trip, too, he returned to London with a mind full of new impressions and new ideas; for he had traveled—like a young man —with his eyes and the pores of his intellect wide open. He was not one of the old men in MacLeish's poem who "go but have not gone," who merely "sail to the seabeach they have left behind."

Johnson speaks in grand, general terms. How often he will begin, "A man, Sir . . ." or "Mankind, Sir, will . . ." Each man hammers out truth on his own anvil, and so Johnson's observations are on age and youth as he saw them, but not as he instinctively lived them. A sick man, he observes, can easily become a scoundrel.[2] He apparently did not. Youth is honest and intolerant. He was. Men grow less tender as they grow older.[3] Johnson certainly did not. Age had better not vie with youth.[4] Johnson did, but he triumphed on the battleground of his own choosing. At the end, his talk was still terse and vigorous; and just before his death he refused opiates because he wanted to die with his mind still clear. There was nothing of the old man in all this.

Johnson on youth and age voices very ordinary truths, but voices them with such clarity and vigor that they seem as fresh as tomorrow morning.

The first years of man must make provision for the last. [Ras.

17

---

[2] Letter to Hill Boothby.   [3] Ram. 78.   [4] Ram. 50.

He that cannot live well to-day . . . will be less qualified to live well to-morrow . . . yet, instead of living, [we] let year glide after year in preparations to live. [Adv. 108

Life is not long, and not too much of it must be spent in idle deliberation *how* it shall be spent. [Letter to Bos., Aug. 1766

Rasselas rose next day, and resolved to begin his experiments upon life. "Youth," cried he, "is the time of gladness: I will join myself to the young men" . . . but a few days brought him back weary and disgusted. Their mirth was without images, their laughter without motive; their pleasures were gross and sensual, in which the mind had no part; their conduct was at once wild and mean: they laughed at order and at law, but the frown of power dejected, and the eye of wisdom abashed them. [Ras. 17

Sir, I love the acquaintance of young people; because, in the first place, I don't like to think myself growing old. In the next place, young acquaintances must last longest, if they do last; and then, Sir, young men have more virtue than old men; they have more generous sentiments in every respect. I love the young dogs of this age: they have more wit and humour and knowledge of life than we had; but then the dogs are not so good scholars. [Bos. 21 July 1763

Among other pleasing errours of young minds, is the opinion of their own importance. He that has not yet remarked how little attention his contemporaries can spare from their own affairs, conceives all eyes turned upon himself, and imagines every one that approaches him to be an enemy or a follower, an admirer or a spy. He therefore considers his fame as involved in the event of every action. Many of the virtues and vices of youth proceed from this quick sense of reputation.

This it is that gives firmness and constancy, fidelity and disinterestedness, and it is this that kindles resentment for slight injuries, and dictates all the principles of sanguinary honour. [Ram. 196

You have hitherto done nothing to diminish my good will, and though you had done much more than you have supposed imputed to you, my good will would not have been diminished.

I write thus largely on this suspicion which you have suffered to enter your mind, because in youth we are apt to be too rigorous in our expectations, and to suppose that the duties of life are to be performed with unfailing exactness and regularity; but in our progress through life, we are forced to abate much of our demands, and to take friends such as we can find them, not as we would make them.

These concessions every wise man is more ready to make to others as he knows that he shall often want them himself; and when he remembers how often he fails in the observance or cultivation of his best friends, is willing to suppose that his friends may in their turn neglect him without any intention to offend him. [Letter to Geo. Strahan, July 1763

. . . every age and every condition indulges in some darling fallacy; every man amuses himself with projects which he knows to be improbable, and which, therefore, he resolves to pursue without daring to examine them. [Adv. 69

It is however certain, that no estimate is more in danger of erroneous calculations than those by which a man computes the force of his own genius. It generally happens at our entrance into the world, that, by the natural attraction of similitude, we associate with men like ourselves, young, sprightly, and ignorant, and rate our accomplishments by comparison with theirs: when we have once obtained an acknowledged superiority over our acquaintances, imagination and desires easily extend it over the rest of mankind; and if no accident forces us into new emulations, we grow old, and die in admiration of ourselves. [Ram. 154

So different are the colours of life as we look forward to the future, or backward to the past . . . that the conversation of the old and young ends generally with contempt or pity on either side. To a young man entering the world with fullness of hope, and ardour of pursuit, nothing is so unpleasant as the cold caution, the faint expectations, the scrupulous diffidence, which experience and disappointments certainly infuse; and the old man wonders in his turn that the world can never grow wiser, that neither precepts, nor testimonies, can cure boys of their credulity and sufficiency; and that not one can be convinced that snares are laid for him, till he finds himself entangled. [Ram. 69

. . . a man commonly grew wickeder as he grew older (he said); at least he but changed the vices of youth, headstrong passion and wild temerity, for treacherous caution and desire to circumvent. I am (said he) always on the young people's side, when there is a dispute between them and the old ones: for you have at least a chance for virtue till age has withered its very root. [Pioz. Anec.

. . . in the decline of life, shame and grief are of short duration. [Ras. 4

. . . let the gay and vigorous expect pleasure in their excursions: it is enough that age can obtain ease. [Ras. 45

In youth, it is common to measure right and wrong by the

opinion of the world, and, in age, to act without any measure but interest, and to lose shame without substituting virtue. [Ram. 196

To play with important truths, to disturb the repose of established tenets, to subtilise objections, and elude proof is too often the sport of youthful vanity, of which maturer experience commonly repents. There is a time when every man is weary of raising difficulties only to task himself with the solution, and desires to enjoy truth without the labour or hazard of contest. [Browne

. . . our tastes greatly alter. The lad does not care for the child's rattle, and the old man does not care for the young man's whore . . . as we advance in the journey of life, we drop some of the things which have pleased us; whether it be that we are fatigued and don't choose to carry so many things any farther, or that we find other things which we like better. [Bos. Spring 1776

The old man trusts wholly to slow contrivance and gradual progression; the youth expects to force his way by genius, vigour, and precipitance. The old man pays regard to riches, and the youth reverences virtue. The old man deifies prudence: the youth commits himself to magnanimity and chance. The young man, who intends no ill, believes that none is intended, and therefore acts with openness and candour: but his father, having suffered the injuries of fraud, is impelled to suspect, and too often allured to practise it. Age looks with anger on the temerity of youth, and youth with contempt on the scrupulosity of age. [Ras. 26

In my younger days it is true I was much inclined to treat mankind with asperity and contempt; but I found it answered no good end. I thought it wiser and better to take the world as it goes. Besides, as I have advanced in life I have had more reason to be satisfied with it. Mankind have treated me with more kindness, and, of course, I have more kindness for them. [Miss Reynolds

Every old man complains of the growing depravity of the world, of the petulance and insolence of the rising generation. He recounts the decency and regularity of former times, and celebrates the discipline and sobriety of the age in which his youth was passed; a happy age, which is now no more to be expected, since confusion has broken in upon the world and thrown down all the boundaries of civility and reverence. [Ram. 50

He that would pass the latter part of his life with honour and decency must, when he is young, consider that he shall one day be old; and remember when he is old that he has once been young. In youth he must lay up knowledge for his support, when his powers of acting shall forsake him; and in age forbear to animadvert with rigour on faults which experience only can correct. [Ram. 50

Peevishness is generally the vice of narrow minds, and except when it is the effect of anguish and disease . . . proceeds from an unreasonable persuasion of the importance of trifles. . . . He that resigns his peace to little casualties, and suffers the course of his life to be interrupted by fortuitous inadvertancies, or offences, delivers up himself to the direction of the wind, and loses all that constancy and equanimity, which constitutes the chief praise of a wise man. [Ram. 112

Sir, as a man advances in life, he gets what is better than

admiration—judgement, to estimate things at their true value
. . . admiration and love are like being intoxicated with cham-
pagne; judgement and friendship are like being enlivened. [Bos.
16 April 1775

Thus we find old age, upon which suspicion has been strongly
impressed, by long intercourse with the world, inflexible and
severe, not easily softened by submission, melted by complaint,
or subdued by supplication. Frequent experience of counter-
feited miseries, and dissembled virtue, in time overcomes that
disposition to tenderness and sympathy, which is so powerful
in our younger years; and they that happen to petition the old
for compassion or assistance, are doomed to languish without
regard, and suffer for the crimes of men who have formerly been
found undeserving or ungrateful. [Ram. 79

The world . . . is chiefly unjust and ungenerous in this, that
all are ready to encourage a man who once talks of leaving it,
and few things do really provoke me more, than to hear people
prate of retirement, when they have neither skill to discern
their own motives, or penetration to estimate the consequences:
but while a fellow is active to gain either power or wealth . . .
every body produces some hindrance to his advancement, some
sage remark, or some unfavourable prediction; but let him once
say slightly, I have had enough of this troublesome bustling
world . . . Ah, dear Sir! cries the first old acquaintance he meets,
I am glad to find you in this happy disposition: yes, dear friend!
do retire and think of nothing but your own ease . . . Miss
Dolly makes the charmingest chicken broth in the world, and
the cheesecakes we eat of her's once, how good they were: I
will be coming every two or three days myself to chat with you
in a quiet way; *so snug!* . . . [Thus he] lays himself down a
voluntary prey to his own sensuality and sloth, while the am-

bition and avarice of the nephews and nieces, with their rascally adherents, and coadjutors, reap the advantage, while they fatten their fool. [Pioz. Anec.

A man grows better humoured as he grows older. He improves by experience. When young, he thinks himself of great consequence and every thing of importance. As he advances through life, he learns to think himself of no consequence and little things of little importance; and so he becomes patient and better pleased. All good humour and complaisance are acquired. [Tour 14 September

As I know more of mankind I expect less of them, and am ready now to call a man *a good man,* upon easier terms than I was formerly. [Bos. Sept. 1783

He . . . lay down on his couch peevish and restless, rather afraid to die than desirous to live. [Ram. 190

The most usual support of old age is wealth. He whose possessions are large, and whose chests are full, imagines himself fortified against invasions on his authority. If he has lost all other means of government, if his strength and his reason fail him, he can at last alter his will; and, therefore, all that have hopes must likewise have fears, and he may still continue to give laws to such as have not ceased to regard their own interest.

This is indeed too frequently the citadel of the dotard, the last fortress to which age retires. [Ram. 69

[Swift] could make little use of books in his later years; his ideas, therefore, being neither renovated by discourse, nor increased by reading, wore gradually away, and left his mind vacant to the vexations of the hour, till, at last, his anger was heightened into madness. [L.P., Swift

If dotards will contend with boys in those performances in which boys must always excel them; if they will . . . endeavour at gaiety with faltering voices, and darken assemblies of pleasure . . . they may well expect those who find their diversions obstructed will hoot them away; and that if they descend to competition with youth, they must bear the insolence of successful rivals. [Ram. 50

. . . it cannot surely be supposed that old age, worn with labours, harassed with anxieties, and tortured with diseases, should have any gladness of its own, or feel any satisfaction from the contemplation of the present. All the comfort that can now be expected must be recalled from the past, or borrowed from the future; the past is very soon exhausted, all the events or actions of which the memory can afford pleasure are quickly recollected; and the future lies beyond the grave, where it can be reached only by virtue and devotion. [Ram. 69

. . . an old man should not resign himself to the management of any body. [Tour 30 September

. . . at seventy-seven it is time to be in earnest. [Journey, Coll

Health begins after seventy—and often long before—to have a different meaning from that which it had at thirty. But it is culpable to murmur at the established order of creation as it is vain to oppose it. He that lives, must grow old; and he who would rather grow old than die, has God to thank for the infirmities of age. [Letter to Bos., December 1782

Of the uncertainties of our present state, the most dreadful and alarming is the uncertain continuance of reason. [Ras. 43

> In life's last scene what prodigies surprise,
> Fears of the brave, and follies of the wise?
> From Marlb'rough's eyes the streams of dotage flow,
> And Swift expires a driv'ler and a show.
>
> [Van. H. Wishes

It is a man's own fault, it is from want of use, if his mind grows torpid in old age. [Bos. 9 April 1778

. . . nothing more certainly offended Mr. Johnson, than the idea of a man's faculties decaying by time. "It is not true, Sir (would he say); what a man could once do, he would always do, unless indeed by dint of vicious indolence, and compliance with the nephews and nieces who crowd round the old fellow, and help to tuck him in, till he, contented with the exchange of fame for ease, e'en resolves to let them set the pillows at his back, and gives no further proof of his existence than just to suck the jelly that prolongs it." [Pioz. Anec.

There must be a diseased mind, where there is a failure of memory at seventy. A man's head, Sir, must be morbid, if he fails so soon. [Bos. 22 Sept. 1777

To be told that any man has attained a hundred years gives hope and comfort to him who stands trembling on the brink of his own climacteric. [Journey, Ostig

A lady he thought well of, was disordered in her health . . . "What is her disease?" enquired Johnson. Oh, nothing positive [was the reply], rather a gradual and gentle decline. "She will die, then, pretty dear (answered he)! When Death's pale horse runs away with persons on full speed, an active physician may possibly give them a turn; but if he carries them on an even slow pace, down hill too! no care nor skill can save them!" [Pioz. Anec.

Thus every period of life is obliged to borrow its happiness from the time to come. In youth we have nothing past to entertain us, and in age we derive little from retrospect but hopeless sorrow. Yet the future likewise has its limits, which the imagination dreads to approach, but which we see to be not far distant. The loss of our friends and companions impresses hourly upon us the necessity of our own departure; we know that the schemes of man are quickly at an end, that we must soon lie down in the grave with the forgotten multitudes of former ages, and yield our place to others, who, like us, shall be driven a while, by hope or fear, about the surface of the earth, and then like us be lost in the shades of death. [Ram. 203

A person mentioned his having seen a noble person driving and looking exceedingly well notwithstanding his great age. Johnson said:

Ah, Sir; that is nothing. Bacon observes, that a stout healthy old man is like a tower undermined. [Bos. 16 May 1784

I confirmed all that the Doctor had been saying, how no present danger could be expected; but that his age . . . must naturally accelerate the arrival of the hour that can be escaped by none [writes Mrs. Thrale]. "And this (says Johnson, rising in great anger) is the voice of female friendship I suppose, when the hand of the hangman would be softer." [Pioz. Anec.

. . . men may be generally observed to grow less tender as they advance in age. He who, when life was new, melted at the loss of every companion, can look in time, without concern, upon the grave into which his friend was thrown, and into which himself is ready to fall; not that he is more willing to die than formerly, but that he is more familiar to the death of others, and therefore is not alarmed so far as to consider how much nearer he approaches to his end. [Ram. 78

Praise . . . is to an old man an empty sound. I have neither mother to be delighted with the reputation of her son, nor wife to partake the honours of her husband. I have outlived my friends and my rivals. Nothing is now of much importance; for I cannot extend my interest beyond myself. [Ras. 45

. . . what is success to him that has none to enjoy it? Happiness is not found in self-contemplation; it is perceived only when it is reflected from another. [Idl. 41

Sir, there comes a time in life when a man requires the repairs of the table. [Cradock, Johnsoniana

There is nothing against which an old man should be so much upon his guard as putting himself to nurse. Innumerable have been the melancholy instances of men once distinguished for firmness, resolution, and spirit, who in their latter days have been governed like children, by interested female artifice. [Bos. 26 March 1776

. . . to a man who has survived all the companions of his youth . . . this full-peopled world is a dismal solitude. He stands forlorn and silent, neglected or insulted, in the midst of multitudes, animated with hopes which he cannot share, and employed in business which he is no longer able to forward or retard; nor can he find any to whom his life or his death are of importance, unless he has secured some domestic gratifications, some tender employments, and endeared himself to some whose interest and gratitude may unite them to him. [Ram. 69

There are few things . . . that we so unwillingly give up, even in advanced age, as the supposition that we have still the power of ingratiating ourselves with the Fair Sex. [Steevens, John. Misc.

I value myself upon this, that there is nothing of the old man in my conversation. [Bos. 30 April 1778

Piety is the only proper and adequate relief of decaying man. He that grows old without religious hopes, as he declines into imbecility, and feels pains and sorrows incessantly crowding upon him, falls into a gulf of bottomless misery, in which every reflection must plunge him deeper, and where he finds only new graduations of anguish, and precipices of horror. [Ram. 69

It matters not how a man dies, but how he lives. [Bos. 26 Oct. 1769

On God, Religion, and
Man's Salvation

*There are many good men whose fear of God pre-
dominates over their love.*

Bos. March 1778

In matters of religion Johnson was at once a skeptic and a
believer, surprisingly tolerant and at times brutally intolerant.
He could make allowances for different religions and—up to a
point—for different sects in the great family of Christianity.
He was, on the whole, a convinced Christian. But somehow
one gets the impression that, like Tillich, he recognized that in
all faith there is an element of doubt. Johnson reasoned himself
into his belief; he hated feelers.

He believed that one's religion needed to be strengthened by
every possible external support. "To be of no church is dangerous," he wrote of Milton. He knew men well enough to
know that they needed to be continually reminded of their
duty; but more, that their limited thinking always needed to
be nourished and deepened by the long experience of a great
tradition. He attended services regularly at St. Clement Danes
in the Strand, and the spot directly above the pulpit, where he
was accustomed to sit, is now marked. Three times a year—on
his birthday, at New Year's, and on Easter Sunday—he would
solemnly resolve to amend his life, would compose a prayer for

divine help, and take the Sacrament. The attempts at amendment came to nothing, but for decades he persisted because, he
wrote, "Reformation is necessary, and despair is criminal."[1]
Johnson's terror of death was a strange compound of belief in
God's judgment and conviction of his own sinfulness. He believed, I suppose, in God's mercy; but his faith never came easy.
He had hope, but hope shadowed by fear, and the fear was
never far in the background.

For Whigs in politics he had only violent hatred; for dis-
senters in religion he could feel something like toleration,
though Quaker, Baptist, Congregationalist, and Methodist are
not in his Dictionary. He could even praise the preaching of
Wesley; he had, however, less than praise for Whitefield. One
of his severest blasts was for a young lady who had quit the
Church of England to become a Quaker; one wonders if he was
angry not because she had changed, but because he could not
believe she had thought her way into her new sect. "She knew
no more," he said, "of the Church which she left and that
which she embraced, than she did of the difference between the
Copernican and Ptolemaick systems"[2]

The fact is that Johnson in matters of religion was, as he was
in most other matters, violent, rational if not reasonable, and
little troubled by consistency—that bugbear of petty minds.

[In my youth] I then became a sort of lax *talker* against religion, for I did not much *think* against it; and this lasted till
I went to Oxford . . . I took up Law's "Serious Call to a Holy
Life," expecting to find it a dull book and perhaps to laugh at
it. But I found Law quite an overmatch for me; and this was
the first occasion of my thinking in earnest of religion. [Bos.
1729

[1] Prayers and Meditations, April 1775.
[2] Bos. 15 April 1778.

I must always doubt of that which has not yet happened. [More, John. Misc.

Soul: The immaterial and immortal spirit of man. [Dict.

I think all Christians, whether Papists or Protestants, agree in the essential articles, and that their differences are trivial, and rather political than religious. [Bos. 25 June 1763

Papist: One that adheres to the communion of the pope and church of Rome. [Dict.

Presbyterian: An abettor of presbytery or Calvinistal doctrine.
Presbytery: Body of elders, whether priests or laymen . . .
    "Flea-bitten synod, an assembly brewed
    Of clerks and elders and, like the rude
    Chaos of presbytery, where laymen guide
    With the tame woolpack clergy at their side."
                                    [Dict.

Protestant: One of those who adhere to them, who, at the beginning of the reformation, protested against the errours of the church of Rome. "This is the first example of any protestant subjects that have taken up arms against their king, a *protestant.*" [Dict.

[As apostolic ordination] was an apostolick institution, I think it is dangerous to be without it. And, Sir, the Presbyterians have no publick worship; they have no form of prayer in which they know they are to join. They go to hear a man pray, and are to judge whether they will join with him. [Bos. 26 Oct. 1769

To be of no church is dangerous. Religion, of which the rewards are distant, and which is animated only by Faith and Hope, will glide by degrees out of the mind unless it be invigorated and reimpressed by external ordinances, by stated calls to worship, and by the salutary influence of example. [L.P., Milton

The great art therefore of piety, and the end for which all the rites of religion seem to be instituted, is the perpetual renovation of the motives to virtue, by a voluntary employment of our mind in the contemplation of its excellence, its importance, and its necessity, which, in proportion as they are more frequently and more willingly revolved, gain a more forcible and permanent influence, till in time they become the reigning ideas, the standing principles of action, and the test by which every thing proposed to the judgement is rejected or approved. [Ram. 7

[Our first reformers] were not burnt for not believing bread and wine to be CHRIST, but for insulting those who did believe it. [Bos. 7 May 1773

The heathens were easily converted, because they had nothing to give up; but we ought not, without very strong conviction indeed, to desert the religion in which we have been educated. [Bos. 15 April 1778.

A man who is converted from Protestantism to Popery, may be sincere: he parts with nothing: he is only superadding to what he already had. But a convert from Popery to Protestantism, gives up so much of what he has held as sacred as any thing that he retains; there is so much *laceration of mind* in such a conversion, that it can hardly be sincere and lasting. [Bos. 26 Oct. 1769

Of the Roman Catholic religion:

If you join the Papists externally, they will not interrogate you strictly as to your belief in their tenets. No reasoning Papist believes every article of their faith. There is one side on which a good man might be persuaded to embrace it. A good man of a timorous disposition, in great doubt of his acceptance with God, and pretty credulous, might be glad to be of a church where there are so many helps to get to Heaven. I would be a Papist if I could. I have fear enough; but an obstinate rationality prevents me. I shall never be a Papist, unless on the near approach of death, of which I have a very great terrour. I wonder that women are not all Papists. [Bos. 10 June 1784

All theory is against freedom of the will; all experience for it. [Bos. 15 April 1778

. . . belief ought to be proportioned to evidence or probability. . . . Whatever is true will bear to be related, whatever is rational will endure to be explained. [Adv. 69

None would have recourse to an invisible power, but that all other subjects have eluded their hopes. None would fix their attention upon the future, but that they are discontented with the present. If the senses were feasted with perpetual pleasure, they would always keep the mind in subjection. Reason has no authority over us, but by its power to warn us against evil. [Idl. 89

As to the Christian religion, Sir, besides the strong evidence which we have for it, there is a balance in its favour from the number of great men who have been convinced of its truth, after a serious consideration of the question. Grotius was an acute man, a lawyer, a man accustomed to examine evidence, and he was convinced. Grotius was not a recluse, but a man of the world . . . Sir Isaac Newton set out an infidel, and came to be a very firm believer. [Bos. 28 July 1763

Patience and submission are very carefully to be distinguished from cowardice and indolence. We are not to repine, but we may lawfully struggle; for the calamities of life, like the necessities of nature, are calls to labour and exercises of diligence. When we feel any pressure of distress, we are not to conclude that we can only obey the will of Heaven by languishing under it, any more than when we perceive the pain of thirst, we are to imagine that water is prohibited. Of misfortune it never can be certainly known whether, as proceeding from the hand of God, it is an act of favour or of punishment; but since all the ordinary dispensations of Providence are to be interpreted according to the general analogy of things, we may conclude that we have a right to remove one inconvenience as well as another; that we are only to take care lest we purchase ease with guilt; and that our Maker's purpose, whether of reward or severity, will be answered by the labours which He lays us under the necessity of performing. [Ram. 32

The precepts of *Epicurus*, who teaches us to endure what the laws of the universe make necessary, may silence, but not content us. The dictates of *Zeno*, who commands us to look with indifference on external things, may dispose us to conceal our sorrow, but cannot assuage it . . . Philosophy may infuse stubbornness, but Religion only can give patience. [Idl. 41

. . . whatever enlarges hope will exalt courage. [Journey, Edinburgh

Hope is itself a species of happiness, and, perhaps, the chief happiness which this world affords: but, like all other pleasures immoderately enjoyed, the excesses of hope must be ex-

piated by pain; and expectations improperly indulged, must
end in disappointment. [Bos. 8 June 1762

To enumerate the various modes of charity . . . as it is difficult, would be useless. They are as extensive as want, and as
various as misery. [Sermon XIII

The principle upon which extemporary prayer was originally
introduced is no longer admitted. The minister formerly, in
the effusion of his prayer, expected immediate, and perhaps
perceptible inspiration, and therefore thought it his duty not
to think before what he should say. It is now universally confessed, that men pray as they speak on other occasions, according to the general measure of their abilities and attainments. Whatever each may think of a form prescribed by
another, he cannot but believe that he can himself compose
by study and meditation a better prayer than will rise in his
mind at a sudden call; and if he has any hope of supernatural
help, why may he not as well receive it when he writes as when
he speaks? [Journey, Ostig

I am myself fully convinced that a form of prayer for publick
worship is in general most decent and edifying. *Solennia verba*
have a kind of prescriptive sanctity, and make a deeper impression on the mind than extemporaneous effusions, in which, as
we know not what they are to be, we cannot readily acquiesce.
Yet I would allow also of a certain portion of extempore address, as occasion may require. This is the practice of the French
Protestant churches. And although the office of forming sup-
plications to the throne of Heaven is, in my mind, too great a
trust to be indiscriminately committed to the discretion of
every minister, I do not mean to deny that sincere devotion
may be experienced when joining in prayer with those who use
no Liturgy. [Tour 27 October

Reason and truth will prevail at last. The most learned of the Scottish doctors would now gladly admit a form of prayer, if the people would endure it. The zeal or rage of congregations has its different degrees. In some parishes the Lord's prayer is suffered: in others it is still rejected as a form; and he that should make it part of his supplication would be suspect of heretical pravity. [Journey, Ostig

Sir, you must consider that we have perfect and imperfect obligations. Perfect obligations, which are generally not to do something, are clear and positive; as, "thou shalt not kill." But charity, for instance, is not definable by limits. It is a duty to give to the poor; but no man can say how much another should give to the poor, or when a man has given too little to save his soul. [Bos. 7 May 1773

Of him, to whom much is given, much shall be required. Those, whom God has favoured with superiour faculties, and made eminent for quickness of intuition, and accuracy of distinctions, will certainly be regarded as culpable in his eye, for defects and deviations which, in souls less enlightened, may be guiltless. But, surely, none can think without horrour on that man's condition, who has been more wicked in proportion as he had more means of excelling in virtue, and used the light imparted from Heaven only to embellish folly, and shed lustre upon crimes. [Ram. 77

For true charity arises from faith in the promises of God, and expects rewards only in a future state. To hope for our recompense in this life, is not beneficence, but usury. [Sermon IV

Others . . . frequently delight to dwell upon the excellency of charity, and profess themselves ready to comply with its precepts, whenever proper objects shall be proposed, and opportunity of proper application shall be found; but they pretend that they are so well informed, with regard to the perversion of charity, and discover so many ill effects of indistinguishing and careless liberality, that they are not easily satisfied with the occasions which are offered them. They are sometimes afraid of encouraging idleness, and sometimes of countenancing imposture, and so readily find objections to every method of charity that can be mentioned to them, that their good inclinations are of very little advantage to the rest of mankind; but, however, they congratulate themselves upon their merit, and still applaud that generosity by which calamity was never softened, and by which want never was relieved. [Sermon XIX

To do the best, can seldom be the lot of man: it is sufficient if, when opportunities are presented, he is ready to do good. How little virtue could be practised if beneficence were to wait always for the most proper objects, and the noblest occasions; occasions that may never happen, and objects that may never be found? [Intro. Proceedings of Committee

Whoever steadily perseveres in the exertion of all his faculties, does what is great with respect to himself; and what will not be despised by Him, who has given all created beings their different abilities: he faithfully performs the task of life, within whatever limits his labours may be confined, or how soon soever they may be forgotten. [Adv. 128

When we act according to our duty, we commit the event to Him by whose laws our actions are governed, and who will suffer none to be finally punished for obedience. When, in prospect of some good, whether natural or moral, we break the rules prescribed us, we withdraw from the direction of superiour wisdom, and take all consequences upon ourselves . . . When we . . . attempt to find a nearer way to good, by overleaping settled boundaries of right and wrong, we cannot be happy even by success, because we cannot escape the consciousness of our fault; but if we miscarry, the disappointment is irremediably embittered. [Ras. 34

Charity, or tenderness for the poor, which is now justly considered, by a great part of mankind, as inseparable from piety, and in which almost all the goodness of the present age consists, is, I think, known only to those who enjoy, either immediately or by transmission, the light of revelation. [Idl. 4

Speaking of *inward light*, to which some methodists pretended, he said, it was a principle utterly incompatible with social or civil security. "If a man (said he) pretends to a principle of action of which I can know nothing, nay, not so much as that he has it, but only that he pretends to it; how can I tell what that person may be prompted to do? When a person professes to be governed by a written ascertained law, I can then know where to find him." [Bos. 1770

In order to the right conduct of our lives, we must remember, that we are not born to please ourselves. He that studies simply his own satisfaction, will always find the proper business of his station too hard or too easy for him. But if we bear continually in mind our relation to the Father of Being, by whom we are placed in the world, and who has allotted us the part which we are to bear in the general system of life, we shall be easily persuaded to resign our own inclinations to Unerring Wisdom, and do the work decreed for us with cheerfulness and diligence. [Adv. 128

Resentment gratifies him who intended an injury, and pains him unjustly who did not intend it. [Bos. 9 Sept. 1784

The miseries of life may, perhaps, afford some proof of a future state, compared as well with the mercy as the justice of God. It is scarcely to be imagined that Infinite Benevolence would create a being capable of enjoying so much more than is here to be enjoyed, and qualified by nature to prolong pain by remembrance, and anticipate it by terrour, if he was not designed for something nobler and better than a state, in which many of his faculties can serve only for his torment; in which he is to be importuned by desires that can never be satisfied, to feel many evils which he has no power to avoid, and to fear many which he shall never feel: there will surely come a time, when every capacity of happiness shall be filled, and none shall be wretched but by his own fault. [Adv. 120

Every sin, if persisted in, will become heinous. Whoremonger is a dealer in whores, as an ironmonger is a dealer in iron. But as you don't call a man an ironmonger for buying or selling a pen-knife; so you don't call a man a whoremonger for getting one wench with child. [Bos. 5 April 1772

Mr. Johnson had indeed a real abhorrence of a person that had ever before him treated a little thing like a great one: and he quoted this scrupulous person with his packthread very often, in ridicule of a friend who, looking out on Streatham Common from our windows one day, lamented the enormous wickedness of the times, because some bird-catchers were busy there one fine Sunday morning. "While half the Christian world is permitted (said he) to dance and sing, and celebrate Sunday as a day of festivity, how comes your puritanical spirit so offended with frivolous and empty deviations from exactness? Whoever loads life with unnecessary scruples, Sir (continued he), provokes the attention of others on his conduct, and incurs the censure of singularity, without reaping the reward of superior virtue." [Pioz. Anec.

... gloomy penitence is only madness turned upside down. A man may be gloomy, till, in order to be relieved from gloom, he has recourse again to criminal indulgences. [Bos. 10 April 1776

Scruples made many men miserable, but few men good. [Hoole, John. Misc.

Truth is scarcely to be heard, but by those from whom it can serve no interest to conceal it. [Ram. 150

Truth, such as is necessary to the regulation of life, is always found where it is honestly sought. Change of place is no natural cause of the increase of piety, for it inevitably produces dissipation of mind. [Ras. 11

If obedience to the will of God be necessary to happiness, and knowledge of His will necessary to obedience, I know not how he who withholds this knowledge or delays it can be said to love his neighbour as himself. He that voluntarily continues ignorance is guilty of all the crimes which ignorance produces; as to him that should extinguish the tapers of a lighthouse might justly be imputed the calamities of shipwrecks. [Letter to Wm. Drummond, Aug. 1766

All unnecessary vows are folly, because they suppose a prescience of the future that has not been given us. They are, I think, a crime because they resign that life to chance which God has given us to be regulated by reason; and superinduce a kind of fatality from which it is the great privilege of our Nature to be free. [Letter to Mrs. T., May 1773

Non-Conformist: One who refuses to join in the established worship. "On his deathbed he declared himself a *non-conformist* and had a fanatick preacher to be his spiritual guide." [Dict.

I do not like much to see a Whig in any dress; but I hate to see a Whig in a parson's gown. [Tour 24 September

Asked why he did not accept a church living that was offered to him, Johnson replied:

Sir, I have not the requisites for the office, and I cannot in my conscience shear a flock which I am unable to feed. [Hawkins

That man is little to be envied whose patriotism would not gain force upon the plain of Marathon, or whose piety would not grow warmer among the ruins of Iona. [Journey, Iona

. . . when I find Tully confessing of himself, that he could not forbear at Athens to visit the walks and houses which the old philosophers had frequented or inhabited, and recollect the reverence which every nation, civil and barbarous, has paid to the ground where merit has been buried, I am afraid to declare against the general voice of mankind, and am inclined to believe, that this regard, which we involuntarily pay to the meanest relic of a man great and illustrious, is intended as an incitement to labour and an encouragement to expect the same renown, if it be sought by the same virtues. [Ram. 83

. . . religion will appear as the voice of reason and morality the will of God. [Pref. Preceptor

. . . our duty is made apparent by its proximate causes. [Idl. 37

. . . whatever now hinders us from doing that which our reason and conscience declare necessary to be done, will equally

obstruct us in times to come. It is easy for the imagination . . .
to please itself with scenes of unmingled felicity, or plan out
courses of uniform virtue; but good and evil are in real life
inseparably united; habits grow stronger by indulgence; and
reason loses her dignity, in proportion as she has oftener yielded
to temptation: "he that cannot live well to-day," says Martial,
"will be less qualified to live well to-morrow." [Adv. 108

"That [God] is infinitely good, as far as the perfection of
his nature will allow, I certainly believe; but it is necessary for
good upon the whole, that individuals should be punished. As
to an *individual*, therefore, he is not infinitely good; and as I
cannot be *sure* I have fulfilled the conditions on which salvation
is granted, I am afraid I may be one of those who shall be
damned" (looking dismally). *Dr. Adams.* "What do you mean
by damned?" *Johnson.* . . . . "Sent to Hell, Sir, and punished
everlastingly." *Dr. Adams.* "I don't believe that doctrine."
Johnson. "Hold, Sir; do you believe that some will be punished
at all?" *Dr. Adams.* "Being excluded from Heaven will be a punishment . . ." *Johnson.* "Well, Sir; but, if you admit any degree
of punishment, there is an end of your argument for infinite
goodness simply considered . . . A man may have such a degree
of hope as to keep him quiet. You see I am not quiet, from the
vehemence with which I talk; but I do not despair . . . I do not
forget the merits of my Redeemer; but my Redeemer has said
that he will set some on his right hand and some on his left."
[Bos. 12 June 1784

. . . if he who considers himself as suspended over the abyss
of eternal perdition only by the thread of life, which must
soon part by its own weakness, and which the wing of every
minute may divide, can cast his eyes round him without shud-
dering with horrour, or panting with security; what can he judge

of himself, but that he is not yet awakened to sufficient conviction. [Ram. 110

Some people are not afraid [of death], because they look upon salvation as the effect of an absolute decree, and think they feel in themselves the marks of sanctification. Others, and those the most rational in my opinion, look upon salvation as conditional; and as they never can be sure that they have complied with the conditions, they are afraid. [Bos. 17 May 1784

Do not disturb your mind . . . with other hopes or fears than reason may suggest: if you are pleased with prognostics of good, you will be terrified likewise with tokens of evil, and your whole life will be a prey to superstition. [Ras. 13

It has been the boast of some swelling moralists, that every man's fortune was in his own power, that prudence supplied the place of all other divinities, and that happiness is the unfailing consequence of virtue. But, surely, the quiver of Omnipotence is stored with arrows, against which the shield of human virtue, however adamantine it has been boasted, is held up in vain: we do not always suffer by our crimes; we are not always protected by our innocence. [Adv. 120

There is nothing which we estimate so fallaciously as the force of our own resolutions, nor any fallacy which we so unwillingly and tardily detect. [Idl. 27

Repentance, however difficult to be practised is, if it be explained without superstition, easily understood. *Repentance is the relinquishment of any practise, from the conviction that it has offended God.* Sorrow and fear, and anxiety, are properly not parts, but adjuncts of repentance; yet they are too closely connected with it to be easily separated; for they not only mark its sincerity, but promote its efficacy. [Ram. 110

Trust in God, that trust to which perfect peace is promised, is to be obtained only by repentance, obedience, and supplication, not by nourishing in our own hearts a confused idea of the goodness of God, or a firm persuasion that we are in a state of grace; by which some have been deceived, as may be feared, to their own destruction. We are not to imagine ourselves safe, only because we are not harassed with those anxieties about our future state with which others are tormented, but which are so far from being proofs of reprobation, that though they are often mistaken by those that languish under them, they are more frequently evidences of piety, and a sincere and fervent desire of pleasing God. [Sermon XIV

Nothing can be great which is not right. Nothing which reason condemns can be suitable to the dignity of the human mind. To be driven by external motives from the path which our own heart approves; to give way to any thing but conviction; to suffer the opinion of others to rule our choice, or overpower our resolves; is to submit tamely to the lowest and most ignominious slavery, and to resign the right of directing our own lives. [Ram. 185

. . . it is to be remembered that the laws of mere morality have no coercive power; and, however they may, by conviction of their fitness, please the reasoner in the shade, when the passions stagnate without impulse, and the appetites are secluded from their objects, they will be of little force against the ardour of desire and the vehemence of rage amidst the pleasures and tumults of the world. To counteract the power of temptations, hope must be excited by the prospects of reward and fear by the expectation of punishment; virtue may owe her panegyricks to morality, but must derive her authority from religion. [Pref. Preceptor

Nothing is more unjust, however common, than to charge with hypocrisy him that expresses zeal for those virtues which he neglects to practise; since he may be sincerely convinced of the advantages of conquering his passions, without having yet obtained the victory, as a man may be confident of the advantages of a voyage, or a journey, without having courage or industry to undertake it, and may honestly recommend to others those attempts which he neglects himself. [Ram. 14

Hypocrisy is the necessary burthen of villainy, affectation part of the chosen trappings of folly; the one completes the villain, the other only finishes the fop. Contempt is the proper punishment of affectation, and detestation the just consequence of hypocrisy. [Ram. 20

". . . religion and morality," said Kames, "are stamped on [man's] heart; and none can be ignorant of them, who attend to their own perceptions."
"Now [answered Johnson], after consulting our own hearts all we can, and with all the helps we have, we find how few of us are virtuous." [Bos. 13 May 1778

To dread no eye, and to suspect no tongue, is the great prerogative of innocence; an exemption granted only to invariable virtue. But guilt has always its horrours and solicitudes: and to make it yet more shameful and detestable, it is doomed often to stand in awe of those, to whom nothing could give influence or weight, but their power of betraying. [Ram. 68

. . . there is very little hypocrisy in the world; we do not so

often endeavour or wish to impose on others as on ourselves.
[Idl. 27

Sir, are you so grossly ignorant of human nature, as not to
know that a man may be very sincere in good principles, without having good practise? [Tour 25 October

The great task of him who conducts his life by the precepts
of religion, is to make the future predominate over the present,
to impress upon his mind so strong a sense of the importance
of obedience to the Divine will, of the value of the reward
promised to virtue, and the terrours of the punishment denounced against crimes, as may overbear all temptations which
temporal hope or fear can bring in his way, and enable him
to bid equal defiance to joy and sorrow, to turn away at one
time from the allurements of ambition, and push forward at
another against the threats of calamity. [Ram. 7

Life is not the object of science: we see a little, very little;
and what is beyond we can only conjecture. If we inquire of
those who have gone before us, we receive small satisfaction;
some have travelled life without observation, and some willingly mislead us. The only thought, therefore, on which we can
repose with comfort, is that which presents to us the care of
Providence, whose eye takes in the whole of things, and under
whose direction all involuntary errours will terminate in happiness. [Adv. 107

Learn that the present hour alone is ours. [Irene

Man cannot so far know the connection of causes and events,
as that he may venture to do wrong in order to do right. [Ras.
34

For surely, nothing can so much disturb the passions, or perplex the intellects of man as the disruption of his union with visible nature; a separation from all that has hitherto delighted and engaged him; a change not only of the place, but of the manner of his being; an entrance into a state not simply which he knows not, but which perhaps he has no faculties to know; an immediate and perceptible communication with the Supreme Being, and, what is above all distressful and alarming, the final sentence and unalterable allotment. [Ram. 78

Write to me no more about *dying with a grace;* when you feel what I have felt in approaching eternity—in fear of soon hearing the sentence of which there is no revocation, you will know the folly. [Bos. 12 June 1784

Of death Boswell remarked that "it is unreasonable for a man to wish to continue in the show-room, after he has seen it. Let him go cheerfully out, and give place to other spectators":

Yes, sir, if he is sure he is to be well, after he goes out of it. But if he is to grow blind after he goes out of the show-room, and never see any thing again; or if he does not know whither he is to go next, a man does not go cheerfully out of a show-room. No wise man will be contented to die, if he thinks he is to go into a state of punishment. Nay, no wise man will be contented to die if he thinks he is to fall into annihilation; for however unhappy any man's existence may be, he yet would rather have it, than not exist at all. No; there is no rational principle by which a man can die contented but a trust in the mercy of GOD, through the merits of Jesus Christ." [Tour 12 September

In general no man can be sure of his acceptance with GOD; some, indeed, may have had it revealed to them. St. Paul, who wrought miracles, may have had a miracle wrought on himself, and may have obtained supernatural assurance of pardon, and mercy, and beatitude; yet St. Paul, though he expresses strong hope, also expresses fear, lest having preached to others, he himself should be a cast-away. [Bos. 3 June 1781

. . . keep this thought always prevalent, that you are only one atom of the mass of humanity, and have neither such virtue nor vice as that you should be singled out for supernatural favours or afflictions. [Ras. 46

He that in the latter part of his life too strictly inquires what he has done, can very seldom receive from his own heart such an account as will give him satisfaction. [Idl. 88

To convince any man against his will is hard, but to please him against his will is justly pronounced by Dryden to be above the reach of human abilities. [Ram. 93

He that lives well in the world is better than he that lives well in a monastery. But, perhaps, everyone is not able to stem the temptations of publick life; and, if he cannot conquer, he may properly retreat. Some have little power to do good, and have likewise little strength to resist evil. Many are weary of their conflicts with adversity, and are willing to eject those passions which have long busied them in vain. And many are dismissed by age and diseases from the more laborious duties of society. In monasteries the weak and timorous may be happily sheltered, the weary may repose, and the penitent may meditate. [Ras. 47

But surely . . . it cannot be allowed that flight [from life] is victory; or that he fills his place in creation laudably, who does no ill, *only* because he does nothing. [Sermon iII

The life of a solitary man will be certainly miserable, but not certainly devout. [Ras. 21

Piety practised in solitude, like the flower that blooms in the desert, may give its fragrance to the winds of Heaven, and delight those unembodied spirits that survey the works of God and the actions of men; but it bestows no assistance upon earthly beings, and however free from taints of impurity, yet wants the sacred splendour of beneficence. [Adv. 126

Of him that hopes to be forgiven, it is indispensably required that he forgive. It is therefore superfluous to urge any other motive. On this great duty eternity is suspended: and to him that refuses to practise it, the throne of mercy is inaccessible, and the Saviour of the world has been born in vain. [Ram. 185

But as it is necessary not to invite robbery by supineness, so it is our duty not to suppress tenderness by suspicion; it is better to suffer wrong than to do it, and happier to be sometimes cheated than not to trust. [Ram. 79

... it is better to *live* rich than to *die* rich. [Bos. 1778

A wicked fellow is the most pious when he takes to it. He'll beat you all at piety. [Bos. 10 June 1784

Campbell is a good man, a pious man. I am afraid he has not been in the inside of a church for many years, but he never passes a church without pulling off his hat. This shows that he has good principles. [Bos. 1 July 1763

No saint, however, in the course of his religious warfare, was more sensible of the unhappy failure of pious resolves than

Johnson. He said one day . . . "Sir, Hell is paved with good intentions." [Bos. 16 April 1775

. . . most men may review all the lives that have passed within their observation, without remembering one efficacious resolution, or being able to tell a single instance of a course of practice suddenly changed in consequence of a change of opinion, or an establishment of determination. Many indeed alter their conduct, and are not at fifty what they were at thirty; but they commonly varied imperceptibly from themselves, followed the train of external causes, and rather suffered reformation than made it. [Idl. 27

Where there is yet shame there may in time be virtue. [Journey, St. Andrews

He that once turns aside to the allurements of unlawful pleasure can have no security that he shall ever regain the paths of virtue. [Ram. 178

Once, indeed (said he), I was disobedient; I refused to attend my father to Uttoxeter market. Pride was the source of that refusal, and the remembrance of it was painful. A few years ago, I desired to atone for this fault; I went to Uttoxeter in very bad weather, and stood for a considerable time bareheaded in the rain, on the spot where my father's stall used to stand. In contrition I stood, and I hope the penance was expiatory. [Bos. Nov. 1784

No man, therefore, who smarted from the ingratitude of his friends found any sympathy from [Johnson]. "Let him do good on higher motives next time," would be the answer; "he will then be sure of his reward." [Pioz. Anec.

Of Thomas Hollis, who Mrs. Carter feared might be an atheist, Johnson said:

I don't know that. He might perhaps have become one, if he had had time to ripen (smiling). He might have *exuberated* into an Atheist. [Bos. 20 April 1781

Of Foote:

I do not know, Sir, that the fellow is an infidel; but if he be an infidel, he is an infidel as a dog is an infidel; that is to say, he has never thought upon the subject. [Bos. 19 Aug. 1769

. . . the superstitious are often melancholy, and the melancholy almost always superstitious. [Ras. 46

This merriment of parsons is mighty offensive. [Bos. March 1781

I saw not one [minister] in the islands whom I had reason to think either deficient in learning, or irregular in life; but found several with whom I could not converse without wishing, as my respect increased, that they had not been Presbyterians. [Journey, Ostig

It may be observed, in general, that the future is purchased by the present. It is not possible to secure distant or permanent happiness but by the forbearance of some immediate gratification. This is so evidently true with regard to the whole of our existence, that all the precepts of theology have no other tendency than to enforce a life of faith; a life regulated not by our senses but our belief; a life in which pleasures are to be refused for fear of invisible punishments, and calamities sometimes to be sought, and always endured, in hope of rewards that shall be obtained in another state.

Even if we take into our view only that particle of our duration which is terminated by the grave, it will be found that we cannot enjoy one part of life beyond the common limitations of pleasure, but by anticipating some of the satisfaction which should exhilarate the following years. The heat of youth may spread happiness into wild luxuriance; but the radical vigour requisite to make it perennial is exhausted, and all that can be hoped afterwards is languor and sterility. [Ram. 178

Seward remarked that one would think that sickness and the view of death make more men religious:

Sir, they do not know how to go about it; they have not the first notion. A man who has never had religion before, no more grows religious when he is sick, than a man who has never learnt figures can count when he has need of calculation. [Bos. 30 April 1783

About the responsibility for teaching religion, Johnson said:

"Consider, Sir; if you have children whom you wish to educate in the principles of the Church of England, and there comes a Quaker who tries to pervert them to his principles, you would drive away the Quaker. You would not trust the predomination of right, which you believe is in your opinions; you would keep wrong out of their heads. Now the vulgar are the children of the State. If any one attempts to teach them doctrines contrary to what the State approves, the magistrate may and ought to restrain him." *Seward.* "Would you restrain private conversation, Sir?" *Johnson.* "Why, Sir, it is difficult to say where private conversation begins, and where it ends. If we three should discuss even the great question concerning the existence of a Supreme Being by ourselves, we should not be restrained; for that would be to put an end to all improvement. But if we should discuss it in the presence of ten boarding-school girls, and as many boys, I think the magistrate would do well to put us in the stocks, to finish the debate there." [Bos. 30 April 1783

On Easter day, 1765, Johnson went to morning service at St. Clement Danes in the Strand. He made resolves for the coming year and prayed—"with some distraction of mind":

Almighty and most merciful Father . . . look down with mercy upon me, and grant that I may turn from my wickedness and live. Forgive the days and years which I have passed in folly, idleness, and sin. Fill me with such sorrow for the time misspent, that I may amend my life according to thy holy word; strengthen me against habitual idleness, and enable me to direct my thoughts to the performance of every duty; that while I live I may serve thee in the state to which thou shalt call me, and at last by a holy and happy death be delivered from the struggles and sorrows of this life, and obtain eternal happiness by thy mercy . . . O God have mercy on me.

[In his journal he adds:] I invited home with me the man whose pious behaviour I had for several years observed on this day, and found him a kind of Methodist, full of texts, but ill-instructed. I talked to him with temper, and offered him twice wine, which he refused. I suffered him to go without the dinner which I had purposed to give him. I thought this day that there was something irregular and particular in his look and gesture; but having intended to invite him to acquaintance, and having a fit opportunity . . . I did what I first designed, and am sorry to have been so much disappointed. Let me not be prejudiced hereafter against the appearance of piety in mean persons, who, with indeterminate notions, and perverse or inelegant conversation, perhaps do all they can. [Prayers and Meditations

Prayer on beginning The Rambler:

Almighty God, the giver of all good things, without whose help all labour is ineffectual, and without whose grace all wisdom is folly; grant, I beseech thee, that in this my undertaking, thy Holy Spirit may not be withheld from me, but that I may promote thy glory, and the salvation both of myself and others: grant this, O Lord, for the sake of Jesus Christ, Amen.

Prayer during the course of the work on the Dictionary:

O God who has hitherto supported me, enable me to proceed in this labour, and in the whole task of my present state; that when I shall render up, at the last day, an account of the talent committed to me, I may receive pardon, for the sake of Jesus Christ. [Prayers and Meditations

On March 28, 1782, Johnson wrote:

This is the day on which, in 1752, dear Tetty died. I have now uttered a prayer of repentance and contrition; perhaps Tetty knows that I prayed for her. Perhaps Tetty is now praying for me. God help me. . . . We were married almost seventeen years and have now been parted thirty. [Prayers and Meditations

About a month after his wife's death, he prayed:

O Lord, Governour of heaven and earth, in whose hands are embodied and departed spirits, if Thou hast ordained the souls of the Dead to minister to the living and appointed my departed Wife to have care of me, grant that I may enjoy tl e good effects of her attention and ministration, whether exer cised by appearance, impulses, dreams or in any other manner agreeable to thy Government. Forgive my presumption, enlighten my ignorance, and however meaner agents are employed, grant me the blessed influences of thy holy Spirit, through Jesus Christ our Lord.

[And two years later he prayed:] Almighty God, vouchsafe to sanctify unto me the reflections and resolutions of this day, let not my sorrow be unprofitable; let not my resolutions be vain. Grant that my grief may produce true repentance, so that I may live to please thee; and when the time shall come when I must die like her whom Thou hast taken from me, grant me eternal happiness in Thy presence, through Jesus Christ our Lord. [Prayers and Meditations

In April 1781 Henry Thrale died, and Johnson "looked for the last time upon the face that for fifteen years had never been turned upon me but with respect and benignity." About eighteen months later, Johnson left forever the Thrale villa at Streatham which for so long had been a second home to him. His prayer at leaving is as follows:

Almighty God, Father of all mercy, help me by thy grace, that I may, with humble and sincere thankfulness, remember the comforts and conveniences which I have enjoyed at this place; and that I may resign them with holy submission, equally trusting in thy protection when Thou givest, and when Thou takest away. Have mercy upon me, O Lord, have mercy upon me.

To thy fatherly protection, O Lord, I commend this family. Bless, guide, and defend them, that they may so pass through this world, as finally to enjoy in thy presence everlasting happiness, for Jesus Christ's sake. Amen. [Bos. 6 Oct. 1782

Johnson's prayer for strength to accept the burdens of increasing age:

O God, most merciful Father, Who by many diseases hast admonished me of my approach to the end of life, and by this gracious addition to my days hast given me an opportunity of appearing once more in Thy presence to commemorate the sacrifice by which Thy Son Jesus Christ has taken away the sins of the world, assist me in this commemoration by Thy Holy Spirit that I may look back upon the sinfulness of my life with pious sorrow, and efficacious Repentance, that my resolutions of amendment may be rightly formed and diligently exerted, that I may be freed from vain and useless scruples, and that I may serve Thee with Faith, Hope, and Charity for the time which Thou shalt yet allow me, and finally be received to Everlasting Happiness, for the sake of Jesus Christ, our Lord. Amen. [Prayers and Meditations

Johnson died on Monday, 13 December 1784. A few days before his death he received the Holy Sacrament in his apartment, composed and fervently uttered this, his last prayer:

Almighty and most merciful Father, I am now, as to human eyes it seems, about to commemorate for the last time, the death of thy Son JESUS CHRIST, our Saviour and Redeemer. Grant, O LORD, that my whole hope and confidence may be in his merits, and thy mercy; enforce and accept my imperfect repentance; make this commemoration available to the confirmation of my faith, the establishment of my hope, and the enlargement of my charity; and make the death of thy Son JESUS CHRIST effectual to my redemption. Have mercy upon me, and pardon the multitude of my offences. Bless my friends; have mercy upon all men. Support me, by thy Holy Spirit, in the days of weakness, and at the hour of death; and receive me, at my death, to everlasting happiness, for the sake of JESUS CHRIST. Amen. [Bos. 13 Dec. 1784

One of the most moving episodes in Johnson's life was his journey to Lichfield in October 1767 to be at the bedside of Catherine Chambers, once his mother's maid, who lay dying. His own journal tells the story:

I . . . told her that we were to part for ever, that as Christians, we should part with prayer, and that I would, if she was willing, say a short prayer beside her. She expressed great desire to hear me; and held up her poor hands, as she lay in bed, with great fervour, while I prayed, kneeling by her . . .

"Almighty and most merciful Father, whose loving kindness is over all thy works, behold, visit, and relieve this thy servant, who is grieved with sickness. Grant that the sense of her weakness may add strength to her faith, and seriousness to her repentance. And grant that by the help of thy Holy Spirit, after the pains and labours of this short life, we may all obtain everlasting happiness, through JESUS CHRIST our Lord; for whose sake hear our prayers . . ."

I then kissed her. She told me, that to part was the greatest pain that she had ever felt, and that she hoped we should meet again in a better place. I expressed, with swelled eyes, and great emotion of tenderness, the same hopes. We kissed and parted. I humbly hope to meet again, and part no more. [Bos. 18 Oct. 1767

In this state of universal uncertainty, where a thousand dangers hover about us, and none can tell whether the good that he pursues is not evil in disguise, or whether the next step will lead him to safety or destruction, nothing can afford any rational tranquility, but the conviction that, however we amuse ourselves with unideal sounds, nothing in reality is governed by chance, but that the universe is under the perpetual superintendance of him who created it; that our being is in the hands of omnipotent goodness, by whom what appears casual to us, is directed for ends ultimately kind and merciful; and that nothing can finally hurt him who debars not himself from the Divine favour. [Ram. 184

On Man and His Conduct
in the World of Men

*You are a philosopher, and will teach me to . . . look
upon the world with indifference.*

Ram. 191

Among his contemporaries Johnson was often referred to as
a philosopher, and what this expression meant—at least to
Boswell—is illustrated in the summer of 1763 when Johnson
and Boswell traveled by coach to Harwich. Johnson was in fine
feather. He spoke to the passengers of Boswell's being an idle
fellow and had something to say about idleness. He defended
the Inquisition to a woman who had expressed horror of it and
distrust of Catholics. He scolded Boswell for tipping the coach-
man a shilling instead of the customary sixpence and had cogent reasons for deploring the departure from custom. At the
inn he said that a man who cared not what he ate would care
for nothing else. In short, he had reasoned and reasonable
opinions on all matters that came within his view. "He now
appeared to me," exclaimed Boswell, "Jean Bull philosophe."[1]

The next day, just before Boswell embarked for Holland, the
pair were discussing Berkeley's "ingenious sophistry" in proving
the nonexistence of matter and showing that everything in the
universe was imaginary. "Johnson answered, striking his foot

[1] Bos. 5–6 Aug. 1763.

with mighty force against a large stone, till he rebounded from it, 'I refute it thus.' "[2] This Boswell recognized as no argument at all, but it was pure Johnson.

Johnson had little patience for speculation that ran counter to common sense. He was no philosopher of abstractions as were Berkeley, Descartes, Kant. He was a moral philosopher, perhaps, a moralist with a clear-eyed understanding of his fellow mortals, a humanist with a moving sympathy for all men, a pragmatist. His genius was for men, not mankind; and he was at home with all sorts of people. He would smile with the wise, dine with the rich, and live with the poor. But "nothing in Johnson," writes Raleigh, "is more admirable than his tolerance of bad characters."[3] This tolerance, of course, is an aspect of his infinite compassion for the destitute, the helpless, the hopeless. His instinct was to find some good in everyone.

Nor did his compassion vapor itself away in mere pity. He sheltered half a dozen indigents in his house. He defended the all but indefensible Savage. He exerted himself—vainly, to be sure—to save the unsavory Dodd from the gallows. He hurried the long distance from Lichfield to London to comfort Mrs. Thrale after the death of her son—comfort which that rather shallow woman did not need.

If Johnson was indeed a philosopher, it was because he was always seeking the truth. Early in the Preface to Shakespeare he wrote that the mind can find rest only in the stability of truth. Without truth, he once told Miss Seward, "there must be a dissolution of society," and he recalled a remark of Sir Thomas Browne's, "Do the devils lie? No; for then Hell could not subsist."[4] Of the passions that hinder a man's seeing or acting the truth, he has much to say. Envy appears very often in his speech and writings, though of that vice no man had less. He has much to say about idleness, and of that vice no man knew more. Pretense in any form he hated, and he was espe-

[2] Bos. 5–6 Aug. 1763.   [3] Raleigh. *Six Essays.*   [4] Bos. 15 April 1778.

cially hard on pedantry. Learning, said the pragmatic Johnson, is worthless unless it is transmuted by living experience into wisdom that can guide a man in living his life.[5] He was quick to discern mere busyness.[6] He did not condemn riches, but he saw how lack or loss of them will obscure virtues that in a perfect world would win and keep friendship.[7] But this, he believed without futile whining or bitterness, is not a perfect world.

It is easy to read "The Vanity of Human Wishes," Rasselas, and some of the essays and decide that to Johnson, as to the Preacher, all is vanity. That is not Johnson; he had too much vitality for such emptiness. He did believe that real satisfaction comes not from achieving but from striving. To satisfy one ambition is only to see others still to be satisfied, or perhaps to learn that an ambition achieved does not give more than fleeting satisfaction. Man lives, he once said, from hope to hope. Nowhere does he want to be supine and let life steamroller over him.

> Must helpless man, in ignorance sedate,
> Roll darkling down the torrent of his fate?

He must strive—and he is not worth his salt if he does not—for a healthful mind, for obedient passions, for patience, and for faith. "The Vanity of Human Wishes" is not mere negativism.

Nor is Rasselas, which ends on quite another note. At the end of the long search which is the story, nothing happens. Having observed the activities of men, Rasselas and Nekayah have not yet decided on a choice of life, the purpose of their leaving the Happy Valley. The inundation of the Nile puts an end to their immediate quest; and when the waters subside, they return to Abyssinia. But they have explored one series of hopes. At home they will find others: for instance, they are

[5] Idl. 34, Ram. 180.   [6] Idl. 18, 48.   [7] Ram. 153.

not yet married. Despite the somewhat disillusioned wisdom of Imlac, they will strive, seek, probably not find, and certainly not yield. After all, they are Johnson's creatures, and only days before his death Johnson said, "I will be conquered, but I will not capitulate."[8]

Johnson, conscious of his own faults and weaknesses, believed that all men had the same faults. His understanding and his somber observation of men confirmed his belief. Thus, out of his experience came the generalizations that make up his philosophy. It is no formulated system; it is not completely consistent. It is the result of reason working honestly on his day-to-day review of the conduct of men, practical wisdom. "If you could contrive to have his fair opinion . . . it was wisdom itself, not only convincing, but overpowering," a friend remarked to Boswell.[9] And Baretti wrote, "His trade is wisdom."[10]

We are to consider mankind not as we wish them, but as we find them, frequently corrupt and always fallible. [Deb. Trade and Navigation

Let us endeavour to see things as they are, and then inquire whether we ought to complain. Whether to see life as it is will give us much consolation, I know not; but the consolation which is drawn from truth, if any there be, is solid and durable; that which may be derived from errour must be, like its original, fallacious and fugitive. [Bos. 21 Sept. 1758

If there were no cowardice, there would be little insolence; pride cannot rise to any great degree, but by the concurrence of blandishment or the sufferance of tameness . . . To those

[8] Bos. Nov. 1784.   [9] Bos. May 1781(n).
[10] Bos. 15 Sept. 1777(n).

who are willing to purchase favour by cringes and compliance, is to be imputed the haughtiness that leaves nothing to be hoped by firmness and integrity. [Ram. 180

. . . courage is reckoned the greatest of all virtues; because, unless a man has that virtue, he has no security for preserving any other. [Bos. 5 April 1775

"It is so *very* difficult (said he, always), for a sick man not to be a scoundrel." [Pioz. Anec.

It being asked whether it was reasonable for a man to be angry at another whom a woman had preferred to him;—*Johnson.* "I do not see, Sir, that it is reasonable for a man to be angry at another, whom a woman has preferred to him; but angry he is . . . and he is loath to be angry at himself." [Bos. 13 May 1775

It is impossible for those that have only known affluence and prosperity, to judge rightly of themselves or others. The rich and powerful live in a perpetual masquerade, in which all about them wear borrowed characters; and we only discover in what estimation we are held, when we can no longer give hopes or fears. [Ram. 75

Fame, like all other things which are supposed to give or to increase happiness, is dispensed with the same equality of distribution. He that is loudly praised will be clamorously censured; he that rises hastily into fame will be in danger of sinking suddenly into oblivion. [Idl. 59

He that gives himself up to his own fancy, and converses with none but such as . . . lull him on the down of absolute authority, soothe him with obsequiousness, and regale him with flattery, soon grows too slothful for the labour of contest, too tender for the asperity of contradiction, and too delicate for the coarseness of truth; a little opposition offends, a little restraint enrages, and a little difficulty perplexes him; having been accustomed to see everything give way to his humour, he soon forgets his own littleness, and expects to find the world rolling at his beck, and all mankind employed to accommodate him and delight him. [Ram. 74

Self-love . . . does not hide our faults from ourselves, but persuades us that they escape the notice of others, and disposes us to resent censures lest we should confess them to be just. We are secretly conscious of defects and vices which we hope to conceal from the public eye, and please ourselves with innumerable impostures, by which, in reality, nobody is deceived. [Ram. 155

Praise is seldom paid with willingness even to incontestable merit, and it can be no wonder that he who calls for it without desert is repulsed with universal indignation. [Ram. 179

The first step in greatness is to be honest. [Essay, Drake

. . . since good or harm must be received for the most part from those to whom we are familiarly known, he whose vices overpower his virtues . . . has no reason to complain that he meets not with affection or veneration, when those with whom he passes his life are more corrupted by his practice than enlightened by his ideas. Admiration begins where acquaintance ceases. [Ram. 77

It is more from carelessness about truth than from intentional lying, that there is so much falsehood in the world. [Bos. 31 March 1778

. . . nobody can live long without knowing that falsehoods of convenience or vanity, falsehoods from which no evil immediately visible ensues, except the general degradation of human testimony, are very lightly uttered, and once uttered are sullenly supported. [L.P., Congreve

Inconsistencies . . . cannot both be right; but, imputed to man, they may both be true. [Ras. 8

It is generally not so much the desire of men sunk into depravity, to deceive the world as themselves; for when no particular circumstances make them dependent on others, infamy disturbs them little, but as it revives their remorse, and is echoed to them from their own hearts. The sentence most dreaded is that of reason and conscience, which they would engage on their side at any price but the labours of duty and the sorrows of repentance. For this purpose every seducement and fallacy is sought, the hopes still rest upon some new experiment till life is at an end; and the last hour steals on unperceived, while the faculties are engaged in resisting reason, and repressing the sense of the Divine disapprobation. [Ram. 76

To charge those favourable representations which men give of their own minds with the guilt of hypocritical falsehood, would show more severity than knowledge. The writer commonly believes himself. Almost every man's thoughts, while they are general, are right; and most hearts are pure, while temptation is away. It is easy to awaken generous sentiments in privacy; to despise death when there is no danger; to glow with benevolence when there is nothing to be given. While such ideas are formed, they are felt; and self-love does not suspect the gleam of virtue to be the meteor of fancy. [L.P., Pope

He, by whose writings the heart is rectified, the appetites

counteracted, and the passions repressed, may be considered as not unprofitable to the great republic of humanity, even though his behaviour should not always exemplify his rules. His instructions may diffuse their influence to regions, in which it will not be inquired, whether the author be *albus an ater*, good or bad; to times, when his faults and all his follies shall be lost in forgetfulness, among things of no concern or importance to the world; and he may kindle in thousands and tens of thousands that flame which burnt but dimly in himself, through the fumes of passion, or the damps of cowardice. The vicious moralist may be considered as a taper, by which we are lighted through the labyrinth of complicated passions, he extends his radiance further than his heat, and guides all that are within view, but burns only those who make too near approaches. [Ram. 77

It may be observed, perhaps without exception, that none are so industrious to detect wickedness, or so ready to impute it as they whose crimes are apparent and confessed. They envy an unblemished reputation, and what they envy they are busy to destroy; they are unwilling to suppose themselves meaner and more corrupt than others, and therefore willingly pull down from their elevations those with whom they cannot rise to an equality. [Ram. 76

We do not indeed so often disappoint others as ourselves. We not only think more highly than others of our own abilities, but we allow ourselves to form hopes which we never communicate, and please our thoughts with employments which none ever will allot us, and with elevations to which we are never expected to rise; and when our days and years have passed away in common business or common amusements, and we find at last that we have suffered our purposes to sleep till the time of action is past, we are reproached only by our own reflections; neither our friends nor our enemies wonder that we live and die like the rest of mankind; that we live without notice, and die without memorial. They know not what task we had proposed [for ourselves] and therefore cannot discern whether it is finished. [Idl. 88

From my experience I have found [mankind] worse in commercial dealings, more disposed to cheat, than I had any notion of; but more disposed to do one another good than I had conceived . . . And really it is wonderful, considering how much attention is necessary for men to take care of themselves, and ward off immediate evils which press upon them, it is wonderful how much they do for others. As it is said of the greatest liar, that he tells more truth than falsehood; so it may be said of the worst man that he does more good than evil. [Bos. 3 April 1778

The world is not so unjust or unkind as it is peevishly represented; those who deserve well seldom fail to receive from others such services as they can perform, but few have much in their power, or are so stationed as to have great leisure from their own affairs, and kindness must be commonly the exuberance of content. The wretched have no compassion; they can do good only from strong principles of duty. [Letter to Mrs. T., April 1781

A literary lady of large fortune was mentioned as one who did good to many . . . [but] acted evidently from vanity. *Johnson.* "I have seen no beings who do as much good from benevolence, as she does, from whatever motive . . . No, Sir, to act from pure benevolence is not possible for finite beings. Human benevolence is mingled with vanity, interest, or some other motive." [Bos. 26 April 1776

We can have no dependance upon that instinctive, that constititional, goodness which is not founded upon principle. I grant you that such a man may be a very amiable member of society. I can conceive him placed in such a situation that he is not much tempted to deviate from what is right; and as every man prefers virtue, when there is not some strong incitement to transgress its precepts, I can conceive him doing nothing wrong. But if such a man stood in need of money, I should not trust him; and I should certainly not like to trust him with young ladies, for *there* there is always temptation. [Bos. 21 July 1763

The most authentic witnesses of any man's character are those who know him in his own family, and see him without any restraint or rule of conduct, but such as he voluntarily prescribes to himself. [Ram. 68

Let us cease to consider what, perhaps, may never happen, and what, when it shall happen, will laugh at human speculation. We will not endeavour to modify the motions of the elements, or to fix the destiny of kingdoms. It is our business to consider what beings like us may perform; each labouring for his own happiness, by promoting within his circle, however narrow, the happiness of others. [Ras. 28

. . . it is maintained that virtue is natural to man, and that if we would but consult our own hearts we should be virtuous. Now after consulting our own hearts all we can, and with all the helps we have, we find how few of us are virtuous. [Bos. 13 May 1778

Combinations of wickedness would overwhelm the world by the advantage which licentious principles afford, did not those

who have long practised perfidy grow faithless to each other.
[L.P., Waller

Writing of prostitutes:

"To wipe all tears from off their faces," is a task too hard
for mortals; but to alleviate misfortunes is often within the
most limited power. Yet the opportunities which every day
affords of relieving the most wretched of human beings are
overlooked and neglected, with equal disregard of policy and
goodness. . . . Surely those whom passion or interest have
already depraved, have some claim to compassion, from beings
equally frail and fallible with themselves. Nor will they long
groan in their present afflictions, if none were to refuse them
relief, but those that owe their exemption from the same
distress only to their wisdom and their virtue. [Ram. 107

Compassion is by some reasoners, on whom the name of
philosophers has been too easily conferred, resolved into an
affection merely selfish, an involuntary perception of pain at
the involuntary sight of a being like ourselves languishing in
misery. But this sensation, if ever it be felt at all from the brute
instinct of uninstructed nature, will only produce effects desultory and transient; it will never settle into a principle of
action, or extend relief to calamities unseen in generations not
yet in being. [Idl. 4

Pity is not natural to man. Children are always cruel. Savages
are always cruel. Pity is acquired and improved by the cultivation of reason. We may have uneasy sensations from seeing a
creature in distress, without pity; for we have not pity unless
we wish to relieve them. [Bos. 20 July 1763

Whatever withdraws us from the power of our senses; whatever makes the past, the distant, or the future predominate over the present, advances us in the dignity of thinking beings. [Journey, Iona

Remember thou! that now faintest under the weight of long-continued maladies, that to thee, more emphatically, the night cometh in which no man can work; and, therefore, say not to him that asketh thee, "Go away now, and to-morrow I will give." To-morrow! to-morrow is to *all* uncertain, to *thee* almost hopeless; to-*day*, if thou wilt hear the voice of God calling thee to repentance, and by repentance to charity, harden not thy heart; but what thou knowest that in thy last moment thou shalt wish done, make haste to do, lest thy last moment be now upon thee. [Sermon IV

It is necessary to the completion of every good, that it be timely obtained. [Ram. 203

Thought is always troublesome to him, who lives without his own approbation. [Sermon III

. . . it is by affliction chiefly that the heart of man is purified . . . Prosperity, allayed and imperfect as it is, has power to intoxicate the imagination, to fix the mind upon the present scene, to produce confidence and elation, and to make him who enjoys affluence and honours forget the hand by which they were bestowed. It is seldom that we are otherwise, than by affliction, awakened to a sense of our own imbecility, or taught to know how little all our acquisitions can conduce to safety or to quiet; and how justly we may ascribe to the superintendence of a higher Power, those blessings which in the wantonness of success we considered as the attainments of our policy or courage . . .

While affliction thus prepares us for felicity, we may console ourselves under its pressures, by remembering, that they are no particular marks of divine displeasure; since all the distresses of persecution have been suffered by those, "of whom the world was not worthy;" and the Redeemer of mankind himself was "a man of sorrows and acquainted with grief!" [Adv. 120

. . . man is not born for happiness. [L.P., Collins

Sorrow is properly that state of mind in which our desires are fixed upon the past, without looking forward into the future, an incessant wish that some thing were otherwise than it has been, a tormenting and harassing want of some enjoyment or possession which we have lost, and which no endeavours can possibly regain. [Ram. 47

Sorrow is a kind of rust of the soul, which every new idea contributes in its passage to scour away. It is the putrefaction of stagnant life, and is remedied by exercise and motion. [Ram. 47

Sadness multiplies itself. Let us do our duty and be cheerful. [Letter to Dr. Taylor, Aug. 1779

Grief is a species of idleness. [Letter to Mrs. T., March 1773

Most of the mortifications that we have suffered, arose from the concurrence of local and temporary circumstances, which can never meet again; and most of our disappointments have succeeded those expectations, which life allows not to be formed a second time. [Idl. 72

The cure for the greatest part of human miseries is not radical, but palliative. Infelicity is involved in corporeal nature, and interwoven with our being; all attempts therefore to decline it wholly are useless and vain; the armies of pain send their arrows against us on every side, the choice is only between those which are more or less sharp, or tinged with poison of greater or less malignity; and the strongest armour which reason can supply, will only blunt their points, but cannot repel them. [Ram. 32

Depend upon it, said he, that if a man *talks* of his misfortunes, there is something in them that is not disagreeable to him; for where there is nothing but pure misery, there never is any recourse to the mention of it. [Bos. 1780

Misery is caused for the most part, not by heavy crush of disaster, but by the corrosion of less visible evils which canker enjoyment and undermine security. The visit of an invader is necessarily rare, but domestic animosities allow no cessation. [Journey, Ostig

Distress will fly to immediate refuge without much consideration of remote consequences. [Ram. 142

. . . it may be doubted whether slavery can ever be supposed the natural condition of men. It is impossible not to conceive that men in their original state were equal; and very difficult to imagine how one would be subjected to another but by violent compulsion. An individual may, indeed, forfeit his liberty by a crime; but he cannot by that crime forfeit the liberty of his children. What is true of a criminal seems true likewise of a captive. A man may accept life from a conquering enemy on condition of perpetual servitude; but [it] is very doubtful whether he can entail that servitude on his descendants, for no man can stipulate without commission for another . . . No man is by nature the property of another . . . The rights of nature must be some way forfeited before they can be justly taken away. [Bos. 23 Sept. 1777

An infallible characteristic of meanness is cruelty. [False Alarm

... slavery is now no where more patiently endured, than in countries once inhabited by the zealots of liberty. [Idl. 11

... how is it that we hear the loudest *yelps* for liberty among the drivers of negroes? [Bos. 25 Sept. 1777

Had only a single traveller related that many nations of the earth were black, we should have thought the accounts of the *Negroes* and of the *Phoenix* equally credible. But of black men the numbers are too great who are now repining under *English* cruelty. [Idl. 87

I am willing to love all mankind, *except an American.* [Bos. 15 April 1778

To love all men is our duty, so far as it includes a general habit of benevolence, and readiness of occasional kindness; but to love all equally is impossible; at least impossible without the extinction of those passions which now produce all our pains and all our pleasures; without the disuse, if not the abolition, of some of our faculties, and the suppression of all our hopes and fears in apathy and indifference. [Ram. 99

Their [the Americans'] numbers at present are not quite sufficient for the greatness which, in some form of government or other, is to rival the ancient monarchies. But by Dr. Franklin's rule of progression, they will in a century and a quarter be more than equal to the inhabitants of Europe. When the Whigs of America are thus multiplied, let the princes of the earth tremble in their palaces. If they should continue to double and double, their own hemisphere will not contain them. [Taxation

The Scots, with a vigilance of jealousy that never goes to sleep, always suspect that an Englishman despises them for their poverty, and to convince him that they are not less rich than their neighbours, are sure to tell him a price [for their purchases] higher than the true. [Journey, Inverary

A Scotsman must be a very sturdy moralist who does not love Scotland better than truth. [Journey, Ostig

When I find a Scotchman, to whom an Englishman is as a Scotchman, that Scotchman shall be as an Englishman to me. [Bos. 1775

Oats: A grain, which in England is generally given to horses, but in Scotland supports the people. [Dict.

I give you leave to say, and you may quote me for it, that there are more gentlemen in Scotland than there are shoes. [Cumberland, John. Misc.

I know not why anyone but a schoolboy in his declamation should whine over the commonwealth of Rome, which grew great only by the misery of the rest of mankind. The Romans, like others, as soon as they grew rich grew corrupt, and, in their corruption, sold the lives and freedoms of themselves and of one another. [Review, *Court of Augustus*

It must, however, be confessed, that a man, who places honour only in successful violence, is a very troublesome and pernicious animal in time of peace; and that the martial character cannot prevail in a whole people, but by the diminution of all other virtues. He that is accustomed to resolve all right into conquest will have very little tenderness or equity. All the friendship in such a life can only be a confederacy of invasion, or alliance of defence. The strong must flourish by force, and the weak subsist by stratagem. [Journey, Ostig

A Frenchman must be always talking, whether he knows any thing of the matter or not; an Englishman is content to say nothing, when he has nothing to say. [Bos. 1780

Johnson, quoting, remarked *For any thing I see, foreigners are fools.*

He said that once, when he had a violent tooth-ache, a Frenchman accosted him thus: *Ah, Monsieur, vous étudiez trop.* [Bos. 1780

. . . we know that for Prisoners of War there is no legal provision; we see their distress and are certain of its cause. We know that they are poor and naked, and poor and naked without a crime. . . . The opponents of this charity [a measure for relief of French prisoners] must allow it to be good and will not easily prove it not to be the best. That charity is best of which the consequences are most extensive: the relief of enemies has a tendency to unite all mankind in fraternal affection. [Intro. Proceedings of Committee

If the world be worth winning, let us enjoy it; if it is to be despised, let us despise it by conviction. But the world is not to be despised but as it is compared with something better . . . *Ex nihilo nihil fit* says the moral as well as the natural philosopher. By doing nothing and by knowing nothing, no power of doing good can be obtained. He must mingle with the world who desires to be useful. [Letter to Mrs. T., June 1775

Men have been wise in very different modes; but they have always laughed the same way. [L.P., Cowley

Conveniences are not missed where they were never enjoyed. [Journey, Ostig

He was no enemy to splendour of apparel or pomp of equipage—"Life (he would say) is barren enough surely with all her trappings; let us therefore be cautious how we strip her." [Pioz. Anec.

Why, Sir, the sense of ridicule is given us, and may be lawfully used. [Bos. 2 April 1779

Boswell. "Perhaps from experience man may be found happier than we suppose." *Johnson.* "No, Sir; the more we enquire, we shall find men the less happy." [Bos. 3 April 1778

Sir, be as wise as you can; let a man be *aliis laetus, sapiens sibi:*

"Though pleas'd to see the dolphins play,
I mind my compass and my way."

You may be wise in your study in the morning, and gay in company at a tavern in the evening. Every man is to take care of his own wisdom and his own virtue, without minding too much what others think. [Bos. 10 Oct. 1779

He that has long lived within sight of pleasures which he could not reach, will need more than common moderation, not to lose his reason in unbounded riot, when they are first put into his power. . . . Let him not be considered as lost in hope-less degeneracy . . . His intoxication will give way in time; the madness of joy will fume imperceptibly away . . . he will re-member that the co-operation of others is necessary to his hap-piness, and learn to conciliate their regard by reciprocal benef-icence. [Ram. 172

. . . advice is commonly ineffectual. If those who follow the call of their desires, without inquiry whither they are going, had deviated ignorantly from the paths of wisdom, and were rushing upon dangers unforeseen, they would readily listen to information that recalls them from their errours, and catch the first alarm by which destruction or infamy is denounced. Few that wander in the wrong way mistake it for the right; they only find it more smooth and flowery, and indulge their own choice rather than approve it: therefore, few are persuaded to quit it by admonition or reproof, since it impresses no new conviction, nor confers any powers of action or resistance. [Ram. 155

It is common for those who have never accustomed them-selves to the labour of inquiry, nor invigorated their confidence by conquests over difficulty, to sleep in the gloomy quiescence of astonishment, without any effort to animate inquiry or dispel obscurity. What they cannot immediately conceive, they con-sider as too high to be reached, or too extensive to be compre-hended; they therefore content themselves with the gaze of folly, forbear to attempt what they have no hopes of perform-ing, and resign the pleasure of rational contemplation to more pertinacious study or more active faculties. [Ram. 137

The folly of allowing ourselves to delay what we know can-not be finally escaped, is one of the general weaknesses, which, in spite of the instruction of moralists and the remonstrances of reason, prevail to a greater or less degree in every mind; even they who most steadily withstand it, find it, if not violent, the most pertinacious of the passions, always renewing its attacks, and, though often vanquished, never destroyed. [Ram. 134

When evils cannot be avoided, it is wise to contract the interval of expectation; to meet the mischiefs which will overtake us if we fly; and suffer only their real malignity, without the conflicts of doubt, and anguish of anticipation. [Ram. 134

If [Cowley] had fixed his habitation in the most delightful part of the new world, it may be doubted whether his distance from the *vanities* of life would have enabled him to keep away the *vexations*. It is common for a man, who feels pain, to fancy that he could bear it better in any other part. Cowley having known the troubles and perplexities of a particular condition, readily persuaded himself that nothing worse was to be found, and that every alteration would bring improvement: he never suspected that the cause of his unhappiness was within, that his own passions were not sufficiently regulated, and that he was harassed by his own impatience, which could never be without something to awaken it, would accompany him over the sea, and finds its way to his American elysium. He would, upon the trial, have been soon convinced, that the fountain of content must spring up in the mind; and that he who has so little knowledge of human nature, as to seek happiness by changing anything but his own dispositions, will waste his life in fruitless efforts, and multiply the griefs which he purposes to remove. [Ram. 6

Tomorrow is an old deceiver, and his cheat never grows stale. [Letter to Mrs. T., May 1773

In nations where there is hardly the use of letters, what is once out of sight is lost for ever. They think but little, and of their few thoughts, none are wasted on the past, in which they are neither interested by fear nor hope. Their only registers are stated observances and practical representations. For this reason an age of ignorance is an age of ceremony. Pageants, and processions, and commemorations, gradually shrink away, as better methods come into use of recording events and preserving rights. [Journey, Raasay

The Roman tyrant was content to be hated, if he was but feared; and there are thousands . . . willing to be thought wicked, if they may be allowed to be wits. It is therefore to be steadily inculcated, that virtue is the highest proof of understanding, and the only solid basis of greatness; and that vice is the natural consequence of narrow thoughts; that it begins in mistake, and ends in ignominy. [Ram. 4

It is not possible to be regarded with tenderness except by a few. That merit which gives greatness and renown, diffuses its influence to a wide compass, but acts weakly on every single breast; it is placed at a distance from common spectators, and shines like one of the remote stars, of which the light reaches us, but not the heat. The wit, the hero, the philosopher, whom their tempers or their fortunes have hindered from intimate relations, die, without any other effect than that of adding a new topic to the conversation of the day. They impress none with any fresh conviction of the fragility of our nature, because none had any particular interest in their lives, or was united to them by a reciprocation of benefits and endearments. [Ram. 78

[Good humor] is the *balm of being*, the quality to which all that adorns or elevates mankind must owe its power of pleasing. Without good-humour, learning and bravery can only confer that superiority which swells the heart of the lion in the desert, where he roars without reply, and ravages without resistance. Without good-humour virtue may awe by its dignity, and amaze by its brightness; but must always be viewed at a distance, and will scarcely gain a friend or attract an imitator. [Ram. 72

. . . such is the constitution of the world, that much of life must be spent in the same manner by the wise and the ignorant, the exalted and the low. Men, however distinguished by external accidents or intrinsick qualities, have all the same wants, the same pains, and, as far as the senses are consulted, the same pleasures. The petty cares and petty duties are the same in every station to every understanding, and every hour brings some occasion on which we all sink to a common level. We are all naked till we are dressed, and hungry till we are fed; and the general's triumph, and the sage's disputation, end, like the humble labours of the smith or plowman, in a dinner or in sleep. [Idl. 51

I have often thought that there has rarely passed a life of which a judicious and faithful narrative would not be useful. For, not only every man has, in the mighty mass of the world, great numbers in the same condition with himself, to whom his mistakes and miscarriages, escapes and expedients, would be of immediate and apparent use; but there is such an uniformity in the state of man, considered apart from adventitious and separable decorations and disguises, that there is scarce any possibility of good or ill, but is common to human kind. A great part of the time of those who are placed at the greatest distance by fortune, or by temper, must unavoidably pass in the same manner; and though, when the claims of nature are satisfied, caprice, and vanity, and accident, begin to produce discriminations and peculiarities, yet the eye is not very heedful or quick, which cannot discover the same causes still terminating their influence in the same effects, though sometimes accelerated, sometimes retarded, or perplexed by multiplied combinations. We are all prompted by the same motives, all deceived by the same fallacies, all animated by hope, obstructed by danger, entangled by desire, and seduced by pleasure. [Ram. 60

This is often the fate of long consideration: he does nothing who endeavours to do more than is allowed to humanity. . . . while you are making the choice of life, you neglect to live. [Ras. 30–31

He to whom many objects of pursuit arise at the same time, will frequently hesitate between different desires till a rival has precluded him, or change his course as new attractions prevail, and harass himself without advancing. He who sees different ways to the same end, will, unless he watches carefully over his own conduct, lay out too much of his attention upon the comparison of probabilities and the adjustment of expedients, and pause in the choice of his road till some accident intercepts his journey. He whose penetration extends to remote consequences, and who, whenever he applies his attention to any design, discovers new prospects of advantage, and possibilities of improvement, will not easily be persuaded that his project is ripe for execution; but will superadd one contrivance to another, endeavour to unite various purposes in one operation, multiply complications, and refine niceties, till he is entangled in his own scheme, and bewildered in the perplexity of various intentions. He that resolves to unite all the beauties of situation in a new purchase, must waste his life in roving to no purpose from province to province. He that hopes in the same house to obtain every convenience, may draw plans and study Palladio, but will never lay a stone. He will attempt a treatise on some important subject, and amass materials, consult authors, and study all the dependent and collateral parts of learning, but never conclude himself qualified to write. He that has abilities to conceive perfection, will not easily be content without it; and since perfection cannot be reached, will lose the opportunity of doing well in the vain hope of unattainable excellence. [Ram. 134

He that compares what he has done with what he has left undone, will feel the effect which must always follow the comparison of imagination with reality; he will look with contempt on his own unimportance, and wonder to what purpose he came into the world; he will repine that he shall leave behind him no evidence of his having been, that he has added nothing to the system of life, but has glided from youth to age among the crowd, without any effort for distinction.

Man is seldom willing to let fall the opinion of his own dignity, or to believe that he does little only because every individual is a very little being. He is better content to want diligence than power, and sooner confesses the depravity of his will than the imbecility of his nature.

From this mistaken notion of human greatness it proceeds, that many who pretend to have made great advances in wisdom so loudly declare that they despise themselves. If I had ever found any of the self-contemners much irritated or pained by the consciousness of their meanness, I should have given them consolation by observing, that a little more than nothing is as much as can be expected from a being, who with respect to the multitudes about him is himself little more than nothing. Every man is obliged by the Supreme Master of the universe to improve all the opportunities of good which are afforded him, and to keep in continual activity such abilities as are bestowed upon him. But he has no reason to repine, though his abilities are small and his opportunities few. He that has improved the virtue, or advanced the happiness of one fellow-creature, he that has ascertained a single moral proposition, or added one useful experiment to natural knowledge, may be contented with his own performance, and, with respect to mortals like himself, may demand, like *Augustus*, to be dismissed at his departure with applause. [Idl. 88

Every man is placed in the present condition by causes which acted without his foresight, and with which he did not always willingly co-operate; and therefore you will rarely meet one who does not think the lot of his neighbour better than his own. [Ras. 16

He that pines with hunger is in little care how others shall be fed. The poor man is seldom studious to make his grandson rich. It may be soon discovered why in a place which hardly supplies the cravings of necessity there has been little attention to the delights of fancy, and why distant convenience is unregarded where the thoughts are turned with incessant solicitude upon every possibility of immediate advantage. [Journey, Mull

The dignity of high birth and long extraction, no man, to whom nature has denied it, can confer upon himself; and, therefore, it deserves to be considered, whether the want of that which can never be gained, may not easily be endured. It is true, that if we consider the triumph and delight with which most of those recount their ancestors, who have ancestors to recount, and the artifices by which some who have risen to unexpected fortune endeavour to insert themselves into an honourable stem, we shall be inclined to fancy that wisdom or virtue may be had by inheritance, or that all the excellencies of a line of progenitors are accumulated on their descendant. Reason, indeed, will soon inform us that our estimation of birth is arbitrary and capricious, and that dead ancestors can have no influence but upon imagination; let it then be examined whether one dream may not operate in the place of another; whether he that owes nothing to forefathers, may not receive equal pleasure from the consciousness of owing all to himself; whether he may not, with a little meditation, find it more honourable to found than to continue a family, and to gain dignity than to transmit it; whether, if he receives no dignity from the virtues of his family, he does not likewise escape the danger of being disgraced by their crimes; and whether he that brings a new name into the world, has not the convenience of playing the game of life without a stake, and opportunity of winning much though he has nothing to lose. [Adv. 111

The gloomy and resentful are always found among those who have nothing to do, or who do nothing. [Idl. 72

The opinion which a man entertains of himself ought to be distinguished . . . as it relates to persons or to things. To think highly of ourselves in comparison with others, to assume by our own authority that precedence which none is willing to grant, must always be invidious and offensive; but to rate our powers high in proportion to things, and imagine ourselves equal to great undertakings, while we leave others in possession of the same abilities, cannot with equal justice provoke censure.

It must be confessed, that self-love may dispose us to decide too hastily in our own favour: but who is hurt by the mistake? If we are incited by this vain opinion to attempt more than we can perform, ours is the labour, and ours is the disgrace. [Adv. 81

We rate ourselves by our fortune rather than our virtues, and exorbitant claims are quickly produced by imaginary merit. [Ram. 172

That kind of life is most happy which affords us more opportunities of gaining our own esteem; and what can any man [heir to name and estates] infer in his own favour from a condition to which, however prosperous, he contributed nothing, and which the vilest and weakest of the species would have obtained by the same right, had he happened to be the son of the same father? [Adv. 111

It is a matter of very melancholy consideration, that all human advantages confer more power of doing evil than good. [Notes to Rich. II

Where our design terminates only in our own satisfaction, the mistake [of trifling away our life] is of no great importance; for the pleasure of expecting enjoyment is often greater than that of obtaining it, and the completion of almost every wish is found a disappointment; but when many others are interested in an undertaking, when any design is formed, in which the improvement or security of mankind is involved, nothing is more unworthy either of wisdom or benevolence, than to delay it from time to time, or to forget how much every day that passes over us, takes away from our power, and how soon an idle purpose to do an action sinks into a mournful wish that it had once been done. [Ram. 71

The reigning errour of mankind is, that we are not content with the conditions on which the goods of life are granted. [Ram. 178

Every man is to take existence on the terms on which it is given to him. To some men it is given on condition of not taking liberties which other men may take without much harm. One man may drink wine, and be nothing the worse for it; on another, wine may have effects so inflammatory as to injure

him both in body and mind, and perhaps make him commit
something for which he may deserve to be hanged. [Bos. May
1776

It sometimes happens that too close an attention to minute
exactness, or a too rigorous habit of examining every thing by
the standard of perfection, vitiates the temper, rather than improves the understanding, and teaches the mind to discern
faults with unhappy penetration . . . let no man rashly determine, that his unwillingness to be pleased is a proof of understanding, unless his superiority appears from less doubtful
evidence; for though peevishness may sometimes justly boast
its descent from learning or from wit, it is much oftener of
base extraction, the child of vanity, and nursling of ignorance.
[Ram. 74

Prudence operates on life in the same manner as rules on
composition: it produces vigilance rather than elevation, rather
prevents loss than procures advantage; and often escapes miscarriages, but seldom reaches either power or honour. It
quenches that ardour of enterprize, by which every thing is
done that can claim praise or admiration; and represses that
generous temerity which often fails and often succeeds. Rules
may obviate faults but can never confer beauties; and prudence
keeps life safe, but does not often make it happy. The world
is not amazed with prodigies of excellence, but when wit
tramples upon rules, and magnanimity breaks the chains of
prudence. [Idl. 57

. . . every one should consider himself as entrusted, not only
with his own conduct, but with that of others; and as account-
able, not only for the duties which he neglects, or the crimes
that he commits, but for that negligence and irregularity which
he may encourage or inculcate . . . for it is possible that for

want of attention, we may teach others faults from which ourselves are free, or, by a cowardly desertion of a cause which we ourselves approve, may pervert those who fix their eyes upon us, and, having no rule of their own to guide their course, are easily misled by the aberrations of that example which they choose for their directions. [Ram. 70

Those who are oppressed with their own reputation will, perhaps, not be comforted by hearing that their cares are unnecessary. But the truth is, that no man is much regarded by the rest of the world. He that considers how little he dwells upon the condition of others will learn how little the attention of others is attracted by himself. While we see multitudes passing before us, of whom, perhaps, not one appears to deserve our notice or excite our sympathy, we should remember, that we likewise are lost in the same throng; that the eye which happens to glance upon us is turned in a moment on him that follows us; and that the utmost which we can reasonably hope or fear is, to fill a vacant hour with prattle, and be forgotten. [Ram. 159

For the hope of happiness . . . is so strongly impressed, that the longest experience is not able to efface it. Of the present state, whatever it be, we feel, and are forced to confess, the misery; yet, when the same state is again at a distance, imagination paints it as desirable. [Ras. 22

What then are the hopes and prospects of covetousness, ambition, and rapacity? Let him that desires most have all his desires gratified, he never shall attain a state which he can for a day and a night, contemplate with satisfaction, or from which, if he had the power of perpetual vigilance, he would not long for periodical separations. [Idl. 32

When [Cowley] was interrupted by company, or fatigued with business, he so strongly imaged to himself the happiness of leisure and retreat, that he . . . forgot, in the vehemence of desire, that solitude and quiet owe their pleasure to those miseries, which he was so studious to obviate: for such are the vicissitudes of the world, through all its parts, that day and night, labour and rest, hurry and retirement, endear each other; such are the changes that keep the mind in action; we desire, we pursue, we obtain, we are satiated: we desire something else, and begin a new pursuit. [Ram. 6

We represent to ourselves the pleasures of some future possession, and suffer our thoughts to dwell attentively upon it, till it has wholly engrossed the imagination . . .

Every man has experienced how much of this ardour has been remitted, when a sharp or tedious sickness has set death before his eyes. The extensive influence of greatness, the glitter of wealth, the praises of admirers . . . have appeared vain and empty things, when the last hour seemed to be approaching . . . We should then find the absurdity of stretching out our arms incessantly to grasp that which we cannot keep, and wearing out our lives in endeavours to add new turrets to the fabric of ambition, when the foundation itself is shaking, and the ground on which it stands is mouldering away. [Ram. 17

Alas, Sir, on how few things can we look back with satisfaction. [Bos. 31 March 1779

No man can form a just estimate of his own powers by unactive speculation. That fortitude which has encountered no dangers, that prudence which has surmounted no difficulties, that integrity which has been attacked by no temptations, can at best be considered but as gold not yet brought to the test, of which therefore the true value cannot be assigned. [Ram. 150

I think there is some reason for questioning whether the body and mind are not so proportioned, that the one can bear all that can be inflicted on the other, whether virtue cannot stand its ground as long as life, and whether a soul well principled will not be separated sooner than subdued. [Ram. 32

This quality of looking forward into futurity, seems the unavoidable condition of a being, whose motions are gradual, and whose life is progressive: as his powers are limited, he must use means for the attainment of his ends, and intend first what he performs last . . . as . . . he is perpetually varying the horizon of his prospects, he must always discover new motives of action, new excitements of fear, and allurements of desire.

The end therefore which at present calls forth our efforts, will be found, when it is once gained, to be only one of the means to some remoter end. The natural flights of the human mind are not from pleasure to pleasure, but from hope to hope. [Ram. 2

Johnson with Extensive View Surveys Mankind...

*He has a peculiar art of drawing characters, which
is as rare as good portrait painting.*

Bos. April 1778

Johnson, wrote Miss Reynolds in her *Memories*, seemed to
delight in drawing characters and, when he did so con amore,
delighted everyone that heard him. "Very few men," wrote Boswell, "had seen greater variety of characters; and none could
observe them better, as was evident from the strong, yet nice
portraits which he often drew . . . The suddenness with
which his accounts of some of them started out in conversation
was not less pleasing than surprising."[1]

This gift grew less out of Johnson's skill in words than out
of his genuine love of human beings. The great body of his
acquaintance ran the gamut from Robert Levett, his strange,
lowly household companion for years, to the Duke of Argyle.
He never dropped a friend; and he made genuine efforts to retain them. Once, when Boswell expressed fear that Langton was
taking ill a hasty expression of Johnson's, Johnson replied,
"What is to become of society, if a friendship of twenty years
is to be broken off for such a cause?"[2] And he called twice upon
Dr. Barnard before the bishop was leaving for his new see in

[1] Bos. 5 April 1776.　　　　　[2] Tour 22 August.

Ireland. "No man," he said, "ever paid more attention to another than he has done to me; and I have neglected him, not wilfully, but from being otherwise occupied."[3]

Yet in all he saw the weaknesses as well as the virtues. He loved the dissolute and all but worthless Savage, memorialized him in a biography that is a little classic; yet his affection did not blind him to Savage's serious faults. He admired his long-time friend Hawkins for his ability and his integrity, but he was not unaware of his friend's harshness and meanness. Of his affection for Mrs. Thrale there can be no doubt, but he saw the shallowness of her nature and her need "to feel her husband's bridle on her neck."

With all their penetration, Johnson's characterizations are uniformly free from pettiness or malice. Of all whom he embalmed in a phrase, only Thomas Sheridan harbored a lifelong grudge[4]—presumably because of what his vanity moved him to think of a slighting remark about his pension. In his final characterization of Lord Chesterfield, Johnson was probably more concerned with turning a phrase than in lampooning a man, a man who, anyway, could not have cared in the slightest degree.

One of the neatest paragraphs in Boswell is Johnson's spoken appraisal of William Fitzherbert, an appraisal which later ends in the postscript of Johnson's comment about his death. Fitzherbert hanged himself. Mrs. Thrale records one of her guests asking in astonishment, "What upon earth could have made [him] hang himself?" "Why," answered Dr. Johnson, "just his having a multitude of acquaintance, and ne'er a friend."[5]

A rather obscure comment on a rather obscure man—one who, like Mr. Edwards, is probably saved from oblivion by his contact with Johnson—is that on Jack Ellis. The statement was made in 1776. Johnson was then at the peak of his fame; his talk famous and his criticism—if Macaulay is to be trusted,

[3] Bos. May 1781.   [4] Bos. 1763.   [5] Bos. 15 Sept. 1777(n).

as he probably is not—was "sufficient to sell off a whole edition
in a day, or to condemn the sheets to the service of the trunk-
maker and pastry cook." It is striking because of its vivid juxta-
position of opposites—money-scrivening and connoisseurship
in literature. "The most literary conversation that I ever enjoyed," said Johnson, "was at the table of Jack Ellis, a money-
scrivener behind the Royal Exchange, with whom I at one
period used to dine generally once a week."[6]

That he really enjoyed exercising his faculty for discerning
character is seen in the Lives of the Poets. In his essays on Milton, Pope, Swift, and Savage—to mention only the obvious—
he fills pages with keen comment and vivid detail. His terse
account of the end of Rochester is quite typical: "Thus in
a course of drunken gaiety, and gross sensuality, with intervals
of study perhaps yet more criminal, with an avowed contempt
of all decency and order, a total disregard to every moral, and a
resolute denial of every religious obligation, he lived worthless
and useless, and blazed out his youth and his health in lavish
voluptuousness; till, at the age of one and thirty, he had exhausted the fund of life, and reduced himself to a state of
weakness and decay . . . He died . . . before he had completed
his thirty-fourth year."[7]

What Johnson said from time to time of Oliver Goldsmith,
if put together in connected form, would make a beautifully
phrased essay, in which criticism and praise would rise to the
conclusive final judgment, "he was a very great man." Falstaff
fascinated him, and his characterization of that cowardly, rascally hero is among Johnson's finest pieces of writing.

A good many years ago James Truslow Adams in an essay,
"The Mucker Pose," complained that the ability to describe
a person's character is one of the lost arts—that "good scout,"
"great guy," "good egg," or some such stereotype is as close as

6 Bos. 5 April 1776.
7 L.P., Rochester.

we come to verbal portraiture. If this is true, then surely Johnson must represent this art at its high tide. A constant seeker after the truth, "he had read"—as he wrote of Addison—"with critical eyes the important volume of human life, and knew the heart of man from the depths of stratagem to the surface of affectation."[8] No man has left so large a gallery of miniatures and full-length portraits, any one of which could serve as a model of pungency and perspicacity.

Of Sir John Hawkins:

As to Hawkins, why really I believe him to be an honest man at bottom; but to be sure he is somewhat mean, and it must be owned he has some degree of brutality and is not without a tendency to savageness that cannot be well defended. But my poor friend Sir John, it cannot well be denied, was an unclubable man. [D'Arblay Diary

Of Bet Flint, "a woman of the town of some eccentrick talents and much effrontery":

Bet (said he) wrote her own Life in verse, which she brought to me, wishing that I would furnish her with a Preface to it. (Laughing.) I used to say of her that she was generally slut and drunkard; occasionally whore and thief. She had, however, genteel lodgings, a spinnet on which she played, and a boy that walked before her chair. Poor Bet was taken up on a charge of stealing a counterpane, and tried at Old Bailey. Chief Justice ———, who loved a wench, summed up favourably, and she was acquitted. After which Bet said, with a gay and satisfied air, "Now that the counterpane is *my own*, I shall make a petticoat of it." [Bos. 8 May 1781

8 L.P., Addison.

Johnson's occasional comments on Goldsmith as a conversationalist fall into a pattern and at the same time tell a great deal else:

The misfortune of Goldsmith in conversation is this: he goes on without knowing how he is to get off. His genius is great, but his knowledge is small. As they say of a generous man, it is a pity he is not rich, we may say of Goldsmith, it is a pity he is not knowing. He would not keep his knowledge to himself. [Bos. 1 July 1772

Goldsmith had no settled notions upon any subject; so he talked always at random. It seemed to be his intention to blurt out whatever was in his mind, and see what would become of it. He was angry too, when catched in an absurdity; but it did not prevent him from falling into another the next minute . . . Goldsmith, however, was a man, who, whatever he wrote, did it better than any other man could do. He deserved a place in Westminster-Abbey, and every year he lived, would have deserved it better. He had, indeed, been at no pains to fill his mind with knowledge. He transplanted it from one place to another; and it did not settle in his mind; so he could not tell what was in his own books. [Bos. 9 April 1778

No man was more foolish when he had not a pen in his hand, or more wise when he had. [Bos. 1780

But let not his frailties be remembered; he was a very great man. [Letter to Langton, 5 July 1774

Of Miss Lucy Porter, his stepdaughter, then in her middle fifties, he said:

She has raised my esteem by many excellencies, very noble and resplendent, though a little discoloured by hoary virginity. [Letter to Mrs. T., 20 July 1767

Of Lord Chesterfield:

This man (said he) I thought had been a Lord among wits; but, I find, he is only a wit among Lords! [Bos. 1754

Of "a fellow in the House of Commons":

He has a mind as narrow as the neck of a vinegar-cruet. [Tour 30 September

. . . the late Earl of Corke . . . was a genteel man, but did not keep up the dignity of his rank. He was so generally civil, that nobody thanked him for it. [Bos. 21 Sept. 1777

Of Lord Mansfield who, though a Scot, had been educated in England:

Much (said he) may be made of a Scotchman, if he be *caught* young. [Bos. Spring 1772

Of Lady Macdonald of Skye:

This woman would sink a ninety-gun ship, she is so dull and heavy. [Tour 3 September

Of Edmund Burke:

You could not stand five minutes with that man beneath a shed while it rained, but you must be convinced you had been standing with the greatest man you had ever yet seen. [Pioz. Anec.

Of Dr. Joseph Warton, headmaster of Winchester:

Sir, he is an enthusiast by rule. [Bos. 1780

Of Polly Carmichael, who was one of his strange household:

I took to Poll very well at first, but she won't do upon closer examination . . . Poll is a stupid slut. I had some hopes for her at first; but when I talked to her tightly and closely, I could make nothing of her. She was wiggle waggle: and I could never persuade her to be categorical. [D'Arblay Diary

Of Foote, the actor:

Foote is quite impartial, for he tells lies of every body. [Bos. 16 March 1776

Of a Welsh "lady of quality, since dead":

That woman (cries Johnson) is like sour small-beer, the beverage of her table, and produce of the wretched country she lives in: like that, she could never have been a good thing, and even that bad thing is spoiled. [Pioz. Anec.

Of a Scotch lady:

. . . she resembled a dead nettle; were she alive (said he), she would sting. [Pioz. Anec.

Of Milton, to a woman who complained that the poet who wrote Paradise Lost could yet write such poor sonnets:

Milton, Madam, was a genius that could cut a Colossus from a rock; but could not carve heads upon cherry-stones. [Bos. 13 June 1784

A Scot, thinking to triumph over Johnson, asked about Buchanan, "Ah, Dr. Johnson, what would you have said of Buchanan had he been an Englishman?"

Why, Sir, . . . I should *not* have said of Buchanan, had he been an *Englishman*, what I will now say of him as a *Scotchman*—that he was the only man of genius his country ever produced. [Bos. 1783

Of Boswell:

I will do you, Boswell, the justice to say, that you are the most *unscottified* of your countrymen. [Bos. 1 May 1773

Of a vain and anxious young author:

Sir (said he), there is not a young sapling upon Parnassus more severely blown about by every wind of criticism. [Bos. June 1784

Of Samuel Richardson:

That fellow Richardson . . . could not be contented to sail quietly down the stream of reputation without longing to taste the froth from every stroke of the oar. [Pioz. Anec.

Of Dr. John Campbell, a political writer:

Campbell is not always rigidly careful of truth in his conversation; but I do not believe there is anything of this carelessness in his books. Campbell is a good man, a pious man. I am afraid he has not been in the inside of a church for many years; but he never passes a church without pulling off his hat. [Bos. 1 July 1763

Of "a very ignorant young fellow":

This fellow's dullness is elastic . . . and all we do is but like kicking at a woolsack. [Pioz. Anec.

Of Dr. William Warburton, Bishop of Gloucester:

The worst of Warburton is, that he has a rage for saying something, when there's nothing to be said. [Bos. 1758

Warburton may be absurd . . . but he will never be weak: he *flounders well.* [Stockdale, John. Misc.

Of George I:

George the First knew nothing, and desired to know nothing; did nothing, and desired to do nothing: and the only good thing that is told of him is, that he wished to restore the crown to its hereditary successor. [Bos. 6 April 1775

Of a Colonel Livingstone, "who talked a bit vaguely":

A mighty misty man, the colonel. [Tour 25 October

Of Sir Alexander Macdonald (probably):

Sir, he has no more the soul of a chief than an attorney who has twenty houses in a street and considers how much he can make by them. [Tour 3 November

Of Richardson:

. . . his perpetual study was to ward off petty inconveniencies and to procure petty pleasures . . . his love of continual superiority was such that he took care to be always surrounded by women who listened to him implicitly, and did not venture to controvert his opinions. [Tour 20 November

Of Thomas Gray:

Sir, he was dull in company, dull in his closet, dull everywhere. He was dull in a new way, and that made many people think him GREAT. [Bos. 28 March 1775

Of a penurious acquaintance, perhaps Garrick:

Sir, he is narrow, not so much from avarice, as from impotence to spend his money. He cannot find in his heart to pour out a bottle of wine; but he would not much care if it should sour. [Bos. 12 April 1776

Of Dean Mudge:

He grasps more sense than he can hold; he takes more corn than he can make into meal; he opens a wide prospect, but it is so distant, it is indistinct. [Bos. 20 April 1781

Of Reynolds and Foote:

When Foote has told me something, I dismiss it from my mind like a passing shadow: when Reynolds tells me something, I consider myself as possessed of an idea the more. [Pioz. Anec.

Of Allen, Viscount Bathurst:

Dear Bathurst . . . was a man to my very heart's content: he hated a fool, and he hated a rogue, and he hated a *whig;* he was a very good *hater.* [Pioz. Anec.

Of James Macpherson:

He wants to make himself conspicuous. He would tumble in a hogstye, as long as you looked at him and called him to come out. [Bos. 14 July 1763

Of Thomas Sheridan:

Why, Sir, Sherry is dull, naturally dull; but it must have taken him a great deal of pains to become what we now see him. Such an excess of stupidity, Sir, is not in Nature. [Bos. 28 July 1763

Of the Rev. Mr. Seward of Lichfield:

Sir, his ambition is to be a fine talker; so he goes to Buxton, and such places where he may find companies to listen to him. And, Sir, he is a valetudinarian, one of those who are always mending themselves. I do not know a more disagreeable character than a valetudinarian, who thinks he may do anything that is for his ease, and indulges himself in the grossest freedoms. Sir, he brings himself to the state of a hog in a stye. [Bos. 16 Sept. 1777

Of a man who had been hired to sit up one night with him in his last illness:

The fellow's an idiot; he is as awkward as a turn-spit when first put into the wheel, and as sleepy as a dormouse. [Bos. Dec. 1784

Of a dull tiresome man:

That fellow seems to me to possess but one idea, and that is a wrong one. [Bos. 1770

Of two minor writers, Derrick and Smart, of whom he had been asked to state which was superior:

Sir, there is no settling the point of precedency between a louse and a flea. [Bos. 1783

Of two disputants:

One has ball without powder; the other powder without ball. [Hawkins

Of Mr. Hawkins, usher at Lichfield School, under whom Johnson began the study of Latin:

A man (said he) very skilful in his little way. [Bos. 1712

Of Mr. Hunter, headmaster of Lichfield:

[He] was very severe and wrong-headedly severe. He used (said he) to beat us unmercifully; and he did not distinguish between ignorance and negligence; for he would beat a boy equally for not knowing a thing, as for neglecting to know it. [Bos. 1712

Of an instructor whom he familiarly called Tom Brown:

[He] published a spelling-book, and dedicated it to the UNIVERSE; but, I fear, no copy of it can now be had. [Bos. 1712

Of Charles Churchill, a poet whose poetry, said Johnson, "had a temporary currency, only from its audacity of abuse":

I called the fellow a blockhead at first, and I will call him a blockhead still. However, I will acknowledge that I have a better opinion of him now than I once had; for he has shewn more fertility than I expected. To be sure, he is a tree that cannot produce good fruit: he only bears crabs. But, Sir, a tree that produces a great many crabs is better than a tree which produces only a few. [Bos. 1 July 1763

Of William Fitzherbert, M.P. of Derbyshire:

There was (said he) no sparkle, no brilliancy in Fitzherbert; but I never knew a man who was so generally acceptable. He made every body quite easy, overpowered nobody by the superiority of his talents, made no man think worse of himself by being his rival, seemed always to listen, did not oblige you to hear much from him, and did not oppose what you said. Every body liked him; but he had no friend, as I understand the word, nobody with whom he exchanged intimate thoughts. People were willing to think well of every thing about him . . . He was an instance of the truth of the observation, that a man will please more upon the whole by negative qualities than by positive; by never offending, than by giving a great deal of delight. [Bos. 15 Sept. 1777

Of Mr. Jorden, his tutor and a fellow of Pembroke:

He was a very worthy man, but a heavy man, and I did not profit much by his instructions. Indeed, I did not attend him much . . . Whenever a young man becomes Jorden's pupil, he becomes his son. [Bos. 31 Oct. 1728

Of Lady Macdonald of Sleat:

. . . she was as bad as negative badness could be, and stood in the way of what was good: that insipid beauty would not go a great way; and . . . such a woman might be cut out of a cabbage, if there was a skilful artificer. [Tour 20 September

Of Garrick's death:

I am disappointed by that stroke of death, which has eclipsed the gaiety of nations, and impoverished the publick stock of harmless pleasure. [Bos. 1731

The above excerpts are all Johnson in speech. In writing he was perhaps less terse, but even more impressive. Of the friend and companion of his Grub Street days, Richard Savage, he wrote:

It cannot be said, that he made use of his abilities for the direction of his own conduct: an irregular and dissipated manner of life had made him the slave of every passion that happened to be excited by the presence of its object, and that slavery to his passions reciprocally produced a life irregular and dissipated. He was not master of his own motions, nor could promise any thing for the next day. . . .

He was compassionate both by nature and principle, and always ready to perform offices of humanity; but when he was provoked (and very small offences were sufficient to provoke him) he would prosecute his revenge with the utmost acrimony till his passion had subsided.

His friendship was, therefore, of little value; for, though he was zealous in the support or vindication of those whom he loved, yet it was always dangerous to trust him, because he considered himself as discharged, by the first quarrel, from all ties of honour or gratitude; and would betray those secrets which, in the warmth of confidence, had been imparted to him. . . .

For his life, or for his writings, none who candidly consider his fortune will think an apology either necessary or difficult. If he was not always sufficiently instructed in his subject, his knowledge was, at least, greater than could have been attained by others in the same state. If his works were sometimes unfinished, accuracy cannot reasonably be expected from a man oppressed with want, which he has no hope of relieving but by a speedy publication. The insolence and resentment of which he is accused were not easily to be avoided by a great mind, irritated by perpetual hardships, and constrained hourly to return the spurns of contempt, and repress the insolence of prosperity; and vanity may surely be readily pardoned in him, to whom life afforded no other comforts than barren praises, and the consciousness of deserving them.

Those are no proper judges of his conduct who have slumbered away their time on the down of plenty; nor will any wise man presume to say, "Had I been in Savage's condition, I should have lived or written better than Savage." [L.P. Savage

Of Milton:

His political notions were those of a surly and acrimonious republican, for which it is not known that he gave any better reason than that *a popular government was the most frugal; for the trappings of a monarchy would set up an ordinary commonwealth.* It is surely very shallow policy that supposes money to be the chief good . . .

Milton's republicanism was, I am afraid, founded in an envious hatred of greatness, and a sullen desire of independence; in petulance impatient of control, and pride disdainful of superiority. He hated monarchs in the state, and prelates in the church; for he hated all whom he was required to obey. . . .

It has been observed, that they who most loudly clamour for liberty, do not most liberally grant it. What we know of Milton's character in domestick relations, is that he was severe and arbitrary. His family consisted of women; and there appears in his books something like a Turkish contempt of females, as subordinates and inferior beings. That his own daughters might not break the ranks, he suffered them to be depressed by a mean and penurious education. He thought women made only for obedience, and man only for rebellion. [L.P., Milton

Of Swift:

Not knowing what to do, he did nothing; and, with the fate of a double-dealer, at last he lost his power, but kept his enemies. [L.P., Swift

However poetry is defined, Johnson's "On the Death of Mr. Robert Levett, a Practicer of Medicine" must be called poetry. Dr. Levett, whom Johnson met about 1745, lived to be one of his oldest friends. It is possible that he first saw Johnson in his capacity as a physician, though his qualifications for that profession were probably very sketchy, and those that he had were obtained mostly by ear. His practice was among the poorest people of the city, people so poor that, if they paid him at all, their pay was not infrequently food and gin. The gin he was accustomed to drink on the spot—perhaps to make transportation so much the easier. At any rate, according to Hawkins' Life, Johnson once said that Levett was the only man he knew who got drunk from motives of prudence.

> Condemn'd to Hope's delusive mine,
>   As on we toil from day to day,
> By sudden blast or slow decline
>   Our social comforts drop away.
>
> Well try'd through many a varying year,
>   See LEVETT to the grave descend;
> Officious, innocent, sincere,
>   Of every friendless name the friend.
>
> Yet still he fills Affection's eye,
>   Obscurely wise, and coarsely kind;
> Nor, letter'd arrogance, deny,
>   Thy praise to merit unrefin'd.
>
> When fainting Nature call'd for aid,
>   And hov'ring Death prepar'd the blow,

His vigorous remedy display'd
  The power of art without the show.

In Misery's darkest cavern known,
  His ready help was ever nigh,
Where hopeless Anguish pour'd his groan,
  And lonely Want retir'd to die.

No summons mock'd by chill delay,
  No pettv gains disdain'd by pride;
The modest wants of every day,
  The toil of ev'ry day supply'd.

His virtues walk'd their narrow round,
  Nor made a pause, nor left a void;
And sure th' Eternal Master found
  His single talent well employ'd.

The busy day, the peaceful night,
  Unfelt, uncounted, glided by;
His frame was firm, his powers were bright,
  Though now his eightieth year was nigh.

Then, with no throbs of fiery pain,
  No cold gradations of decay,
Death broke at once the vital chain,
  And freed his soul the nearest way.
                              [Bos. 20 Jan. 1782

Of Addison:

Of his habits or external manners, nothing is so often mentioned as that timorous or sullen taciturnity, which his friends called modesty by too mild a name. Steele mentions with great tenderness "that remarkable bashfulness, which is a cloak that hides and muffles merit" . . . And Addison, speaking of his own deficiency in conversation, used to say of himself, that, with respect to intellectual wealth, "he could draw bills for a thousand pounds, though he had not a guinea in his pocket."

[Yet] that man cannot be supposed very unexpert in the arts of conversation and practice of life, who, without fortune or alliance, by his usefulness and dexterity, became Secretary of State; and who died at forty-seven, after having not only stood long in the highest rank of wit and literature, but filled one of the most important offices of state. . . .

Under the patronage of Addison [Button] kept a coffee-house on the south side of Russel-street, about two doors from Covent-garden. Here it was that the wits of the time used to assemble. It is said that when Addison suffered any vexation from the Countess [of Warwick, his wife], he withdrew to the company of Button's house.

From the coffee-house, he went . . . to a tavern, where he often sat late and drank too much wine. In the bottle, discontent seeks for comfort, cowardice for courage, and bashfulness for confidence. It is not unlikely that Addison was first seduced to excess by the manumission which he obtained from the servile timidity of his sober hours. He that feels oppression from the presence of those to whom he knows himself superiour, will desire to set loose his powers of conversation; and who that ever asked succours from Bacchus was able to preserve himself from being enslaved by his auxiliary? . . .

His prose is the model of the middle style; on grave subjects not formal, on light occasions not grovelling, pure without scrupulosity, and exact without apparent elaboration; always equable, and always easy, without glowing words or pointed sentences. Addison never deviates from his track to snatch a grace; he seeks no ambitious ornaments, and tries no hazardous innovations. His page is always luminous, but never blazes in unexpected splendour. . . .

. . . What he attempted, he performed; he is never feeble, and he did not wish to be energetick; he is never rapid, and he never stagnates. His sentences have neither studied amplitude, nor affected brevity; his periods, though not diligently rounded, are voluble and easy. Whoever wishes to attain an English style, familiar but not coarse, and elegant but not ostentatious, must give his days and nights to the volumes of Addison. [L.P., Addison

Of Wolsey:

> With age, with cares, with maladies oppress'd
> He seeks the refuge of monastic rest.
> Grief aids disease, remember'd folly stings,
> And his last sighs reproach the faith of kings.
> [Van. H. Wishes

Of Charles XII of Sweden:

> His fall was destin'd to a barren strand,
> A petty fortress, and a dubious hand;
> He left the name at which the world grew pale,
> To point a moral, or adorn a tale.
> [Van. H. Wishes

Of Swift:

[He] shuffles between cowardice and veracity, and talks big when he says nothing. [L.P., Swift

Of the Dutch patriot De Witt:

... all the plans and enterprises of De Witt are now of less importance to the world than that part of his personal character, which represents him as *careful of his health and negligent of his life.* [Ram. 60

Of Edmund Smith:

He was remarkable for the power of reading with great rapidity, and of retaining with great fidelity what he so easily collected. He therefore always knew what the present question required; and when his friends expressed their wonder at his acquisitions, made in a state of apparent negligence and drunkenness, he never discovered [disclosed] his hours of reading or method of study, but involved himself in affected silence, and fed his own vanity with their admiration and conjectures. [L.P., Smith

Of Edmund Burke:

Burke is unequal; he is a lion who lashes himself into a fury with his own tail. [Bos. (Hill-Powell, V, App. D)

Of Richard Savage:

The reigning errour of his life was that he mistook the love for the practice of virtue, and was, indeed, not so much a good man as the friend of goodness. [L.P., Savage

Of Dryden:

He delighted to tread upon the brink of meaning. [L.P., Dryden

Of Flora Macdonald:

A name that will be mentioned in history and if courage and fidelity be virtues, mentioned with honour. [Journey, Dunvegan

Of Gilbert Walmsley:

. . . let me indulge myself in remembrance. I knew him very early; he was one of the first friends that literature procured me, and I hope that at least my gratitude made me worthy of his notice. He was of an advanced age, and I only not a boy; yet he never received my notions with contempt. He was a Whig, with all the virulence and malevolence of his party, yet difference of opinion did not keep us apart. I honoured him, and he endured me.

He had mingled with the gay world, without exemption from its vices and follies; but he never neglected the cultivation of his mind; his belief in Revelation was unshaken; his learning preserved his principles; he grew first regular, then pious. [L.P., Smith

Of Nicholas Rowe:

Few characters can bear the microscopick scrutiny of wit quickened by anger; and perhaps the best advice to authors would be that they should keep out of the way of one another. [L.P., Rowe

Of Richard Blackmore:

Contempt is a kind of gangrene, which, if it seizes one part of a character, corrupts all the rest by degrees. Blackmore, being despised as a poet, was, in time, neglected as a physician; his practice, which was once invidiously great, forsook him in the latter part of his life; but being by nature, or by principle, averse from idleness, he employed his unwelcome leisure in writing books on physick, and teaching others to cure those whom he could himself cure no longer. [L.P., Blackmore

Of Isaac Watts:

By his natural temper he was quick of resentment; but, by his established and habitual practice, he was gentle, modest, and inoffensive. His tenderness appeared in his attention to children and to the poor. To the poor, while he lived in the family of his friend, he allowed the third part of his annual revenue . . . and for children he condescended to lay aside the scholar, the philosopher, and the wit to write little poems of devotion, and systems of instruction, adapted to their wants and capacities, from the dawn of reason through its gradations of advance in the morning of life. Every man acquainted with the common principles of human action, will look with veneration on the writer who is at one time combating Locke and at another making a catechism for children in their fourth year. A voluntary descent from the dignity of science is, perhaps, the hardest lesson that humility can teach. [L.P., Watts

Of Sir Thomas Browne:

He appears indeed to have been willing to pay labour for truth. [Browne

Of Alexander Pope:

The person of Pope is well known not to have been formed on the nicest model. He has, in his account of the Little Club, compared himself to a spider, and, by another, is described as protuberant behind and before.

He was then [in late middle age] so weak as to stand in perpetual need of female attendance; extremely sensible of cold, so that he wore a kind of fur doublet, under a shirt of very coarse warm linen with fine sleeves. When he rose, he was invested in boddice made of stiff canvass, being scarcely able to hold himself erect till they were laced, and he then put on a flannel waistcoat. One side was contracted. His legs were so slender, that he enlarged their bulk with three pairs of stockings, which were drawn on and off by the maid; for he was not able to dress or undress himself, and neither went to bed nor rose without help. His weakness made it very difficult for him to be clean. . . .

That he loved too well to eat, is certain; but that his sensuality shortened his life will not be hastily concluded, when it is remembered that a conformation so irregular lasted six-and-fifty years, notwithstanding such pertinacious diligence of study and meditation.

In all his intercourse with mankind, he had great delight in artifice, and endeavoured to attain all his purposes by indirect and unsuspected methods. "He hardly drank tea without a stratagem." . . . He practised his arts on such small occasions, that lady Bolingbroke used to say, in a French phrase, that he *played the politician about cabbages and turnips*" . . .

In familiar or convivial conversation, it does not appear that he excelled . . . One apothegm only stands upon record. When an objection raised against his inscription for Shakespeare was defended by the authority of Patrick, he replied . . . that "he would allow the publisher of a Dictionary to know the meaning of a single word, but not of two words put together." . . .

. . . His hopes and fears, his joys and sorrows, acted strongly upon his mind; and, if he differed from others, it was not by carelessness; he was irritable and resentful; his malignity to Philips, whom he had first made ridiculous, and then hated for being angry, continued too long. Of his vain desire to make Bentley contemptible, I never heard any adequate reason. He was sometimes wanton in his attacks; and, before Chandos, lady Wortley, and Hill, was mean in his retreat. . . .

The virtues which seem to have had most of his affection were liberality and fidelity of friendship, in which it does not appear that he was other than he describes himself. His fortune did not suffer his charity to be splendid and conspicuous; but he assisted Dodsley with a hundred pounds, that he might open a shop; and, of the subscription of forty pounds a year, that he raised for Savage, twenty were paid by himself. He was accused of loving money; but his love was eagerness to gain, not solicitude to keep it. [L.P., Pope

Of David Mallet:

Having cleared his tongue from his native pronunciation so as to be no longer distinguished as a Scot, he seems inclined to disencumber himself from all adherences of his original, and took upon him to change his name from Scotch *Malloch* to English *Mallet*, without any imaginable reason of preference which the eye or ear can discover. What other proofs he gave

of disrespect to his native country, I know not; but it was remarked of him, that he was the only Scot whom Scotchmen
did not commend . . .

His stature was diminutive, but he was regularly formed; his
appearance, till he grew corpulent, was agreeable, and he suffered it to want no recommendation that dress could give it.
His conversation was elegant and easy. The rest of his character
may, without injury to his memory, sink into silence. [L.P.,
Mallet

Of Falstaff:

But *Falstaff*, unimitated, unimitable *Falstaff*, how shall I
describe thee? Thou compound of sense and vice; of sense
which may be admired but not esteemed, of vice which may
be despised but hardly detested. *Falstaff* is a character loaded
with faults, and with those faults which naturally produce contempt. He is a thief, and a glutton, a coward, and a boaster,
always ready to cheat the weak and prey upon the poor; to
terrify the timorous and insult the defenceless. At once obsequious and malignant, he satirises in their absence those whom
he lives by flattering. He is familiar with the prince only as an
agent of vice, but of this familiarity he is so proud as not only
to be supercilious and haughty with common men, but to think
his interest of importance to the duke of *Lancaster*. Yet the
man thus corrupt, thus despicable, makes himself necessary to
the prince that despises him, by the most pleasing of all qualities, perpetual gaiety, by an unfailing power of exciting laughter, which is the more freely indulged, as his wit is not of the
splendid or ambitious kind, but consists in easy escapes and
sallies of levity, which make sport but raise no envy. [Notes to
Henry IV, Pt. 2

Key to Sources

An asterisk indicates books included in the reading list; "J" indicates works by Johnson; dates in parentheses are publication dates.

Adv. 67	J, *The Adventurer* (1752–1754), No. 67
Boerhaave	J, "Biographical Essays of Eminent Persons," from *The Gentleman's Magazine* (1739)
Bos. 21 March 1783	Boswell's *Life of Johnson*, date of entry
Brain*	Brain, *Reflections on Genius*
Brav. Engl. Soldier	J, *The Bravery of the English Common Soldiers* (1767)
Browne	J, "Biographical Essays," from *Gent. Mag.* (1739)
D'Arblay Diary	*The Diary and Letters of Madame D'Arblay* [Fanny Burney] (1832)
Deb. Engl. Seamen Deb. Indem. Evidence Deb. Trade and Navigation Deb. Walpole	J, Debates in the Senate of Lilliput, from *Gent. Mag.* (1741)
Dedic. Lennox Shakespeare	J, dedication to Mrs. Lennox' *Shakespeare Illustrated* (1753)
Dict.	J, *A Dictionary of the English Language* (1755)

Essay, Drake   J, from *Gent. Mag.* (1740)

False Alarm   J, *The False Alarm* (1770)

For the Defense   *Boswell for the Defense, 1769–1774*, ed. W. K. Wimsatt and F. A. Pottle (New York, McGraw-Hill, 1959)

Hawkins*   Hawkins, *Life of Johnson*

Idl. 58   J, *The Idler* (1758–1760), No. 58

Intro. Proceedings of Committee   J, introduction to *Proceedings of the Committee . . . for Clothing French Prisoners of War* (1760)

Intro. World Displayed   J, introduction to *The World Displayed*, ed. John Newbery (1759)

Irene   J's play *Irene* (written 1737; publ. 1749)

Johnsoniana*   Croker's collection of anecdotes

John. Misc.*   Hill's *Johnsonian Miscellanies*, collection of memoirs and anecdotes

Journey, Skye   J, *Journey to the Western Islands of Scotland* (1775), chap. title

King of Prussia   J, essay from *Literary Magazine* (1756)

Krutch*   Krutch, *Samuel Johnson*

Letter to Mrs. T., March 1763   J, letter to Mrs. Thrale, date of writing. All of J's letters included may be found in Chapman's edition* unless otherwise noted.

L.P., Dryden   J, *Lives of the Poets* (1779–1781)

London   J's poem "London" (1738)

Lucas*	Lucas, *In Search of Good Sense*
Miss Boothby*	Miss Hill Boothby, *An Account*
Miss Reynolds	Miss Frances Reynolds, *Recollections of Dr. Johnson* (London, 1835)
Murphy*	Murphy, *Life and Genius*
Notes to Rich. II (etc.)	From J's edition of Shakespeare (1765)
Pioz. Anec.*	Mrs. Piozzi [Thrale], *Anecdotes*
Prayers and Meditations*	J's prayers publ. by Strahan
Pref. Dict.	J, preface to his *English Dictionary*
Pref. Preceptor	J, preface to *The Preceptor*, ed. Robert Dodsley (1748–9)
Pref. Rolt's Comm'l. Dict.	J, preface to Rolt's *Dictionary of Trade and Commerce* (1761)
Pref. Shakespeare	J, preface to his edition of Shakespeare
Prol. Opening Drury Lane	J's poem "Prologue Spoken by Mr. Garrick, At the Opening of the Theatre in Drury Lane, 1747"
Raleigh*	Raleigh, *Six Essays*
Ram. 194	J, *The Rambler* (1750–1752), No. 194
Ras. 17	J, *Rasselas* (1759), Chap. 17
Review, A Free Inquiry	J, review of Soame Jenyns' *A Free Inquiry into the Nature and Origins of Evil*, from *Lit. Mag.* (1757)
Review, Court of Augustus	J, review of Thomas Blackwell's *Memoirs of the Court of Augustus*, from *Lit. Mag.* (1756)

Review, *Eight Days' Journey*	J, review of Jonas Hanway's journal, from *Lit. Mag.* (1757)
Review, *Evidence against Queen of Scots*	J, review of Alexander Tytler's *History and Critical Inquiry into the Evidence . . . against Mary Queen of Scots*, from *Gent. Mag.* (1760)
Sermon	J's sermons, unpubl. in his lifetime; compiled from his diaries and journals; those included here taken from the 1825 Collected Works
State of Affairs	J, from *Lit. Mag.* (1756)
Taxation	J, *Taxation No Tyranny* (1775)
Thraliana*	Mrs. Thrale's *Diary*
Tour 4 November	Boswell's *Tour to the Hebrides* (1786), date of entry
Van. H. Wishes	J's poem "The Vanity of Human Wishes" (1749)
Windham Diary	*Diary of the Right Hon. William Windham* (London, 1866)

Suggested Reading

WORKS OF SAMUEL JOHNSON

The History of Rasselas, Prince of Abyssinia. Edited by Gwin J. Kolb. Crofts Classics. New York: Appleton-Century-Crofts, 1962.

This charming story of a prince and his sister who escape from the Happy Valley, where they have everything, to go in search of discontent, contains some of Johnson's best aphorisms. Probably the most widely read of Johnson's works.

A Journey to the Western Islands of Scotland. London: Chapman and Dodd, 1924.

An unusually well-informed and sensible man's observations on a rude society recently defeated in arms and beginning, perhaps, to question its harsh conditions and the prevailing clan organization. Still good for the general reader.
Johnson's *Journey* has been conveniently issued together with Boswell's *Journal of a Tour to the Hebrides with Samuel Johnson* in Oxford University Press's Oxford Standard Authors series (last printing, 1961).

Letters of Samuel Johnson. Edited by R. W. Chapman. 3 vols. Oxford: Clarendon Press, 1952.

A complete and thoroughly indexed collection of Johnson's correspondence. Interesting, of course, but hardly for the casual reader.

Doctor Johnson's Prayers. Edited by Elton Trueblood. New York: Harper and Brothers, 1947.

A very moving book in which are arranged Johnson's prayers on all sorts of occasions—Easter, New Year's Day, studying law, starting his *Ramblers*, etc. Probably the finest liturgical prose since Cranmer. More of the prayers may be found in any standard edition of Johnson's Collected Works; see especially the new Yale Edition of the Works of Samuel Johnson, vol. I, *Diaries, Prayers, and Annals.*

Prayers and Meditations. Edited by the Rev. George Strahan. London: Cadell, 1785.

Expressions of Johnson's attempts to overcome his manifold sins and shortcomings and his magnificent requests for God's help in doing so. This short collection was published by Johnson's friend Strahan a short time after his death.

Johnson, Prose and Poetry. Selected by Mona Wilson. The Reynard Library. Cambridge: Harvard University Press, 1951.

A well-printed and generous (950 pp.) selection, including "The Vanity of Human Wishes," "London," *Rasselas, A Journey,* the prefaces to the *Dictionary* and the edition of Shakespeare, as well as portions of the *Lives of the Poets,* the periodical essays, reviews, and debates.

Samuel Johnson, Selected Prose and Poetry. Edited by Bertrand H. Bronson. New York: Rinehart and Company, 1952.

Johnson's periodical essays—*Rambler, Idler,* and *Adventurer*—take up three full volumes in the 1823 edition of his works. Tastes in essays vary as much as tastes in lyric poems. Still, in this paperback selection is a handful of the best essays for the general reader which are most representative of Johnson. The volume contains much beside.

BIOGRAPHIES, ANECDOTES, MEMOIRS

Boothby, Miss Hill. *An Account of the Life of Dr. Samuel Johnson from His Birth to His Eleventh Year.* London: Richard Phillips, 1805.

A unique little book. Miss Boothby asked Johnson to write letters to her recounting his earliest days. He did so, and this book is her editing of these letters. Not generally available.

Boswell, James. *The Life of Samuel Johnson, LL.D.* Edited by George Birkbeck Hill, revised by L. F. Powell. 6 vols. Oxford: Clarendon Press, 1934–1950.

Any reading in Johnson begins with Boswell. The Hill-Powell edition really covers the ground, with a mass of notes as copious and as interesting as the text; vols. V and VI contain Boswell's *Tour to the Hebrides,* Johnson's short diary of *A Journey into North Wales,* and useful indices to the *Life.*

Boswell, James. *The Life of Samuel Johnson.* Edited by Roger Ingpen. Boston: C. E. Lauriat Co., 1925.

This is the Boswell life in an unhandy, three-volume edition, adequately indexed, profusely illustrated. Better for reference than for casual reading.

———— *Boswell's Life of Johnson.* Edited and abridged by Charles Grosvenor Osgood. Modern Student's Library. New York, Chicago, etc.: Charles Scribner's Sons, 1917.

This handy volume of 570 pages is more than adequate for the beginning reader of Johnson. It contains the famous passages and is carefully edited and well indexed.

———— *Tour to the Hebrides with Samuel Johnson, LL.D.* Edited by Frederick A. Pottle and Charles H. Bennett. New York: Viking Press, 1936 (new ed., McGraw-Hill, 1961).

A gossipy, interesting book in which Boswell follows the method he was later to use in the *Life.* Describes in day-by-day detail the trip of this highly civilized pair through the rough clan country of northwest Scotland.

Hawkins, Sir John. *The Life of Samuel Johnson, LL.D.* London, 1787.

Hawkins knew Johnson before either Boswell or Mrs. Thrale. He is authoritative about the fifteen years before 1762, accurate to a decimal point, discursive and oddly uninteresting.

———— *The Life of Samuel Johnson, LL.D.* Edited by Bertram H. Davis. New York: Macmillan, 1961.

This recent work cuts out much of the irrelevant material that was in the original. The trouble is that the irrelevant material was not quite irrelevant and that the dreariness of the original has been little lessened by the excisions.

Johnsonian Miscellanies. Edited by George Birkbeck Hill. 2 vols. Oxford: Clarendon Press, 1897.

Contains most of the Piozzi *Anecdotes,* all of Murphy's *Life* and some of Hawkins', selections from numerous contemporary memoirs, and all kinds of obscure Johnsonisms. Not generally available.

Johnsoniana; or, Supplement to Boswell: Being Anecdotes and Sayings of Dr. Johnson. Edited by J. Wilson Croker. Philadelphia: Carey and Hart, 1842.

This volume, long out of circulation, is a less scholarly work than *Johnsonian Miscellanies* but the same kind of thing. Contains excerpts from the works of two dozen writers who recorded anecdotes and even the words of Johnson. Interesting for the desultory reader.

Murphy, Arthur. *The Life and Genius of Samuel Johnson, LL.D.* London: Longman, etc., 1793.

Really no more than an essay, this slight volume is not as interesting as Piozzi and Boswell, and gives little that they do not.

Piozzi, Hester Lynch [Mrs. Thrale]. *Anecdotes of the Late Samuel Johnson, LL.D.* London: Cadell, 1786.

This small volume by Johnson's Mrs. Thrale is more concentrated Johnson than Boswell is and, though narrower in scope, is no less interesting. Well worth reading but hard to find.

MODERN BIOGRAPHIES

Clifford, James L. *Young Samuel Johnson.* New York: McGraw-Hill, 1955.

A full biography of Johnson's early years, it ends at about 1750—long before the Boswell and Thrale era and but three years after the Ivy Lane Club and John Hawkins.

Krutch, Joseph Wood. *Samuel Johnson.* New York: Henry Holt, 1944.

A full and splendid biography in the modern idiom, solid in scholarship, easy and readable in style, spiced with much of the best that Johnson said and wrote, and wonderfully indexed.

Norman, Charles. *Mr. Oddity: Samuel Johnson, LL.D.* Drexel Hill, Pa.: Bell Publishing Co., 1951.

A light, very readable life in which the author catches those aspects of Johnson that made Malton, the innkeeper at Edensor Inn, call him *Oddity.* Entertaining book for the general reader.

Pearson, Hesketh. *Johnson and Boswell.* New York: Harper and Brothers, 1959.

An interesting and sound life by a more than competent biographer, who has made full use of the latest information on his subject; more detached than other biographers of Johnson (not to say occasionally acid), Pearson is still highly appreciative of the wit and wisdom of Johnson. Excellent book for the general reader.

SPECIALIZED STUDIES

Bate, Walter Jackson. *The Achievement of Samuel Johnson.* New York: Oxford University Press, 1955.

How much Johnson achieved with so little could be a facile summary of this fascinating work, obviously a labor of love. Especially valuable to the general reader for the opening biographical chapter and the frequent quotations from Johnson's less-known writings.

Brain, Russell. *Some Reflections on Genius.* London: Pitman Medical Publishing Co., 1960.

Of this series of fourteen essays, five have to do especially with Johnson—as a student of science, as a victim of neuroses, and as a subject of a post-mortem examination.

Chase, Peter Pineo. "The Ailments and Physicians of Dr. Johnson." An address to the Beaumont Medical Club, 1950; printed in *Yale Journal of Biology and Medicine,* April 1951.

A Johnson student and physician looks at Johnson's manifold ills. He upsets, in the light of modern knowledge, much earlier theorizing about Johnson's health. A most readable study.

Hopkins, Mary Alden. *Dr. Johnson's Lichfield.* New York: Hastings House, 1952.

A very readable book on the Johnson family and the social groups in and about Lichfield in Johnson's early days and during his later visits. Presupposes some knowledge of Johnson and his circle.

Lucas, F. L. *In Search of Good Sense.* London: Cassell and Company, 1958.

Four essays on eighteenth-century rationalism as represented by Johnson, Boswell, Goldsmith, and Chesterfield. The Johnson piece is especially informative and so full of Johnson as to be a sampler in itself. All essays interesting for the general reader.

McLaren, Murray. *The Highland Jaunt.* London: Jarrolds, 1954.

McLaren undertook only ten years ago to follow the footsteps of Johnson and Boswell through their Hebridean trip. Fast-moving and informative, this volume could be useful either as an adjunct to the *Journey* and the *Tour* or as a guidebook for a summer trip.

Raleigh, Walter. *Six Essays on Johnson.* London: Oxford University Press, 1927.

The first three of these solid essays will appeal to the general reader. One, "Johnson without Boswell," will dispel for him the idea that Boswell was alone in his biographical interest in Johnson. The essays on Johnson's Shakespeare and the *Lives* are for the specialist.

Tinker, Chauncey B. *Young Boswell.* Boston: Atlantic Monthly Press, 1922.

This pleasant work seems less cluttered, more readable, than the series of Boswell books that are still coming out. This is one from which the curious general reader can get much.

Vulliamy, C. E. *Mrs. Thrale of Streatham.* London: Jonathan Cape, 1936.

Interesting and readable, but for the specialist who will get detail that is lacking in Boswell and see the familiar people from a slightly different angle. Presupposes some knowledge of and much interest in the Johnson circle.

———— *Ursa Major: A Study of Dr. Johnson and His Friends.* London: Michael Joseph Ltd., 1946.

This is an interesting and realistic approach to Johnson. It questions much of the contemporary and modern adulation of Johnson, has high praise for Johnson's prose and his wit, less than praise for his conduct. The comments on the people surrounding Johnson are keen, unstereotyped, and provocative.

Voitle, Robert. *Samuel Johnson, The Moralist.* Cambridge: Harvard University Press, 1961.

This book requires more of the reader than mere interest in Johnson. Johnson was a moralist in the general sense of the word, but the author has taken his ideas, erected them into a system, and related them to the philosophical thinking of the eighteenth century.

The general reader might also profit from the *Letters of James Boswell,* edited by Chauncey B. Tinker (Oxford, 1924). These two volumes are still fresh and interesting and worth thumbing through if only for the pleasure of coming upon Boswell's letter to Johnson, written on the Tomb of Melancthon, and his impudent and successful letter begging an interview with Rousseau. The student, the specialist, or the noncasual reader of Johnson eventually finds himself drawn to *Thraliana: The Diary of Hester Lynch Thrale*, 2 vols., edited by Katherine C. Balderston (Oxford, 1942); *Letters of Anna Seward*, 6 vols., 1811; and *The Diary and Letters of Madame D'Arblay*, 3 vols., 1832. In these works, as in Hawkins' *Life*, the general reader has to pan too much gravel for too little gold. He will find much of what they have to say in other places —as in Hill's *Johnsonian Miscellanies* or Croker's *Johnsoniana*.

Index